AMERICAN MILITARY INTERVENTION IN UNCONVENTIONAL WAR

Previous Publications

The Reluctant Superpower: United States Policy in Bosnia, 1991–95 (1997).
The United States, China, and Southeast Asian Security: A Changing of the Guard? (2003).

AMERICAN MILITARY INTERVENTION IN UNCONVENTIONAL WAR

FROM THE PHILIPPINES TO IRAQ

Wayne Bert

First published in 2011
by PALGRAVE MACMILLAN® in the United States – a division of St. Martin's Press LLC,
175 Fifth Avenue, New York, NY 10010.

Where this book is distributed in the UK, Europe and the rest of the world, this is by
Palgrave Macmillan, a division of Macmillan Publishers Limited, registered in England,
company number 785998, of Houndmills, Basingstoke, Hampshire RG21 6XS.

Palgrave Macmillan is the global academic imprint of the above companies and has
companies and representatives throughout the world.

Palgrave® and Macmillan® are registered trademarks in the United States, the United
Kingdom, Europe and other countries.

ISBN 978–0–230–11938–3

Library of Congress Cataloging-in-Publication Data

Bert, Wayne, 1939–
    American military intervention in unconventional war : from the Philippines to
Iraq / Wayne Bert.
        p. cm.
    Includes bibliographical references and index.
    ISBN 978–0–230–11938–3 (hardback)
    1. Asymmetric warfare—United States—Case studies.   2. Asymmetric warfare—
United States—Cost effectiveness—Case studies.   3. United States—Military policy—
Decision making—Case studies.   4. Philippines—History—Philippine American War,
1899–1902.   5. Vietnam War, 1961–1975.   6. Yugoslav War, 1991–1995.   7. Afghan
War, 2001–   8. Iraq War, 2003–   I. Title.
    U163.B375 2011
    355.02'180973—dc22

                                                              2011012940

A catalogue record of the book is available from the British Library.

Design by MPS Limited, A Macmillan Company

First edition: October 2011

10   9   8   7   6   5   4   3   2   1

Printed in the United States of America.

This book is dedicated to

my wife, Kerstin

and my friend, Norma, who died in the crash of American Airlines flight 77 on September 11, 2001

Contents

List of Tables   viii

Preface   ix

I   **Introduction**

1   The New International Environment   3

2   American Policies: Origins and Objectives   15

3   Counterinsurgency and US Adaptation to Fourth Generation War   43

II   **Case Studies**

4   The Philippines—1898–1902   55

5   Vietnam—1945–1973   71

6   Bosnia—1991–1995   103

7   Afghanistan—2001–Present   127

8   Iraq—2003–2010   157

III   **Conclusion**

9   The Perils of Intervention   197

Notes   219

References and Further Reading   235

Index   257

LIST OF TABLES

4.1 US-Philippines war statistics   61

5.1 US-Vietnam war statistics   74

6.1 US-Bosnia war statistics   107

7.1 US-Afghanistan war statistics   129

8.1 US-Iraq war statistics   161

PREFACE

No one starts a war—or rather, no one in his senses ought to do so—without first being clear in his mind what he intends to achieve by that war and how he intends to conduct it.

Carl von Clausewitz

In 1963 while resident in Poland I made the acquaintance of a Polish ornithologist. Democratic in ideology, pro-American in international orientation, he had traveled to both North and South Vietnam in a professional capacity and he had very strong views on the American involvement in Vietnam. The Americans, he said, would never win the war. The government in the south was detached from the people. The leadership presided over a society where the economy was booming in the cities, with a resulting influx of Western consumer goods, but the political elite was out of touch, inequality was great, and the populace exhibited little loyalty to or involvement with the government. In the north, on the other hand, he found both repression by the government and political support from the populace. The government evoked a nationalist mission that struck a responsive chord in the public, which they responded to despite a hard life and a heavy-handed governing style. In the end, my friend maintained, the Vietnamese would opt for the message from the north and the government in the south would go nowhere. He also had some anecdotes about the patience of the Vietnamese and the willingness of the populace to endure frustration, which proved prescient in light of the way the war developed. After returning to the states and the fierce debate over the Vietnam War that followed over the years, I never found a better explanation than my friend's for the dynamic of the war that developed in Vietnam. His analysis was brief and sketchy, but it accurately predicted the outcome, based on arguments that were credible. That experience spawned a question in my mind that has pursued me throughout my professional career: how could a Polish political novice have understood so well the basic dynamics of the situation in Vietnam after only a casual trip there, while the highly educated and politically savvy people in Washington who were in charge of the war and had all the resources of the US government at their disposal seemed oblivious to his insights? Or alternatively, the policy makers understood the situation and realized the policy they were following did not have a good chance of success, but they perceived the overall objective of stopping communism to be so important that they continued the policy rather than taking the risk of adjusting it. This is the conclusion of one popular treatment of the war (Gelb and Betts, 1979:1–6).[1] Or perhaps Lyndon Johnson so feared the domestic threat to his career or so craved the approval of Kennedy supporters that he continued to prosecute the war against his better judgment. In any case, the prosecution of that war led to a foreign policy debacle for the United States and the effective ruin of many a career, not to mention the deaths of 2 to 3 million human beings. The knowledge-able advisers of the presidents intimately and actively involved in the escalation of the war included PhDs in the social sciences and one former "*wunderkind,*" McGeorge Bundy, a dean at Harvard, who became John Kennedy's special assistant for national security (Goldstein, 2008). The "best and the brightest" (Halberstam, 1992) had blown it, but a thought-ful Pole trained to observe birds and with no direct involvement in the war was early on able to predict the outcome of the conflict.

But the debacles of intervention in Iraq and Afghanistan were still to come, and they rivaled Vietnam for the prevalence of misperceptions, bad decisions, and costly policies. What the results of these wars will be it is still too early to say. But the decision-making process in the run-up to the Iraq War seems even less explicable than the decisions that preceded Vietnam. In many ways, the decisions and the decision-making process from the Vietnam War look orderly and thorough compared to the Iraqi process. Further, there is little evidence that those who made the decision had any awareness or took into their calculations the possibility that the United States might be headed into a similar situation, where it would not be able to control events, and the objectives of the policy would for years elude the best attempts to accomplish them. Clearly this case tells us something about the failure of US policy makers to learn from his-tory, as well as their continuing lack of insight into the dynamics of such interventions.

Despite these two failures, however, not all American policy decision making has so badly miscalculated. There is also evidence that the United States has a constructive role to play internationally and that wars can be conducted successfully. These cases are not limited to a more tradi-tional war such as the Gulf War in 1991, when the objective of rolling back the Iraqi invasion of Kuwait was successful at minimal cost to the

United States and its allies. The outcome of the war in Bosnia, although long delayed, can also be viewed as at least moderately successful in fulfilling the objective of the intervention: the cessation of ethnic cleansing and slaughter in the biggest conflict in Europe since World War II (WWII). This war, unlike the Gulf War, involved, in effect, intervention in the internal conflict of what had been the sovereign country of Yugoslavia before it disintegrated. The NATO operation in Kosovo can arguably be deemed a success—in that the objectives of the intervention were accomplished without great cost in lives or material—and perhaps the 1989 invasion of Panama and the intervention in the Philippines to stop a coup d'etat in 1989.[2]

This is a study of US military intervention abroad in wars where unconventional war—under which a variety of descriptions of nontraditional wars: guerrilla war, irregular war, asymmetrical war, low-intensity war, and insurgency can be subsumed—was an important element of the conflict. The United States throughout its history has been involved in many unconventional wars, from the Revolutionary War through the Indian wars to Latin American interventions to leading guerrilla actions in Burma. By unconventional war I mean wars that are often intermittent, asymmetrical in battlefield firepower, with fighters that are indistinguishable from civilians, and fighters that group and fight in ways that are unpredictable and usually calculated by the guerrillas to give their side an advantage. They are wars of maneuver rather than position that allow the insurgent to maximize the advantage against a more powerful antagonist. But above all, the core of unconventional war in the modern world is the quest for the hearts and minds of the people. As Roger Trinquier notes, "The Sina Quo Non of victory in modern warfare is the unconditional support of the population." The political and the military are inextricably intertwined. Further, every insurgency must have a cause. "[I]f no cause exists, it will have to be invented" in order for an insurgency to flourish (Kitson, 1971:29). Many unconventional wars are also civil wars, as were most of the cases examined here. Only the Philippines and Bosnia do not qualify, but even in those cases it depends on the definition given. All of the cases analyzed here involved interventions that resulted in unconventional war, but most of them also, at least from time to time, involved periods of conventional fighting. That is, they involved regular military organizations able to make maximum use of what firepower they possessed with substantial effect on the enemy. For a long time, the United States prevailed in all of its irregular wars, even if it did not get the long-term stability it wanted; for instance, witness the frustratingly long occupations of Nicaragua and Haiti, which did little to stabilize the situation. But in Vietnam it met new conditions where in order to wield influence over the people, short of destroying the country, it required the techniques of counterinsurgency. This book argues a new approach to this kind of war is needed.

I have chosen five cases of intervention to examine, starting with the war to take the Philippines in 1898. The other four are Vietnam—1945–73, Bosnia—1991–95, Afghanistan—2001–ongoing, and Iraq—2003–2010 The latter four cases are the most important US interventions abroad in unconventional war since WWII, in terms of number of troops involved and American lives lost. The interventions in the Dominican Republic (1965), Panama (1989), and Haiti (1994) may have involved as many or more troops as some of my cases, but the number of lives lost was very small and there was a minimal amount of warfare. In Bosnia no lives were lost and the actual American action was minimal. It is also a borderline case inasmuch as it involved considerable conventional war. There was hostage taking and ethnic cleansing, however, which is counted as unconventional war. The most important reason for including it was that at the time both foreign policy elites and the public perceived it as potentially similar to Vietnam and feared a long involvement in a kind of warfare at which the United States has previously come to grief. It also provides a useful contrast to the other cases in terms of the outcome. The Philippines case provides historical perspective and it marks the beginning of the American tradition of major military action abroad. This sample has the advantage of containing the most important cases of US military intervention—especially Vietnam, Afghanistan, and Iraq—that have involved substantial unconventional conflict. There is no question of the significance of the wars in the sample.

The Korean War and the 1991 Gulf War are excluded because they were wars of attrition fought between militaries on mostly conventional battlefields with conventional tactics, in the tradition of WWII. The Gulf War also included an unconventional effort to protect refugees in the Kurdish regions of Iraq following the war. Other important cases of intervention, or cases for potential intervention, existed, but time and space limited the sample. Of those not included, Panama would have been an interesting addition to my sample, and the genocide in Rwanda in 1993 would be a very fruitful study of why intervention for humanitarian, not security reasons, did not take place. I will comment on these other cases occasionally, but I have chosen to limit detailed examination to the cases that were politically and militarily most important.

Three aspects of each case have been examined: the rationale for intervention, implementation of the intervention, and the result of the intervention. In agreement with realists, I am interested in security first. There can be many reasons to intervene in a conflict: the security of the country, humanitarian concerns, concern of a leader about political survival, expansion of power or jurisdiction only tangentially related to security, or promotion of an ideal. But unless security and the survival or welfare of the nation/state are given high priority, other foreign policy objectives may be impossible to carry out. "Basic to all kinds of national self-interest," Robert Osgood states, "is survival or self-preservation, for upon national survival depends the achievement of all other self-interested ends." After the excesses of Vietnam and the Bush administration, I agree with James Kurth that it is time to "make national security once again the principal objective of U.S. foreign policy" (Osgood, 1953:5; Kurth, 2008:110). I have not, however, chosen to evaluate cases solely on whether they contributed to "survival" of the country. Security has many lesser-order aspects short of survival. The possible variety of these is dealt with later in Chapter 2 under "choosing to intervene." Many topics short of sheer survival may constitute security issues, including those of a political and economic as well as military nature.

There can be many legitimate objectives in a foreign policy, and security is only one of them. In some cases, other goals may need to be given priority over the preferred security objectives. Depending on the circumstances this can be appropriate, but in the analysis of foreign policy needs, security is the logical place to start. My purpose here is to evaluate only the security rationale for intervention. If these most pressing objectives do not require intervention, then the case for intervention based on other "second order" factors can legitimately be considered. Further, of the cases being considered here, in all except Bosnia policy makers stressed the security rationale for intervention, which allows me to test that reasoning. If this justification cannot be supported, then the most important rationale for intervention is not substantiated.

If the argument for security as justification for intervening can be substantiated, then a remaining task is to inquire into the success of the implementation and what the results were. The results can be measured by a cost-benefit analysis, discussed below. If the objective can be declared legitimate, and the implementation and the result can be seen as providing more benefit than cost, then the intervention can be viewed as a success from a national security perspective. If, on the other hand, the legitimacy of the intervention on national security grounds cannot be substantiated, then the intervention did not serve a national security purpose. If the intervention is considered illegitimate on national security grounds, as is the situation in most of the cases, this casts considerable doubt on the effectiveness of US policy since I am arguing that some of the most important interventions in the post–WWII period have not been successful.

I also comment considerably on the role of liberal democratic ideals in these five cases and in American foreign policy in general. It is part of the thesis of this book that American ideals play a substantial role in motivating US foreign policy elites and that invoking ideals is effective in mobilizing public opinion. I do not, however, give to that issue the focus that is given to security issues. In the cases of Vietnam, Afghanistan, and Iraq, if US elites had not been able to posit a national security interest, they probably would not have intervened to begin with, and they certainly would not have continued the intervention as long as they did if they had not continued making a national security case. It is not easy to get public support for a potentially costly intervention solely on moral or idealistic grounds, and it is seldom attempted. Support for this assertion is provided by the Bosnian intervention, for which there was only weak public support.

I argue that some of the cases portrayed here reflect idealistic motivation, often in addition to the arguments for intervention on security grounds. Idealistic or, in the US case, liberal democratic justifications for policy can serve to motivate policy makers, or they can serve as rhetoric that policy makers use to garner public support and justify policies. In practice, these two uses are difficult to distinguish, and I believe that such rhetoric has reflected both uses in some of these cases. I have not included an analysis on the legal grounds for intervention for the same reason. Until there is a case that the intervention can be defended on national security grounds, the issue is rather superfluous to the immediate issue of intervention and would render the study unwieldy.

In recent years considerable debate has taken place on the proper definition of security. Whereas security once focused almost solely on security for the state, and comprised essentially military issues, most recently the definition has been broadened to focus on human security and to include other areas such as societal, environmental, and economic security (Buzan et al., 1998). The broadening of the term has had much to do with the increasing importance of third world countries, which sometimes speak of "comprehensive" security, as for example, in Indonesia. Frequently, as Caroline Thomas notes, what is included in such definitions include many things that "are already taken care of" in the more-developed states, "things such as food, health, money and trade." Internal security is often as important as protection against exterior enemies. But as Donald Emerson suggests, the events of 9/11 have, if anything, narrowed the definition of security back closer to the original one (Collins, 2003:8–9). The kind of security referred to here when discussing American security will be primarily state security, since this is what policy makers usually had in mind. This is not to say this

"Eurocentric" definition is the one to be relied on in order to make good policy. While it was probably the view of many foreign policy elites that enhancing the people's security was best done by enhancing state security, as Canada's foreign minister Lord Axworthy wrote in 1999, the US approach to Iraq appears to have enhanced neither (Collins, 2003:4). Many people feel that the intervention there in 2003 actually decreased the security of the United States. This was a CIA finding, based on the assumption that the war had improved the recruiting success of al Qaeda, and one poll done with international relations faculty teaching in four-year American colleges and universities found that 89 percent believed that the war had decreased American security (Maliniak et al., 2007). It also seems clear that much writing in the West has neglected the regional political context of security problems. Joseph Nye and Sean Lynn-Jones commented in 1988 that "[m]any American scholars and policy-makers made recommendations for US policy in the Vietnam War in almost complete ignorance of the politics of Southeast Asia" (Collins, 2003:9).

This study also discusses security in the target states in which the intervention is taking place, primarily in the context of the need to provide security if counterinsurgency is to be successful. The argument is that if US intervention is to take place against failed states or those experiencing substantial levels of insurgency or unconventional war, progress will be made in the war only if adequate security can be provided for the population. In this case, the security required would be of the most comprehensive kind, including not only basic military aspects but political, economic, and societal as well. As the experience in the former Yugoslavia showed, this comprehensive type of security can be in demand not only in the poorest areas of the world, but in the former second world as well (Collins, 2003:10).

This leads to the second important question dealt with here: which means were used to prosecute the intervention and were they appropriate and successful? Were the means used the most efficient at attaining the ends with the least possible cost? Finally, the results of the intervention are examined. Were the results satisfactory? Were they relatively cost free? If not, did the end result of the intervention justify the cost of the intervention? Could better results have been achieved and if so, could they have been obtained at reasonable or justifiable cost?[3] I compare and contrast the five cases with the purpose of drawing some general lessons from and about US intervention abroad, which will be useful in formulating future policy. The five cases can shed light on what seems to work, what doesn't work, and why the cases produced varying responses both from American citizens and on the battlefield. I have chosen the Philippine War as one historical case from another era, but it is in many ways a harbinger of the kinds of cases the United States would become involved in during the post–WWII years.

My purpose here is to provide comparison and analysis of what has happened when the United States has intervened and to give one summary of that experience. On the basis of that experience, I hope to provide some useful normative guidance for the future. Bismarck said the wise man learns from other people's experience, the fool learns from his own. We can learn and benefit from examining history, other people's experience. The focus of the analysis is not primarily theoretical concerns, but rather policy issues. In the discipline of international relations, unfortunately, there is only a very tenuous connection between the two, and theoretical concerns often get priority (Nye, 2009; Jentelson, 2002; Lebow, 2003:xi).[4] This book therefore aims at analysis, using theoretical insights when possible, with insights and guidance for students and policy makers as the end product. Certainly the focus of the work is inductive rather than deductive.

The organization of the book is as follows. Part I, the introduction, has three chapters. Chapter 1 discusses the decline in the frequency of war, the relationship between economics and force, the power of contemporary nationalism, and the new type of war now prevalent in international conflict. Chapter 2 discusses the US response to the environment, including: strategies of containment, focusing on the realist element of US policy during the cold war, and post–cold war policy. American exceptionalism and the national style and other motivations and sources of leadership are also discussed. Finally, appropriate criteria for deciding to intervene are addressed. Chapter 3 briefly summarizes the US bureaucratic response to the new type of warfare and the problems in generating the preferred response of counterinsurgency. Part II is the five case studies and part III is a conclusion.

These case studies, because of space limitations, cannot be comprehensive treatments of the interventions, what transpired there, or what the consequences were. The analysis of the cases is subjective and reflects one person's perspective. In some cases this analysis will convince the reader, in others it will be contested. There are hundreds of books on the wars described here—Vietnam and Iraq especially have resulted in the spilling of vast amounts of ink. Many of these works concentrate on the decision-making process; the series of countless decisions that constitute the policy that justifies the war and the way it is implemented. In my view, the content of the policies often gets slighted in these studies. These books are particularly strong on representing the thinking of the decision makers and the people who influenced them, and for this reason they are useful. But my primary purpose here is to assess policy issues: the content of the decisions taken that affect the entire society and determine the success or failure of foreign policy. My hope is that this book will appeal to a wide variety of readers. General readers, who may be less interested in theoretical issues, should focus on what is most appealing to them, and may prefer to go directly to the case studies and start with them.

I wish to thank Roger Kanet and Ruth Bert, both of whom read an earlier version of the manuscript, as well as several anonymous referees, all of whom provided valuable criticism and suggestions. At Palgrave Macmillan, Robyn Curtis and Farideh Koohi-Kamali were very helpful in navigating and negotiating publication issues, while editing and assistance by Joel Breuklander and Sarah Nathan and the team at Macmillan Publishing Solutions facilitated the production process.

PART I

INTRODUCTION

CHAPTER 1

THE NEW INTERNATIONAL ENVIRONMENT

> One cannot decide whether it is good or bad to intervene at a given time or place without a great deal of concrete empirical analysis.
>
> Hans Morgenthau

Crucial changes in the international system during the past few decades have affected the fundamentals of international politics. Geopolitics has declined in importance as the balance of power concerns that shaped US policy in the twentieth century have diminished. The nuclear revolution and the increasing cost of war have rendered conquest among great powers unthinkable. China is a less plausible threat to Eurasia than Germany in 1917 and 1941 or the Soviet Union after World War II (WWII). Simultaneously, other threats have arisen. The spread of Weapons of Mass Destruction (WMD) and the rise of transnational groups that have the will and the capability to deliver lethal strikes without the surety of retaliation pose new and unsettling danger to the United States and other nation-states. Other threats that pose a global threat and can be fought only through collective action, including global warming, pandemics, cyber attacks and extinction of species, have also become pressing emergencies that require global action. As Stephen Van Evera puts it, never in modern times have the world's major powers had less reason to compete with each other or more reason to cooperate together for the solution to common problems (Van Evera, 2008). This is not to say that geopolitics is not important. The connection of both oil and terrorists to, among other regions, the Middle East, shows regions still matter. But on the other hand, some of the terrorists' most effective work has been done in Europe, and major trends are underway that will, over the long run, diminish the role of oil.

The process of globalization has had a major impact on international politics. Globalized finance enhances the power of the United States compared to other states, and makes going to war less likely because the "macroeconomic discipline demanded by the economic system is incompatible with military adventurism," where war and the risk of war threaten all aspects of this environment (Kirshner, 2008). It is therefore not surprising that the frequency of war seems to be declining in the international system. Moreover when war is fought, the changes in its nature, its impact and the response to it have radically altered. Any analysis of military intervention requires a rethinking of the contemporary nature of war.

DECLINE IN THE FREQUENCY OF WAR

Great powers often experience difficulties in military intervention, in spite of their power. Kenneth Waltz notes that great powers are always Gullivers, more or less "tightly tied." Although they fight more wars than others do, their military strength has "lost much of its usability," and "'non recourse to force' . . . is the doctrine of powerful states" (Waltz, 1979:183–87). According to one view, the main story line of the past 500 years is that strong nations can no longer dominate weak ones at will (Gelb, 2009:6). Further, war in general, and especially war among the great powers, has declined in the second half of the twentieth century. As John Mueller points out, the cold war stands in sharp contrast to the first half of the century, the time of the two most costly wars in history. In his view, the decline in great power war can be attributed to the lessons learned from the carnage of the two world wars, where the advancing level of technology ensured that in war the cost exceeded the benefits. As he put it, most people had gotten the point by 1918, and the rest, especially the Japanese, had gotten it by 1945 (Mueller, 1989:218; 2009). For the past two or three centuries major war between developed countries had gradually "moved toward terminal disrepute because of its perceived repulsiveness and futility" (Mueller, 1989:4). The withdrawal of the Soviet Union from the fray after the cold war changed the world almost overnight. The military and ideological battle between East and West was ended, Eastern Europe regained its independence, and Germany was united:

> All the major problems that had plagued big-country . . . international relations for nearly half a century were resolved with scarcely a shot being fired, a person being executed, or a rock being thrown.

> Mueller, 1995

War has increasingly become the activity of the occupants of countries that are outside the mainstream of the world economy. Moreover, most wars are now internal or civil wars and they are often the result of poor government (Mueller, 2009). These wars are most likely in economic situations where the country is poor, declining, and dependent on natural resource export (Collier, 2005; Holsti, 2006:144).

The frequency with which the United States, the unipolar superpower, is involved in war suggests two insights. On the one hand, it is not surprising that the most powerful country in the world is one of the most frequently involved in conflict. The closer to the top of the international hierarchy, the more likely a power is to believe it necessary to use the military to keep order and make "adjustments" in the international order (Waltz, 1979:187). As we shall see, it is indeed hard to make the case that more than one of the interventions in this study had much of anything to do with what could in any sense be construed as a direct threat to US security. But then one of the characteristics of an imperial power is that it worries less than other countries about its immediate security, and much more about the order it maintains and the more remote threats to that order. On the other hand, the decreasing utility of war for members of the system and the declining number of participants, especially in international wars, raises questions of whether war is the best expenditure of capital, political, economic, and human potential, even for a superpower. Both Mueller and Holsti believe that the norms and values of the international system have changed. War is seen as both very costly and morally repulsive as well. No longer do most people believe, as many prominent individuals did even less than a century ago, that war is an honorable and character-building practice. War is no longer, as according to Toynbee it was for five thousand years, one of "mankind's master institutions" (Mueller, 2009:302).

ECONOMICS AND THE USE OF FORCE

Questions about the utility of war are augmented by the currently fashionable arguments about the progress of globalization and interdependence, the increasing importance of economics, and the vanishing utility of military force. An early argument that encompassed all these points was that of Joseph Nye and Robert Keohane, whose arguments about growing interdependence pointed out that the growing complexity of pervasive economic ties between states also led to increasingly complex bureaucracies that made it even more difficult than in the past to speak of a monolithic or unified government. The testing of their assumptions against Canadian-US relations and US-Australian relations over decades bore out the validity of the argument that the use of force is decreasing and interdependence is growing. Armed conflict is less important and developed nations are economically dependent on trade. The reason is simply that, in a sharp reversal of the past situation, economic development as an end in itself is increasingly seen to be more valuable than military power. As Edward Luttwak suggests, "Geoeconomics is turning geopolitics and all warfare into a provincial phenomenon" (Keohane and Nye, 1977; Rosecrance, 1999; Schweller, 1998:199).[1] The United States, even though it is quite advanced technologically, is no longer dependent on land or conquest as a source of power, and is well on its way to epitomizing a virtual state—the state best adapted to the new economic order—but it is also still a superpower that encompasses political interests and expectations that will involve military intervention for some time to come. Virtual states no longer rely on land for wealth, but rather on high-end services and production. Their economic well-being depends on international economic ties, both trade and investment. War is disruptive to those ties and thus to prosperity. The United States, although highly developed economically, is an intermediate state that is, compared to the leading virtual states, still economically self-contained and politically and culturally introverted (Rosecrance, 1999). Because of its great power, it retains political reasons for intervention.

Jonathan Kirshner, describing globalization as "an array of phenomena that derive from unorganized and stateless forces but that generate pressures that are felt by states," suggests the extent to which the international system has been transformed by these pressures in the past few decades. Foreign assets as a percentage of global products were 17.5 percent in 1914 and 17.7 percent in 1980, but by 1995 they were 56.8 percent. Foreign direct investment, valued at 6 percent of world GDP in 1980, and 9 percent in 1995, was 22 percent in 2003, and of all the trends associated with globalization, the globalization of production is the most unprecedented. The daily turnover in world currency markets, $100 billion in 1979, had reached $400 billion in 1989, 1 trillion dollars in 1994 and nearly 2 trillion in 2004. All of this transnational activity made it twice as likely that a country would experience a financial crisis in the period from 1973–1997 as from 1945 to 1971. Globalization is neither "irresistible nor irreversible." Rather than breeding peace and harmony, it tends to foster conflicts and resentments. At the same time, financial globalization makes the resort to arms by states less likely because the macroeconomic discipline demanded by the economic system is incompatible with military adventurism (Kirshner, 2008).

John Ikenberry has long noted that the "real" international system in the post–WWII period has been the economic system, constructed at

Bretton Woods and led primarily by the United States. The end of the cold war saw a transformation in the structure of the military system, but the break with the past was less than might have been expected because of the importance of and continuity in the underlying economic system (Ikenberry, 1996, 2002; Russett, 1985). All of this ultimately is based on a basic change in culture reflecting the social motivation of individuals, a drastic break with prior centuries when people were motivated primarily by religious doctrine, political ideals, or military expansion. In the modern world, "just about everybody would rather be rich than just about anything else" (Mueller, 1989:221). Most US intervention is in the developing world, and many of the assumptions held around the world are not yet current with the ideas outlined above. As one scholar remarks, "Neoconservative ideas [with their focus on military and disruptive policies] are almost exactly wrong for the new age" (Van Evera, 2008:29). A case in point is the impact of the recent economic downturn, led by the United States but affecting most of the world. Conservatives in particular have been focused on the Chinese military threat as the distribution of power between the United States and China continues to move in China's favor as it upgrades its navy and air force. Focusing on the military balance is futile, however, if a healthy economy cannot be maintained. The United States, now dependent on Chinese financing of its debt, was recently the target of Chinese premier Wen Jiabao's advice that China expects the United States to manage its economy prudently so as to safeguard Chinese investments (Bradsher, 2009). Meanwhile, the Chinese have shown themselves adroit at using their newfound economic influence to bolster their strategic goals.

CONTEMPORARY NATIONALISM AND OTHER CREEDS

An important factor influencing all leaders and their view of the world is the particular ethnocentric perspective and nationalist inclinations that flow from having been socialized into the political culture and norms of a particular nation in the international system. Leaders and citizens in the contemporary United States are prone to underestimate the force of nationalism, a force that is the "most powerful political force on earth today" (Barber, 1996:158; Pei, 2003). The force of nationalism may be strongest in the postcolonial sections of the globe, where a strong reaction to domination by outside powers is palpable. It follows that nationalism will be an important force complicating any attempts at military intervention by outside powers. With the erosion of empires and multinational states, "nationalism has entered a new phase" (Haass, 1994:3). All of the cases in the sample for this study showed evidence of strong nationalist sentiment bolstering the cause of the insurgents. In the Philippines, Vietnam, Afghanistan, and Iraq, the nationalism was directed against the United States, but in Bosnia, where conflicts were primarily over identity, it was directed against neighboring countries. Osama bin Laden, who claimed to speak in the name of Islam, appeared to many to be at least as motivated by politics, and thus potentially by nationalism (Pape, 2005:105–17; Imbrahim, 2007).

People define themselves in terms of the nation to which they belong. "Thus a nation's defeat or victory may be experienced with a sense of personal humiliation or exhilaration by its citizens even though that defeat or victory does not affect them directly" (Andrew Kohut in Hall, 1999:265). For these people, the nation that is imagined is nonetheless as real as anything in their lives. This ability to identify with their government officials as the spokesmen for themselves means that they are extraordinarily sensitive to any perceived affront to their nation's—and hence to their personal—dignity or honor. Many of the countries where US intervention is likely to take place are former colonies. This status only increases and multiplies the concern of citizens there about potential threats to their nation.

The break up of the Sino-Soviet bloc illustrated the appeal and power of nationalism as it has replaced communism as the ideological and organizational glue holding a society together. The disintegration of Yugoslavia and the Soviet Union into constituent nations, and the splitting up of Czechoslovakia into two nations, the Czech Republic and Slovakia, Quebec's struggle to secede from Canada as well as the strains in China as Tibetan, Uighur, and other nationalisms manifest themselves continue to illustrate nationalism's importance. While religion has also become more important in international relations, it is second to nationalist forces.

A NEW KIND OF WAR

The most successful US wars in the twentieth century included WWI, WWII, and the 1991 Gulf War. These were all-out wars where the unambiguous goal was the total military defeat of the enemy, or in the case of the Gulf War, the completion of a specific but more limited objective, that is, throwing Iraq out of Kuwait. These objectives were accomplished through massive production of weaponry and ammunition, training qualified personnel, and enlisting decisive leadership to focus massive firepower on the battlefield. Very few wars since 1945, however, have been that simple.[2] All have had more limited objectives, or at least limited objectives were accepted in the end because the prior objective could not be achieved, as in Korea when a settlement was made on the thirty-eighth parallel. The Vietnam War was an exercise in frustration and a brutal waste of people and resources, resulting in a humiliating withdrawal. Iraq and Afghanistan both became costly and frustrating problems, where the outcome is still not entirely decided. There is a sharp contrast between the success of WWII, with its unlimited goals pursued through a war of attrition, and failure in more recent unconventional wars that the United States was forced to fight on the enemy's terms rather than its own. This reflects a lack of adjustment to the advancement of technology and the development of new methods of war, a failure to adapt to the requirements of what has been termed fourth generation warfare. In addition to the role of technology development, this change is related to the growing power of nationalism, the progress of democratization in governance, and the new emphasis in modern society on individual initiative. In order to prevail in conflicts in the contemporary world, developed countries must revise their perspective on war and how it should be fought.

The first generation of warfare, relying on the smoothbore musket and the tactics of the line and column, reflected not just the development of gunpowder, but changes in the political, economic, and social structures that made possible the transition from a feudal system to the era of monarchical nation-states.[3] The transition, which took centuries, was epitomized by the massive armies of the Napoleonic war machine that triumphed in Europe. Only the nation-state could sustain these large armies.

Second generation warfare was the result of the rifled musket, breechloaders, barbed wire, the machine gun, and indirect fire. The peak of this mode of warfare was WWI, but many of its characteristics were already obvious in the US civil war. It was based on fire and movement, with heavy reliance on indirect fire. Second generation tactics were summarized in the French saying: "the artillery conquers, the infantry occupies." Primary reliance was now on massed firepower rather than massed manpower, and was made possible by the growing reliance on the railroads and the telegraph. The weapons, materials, and supplies required for second generation warfare could only be sustained by the industrialization taking place in nineteenth-century-Europe and the United States and the growing ability of the national governments to tax the accumulating wealth. Nationalism, sustained by the French Revolution and later developments was important in motivating the vast amount of manpower that these war machines required.

Third generation warfare, although a response to developing technology and increasing battlefield firepower, relied more heavily on ideas. It was developed primarily by the Germans after WWI, aware that because of their inferior industrial base they needed new tactics based on maneuver rather than attrition. Third generation warfare relied on penetration to bypass and collapse the enemy's forces, and penetration of the defense was often invited to set the enemy up for a counterattack. In the blitz-krieg, fully developed in WWII and made possible by the tank, was added a new element of mobility and surprise. The Germans regularly and radically critiqued their performance and strategy, constantly learning from past mistakes and converting these insights into new initiatives and strategies. Traditional military thinking in the United States still relies primarily on third generation thinking.

Perhaps the most characteristic fact about fourth generation warfare is that, in Hammes' words, there is a shift from an "Industrial-Age focus on the destruction of the enemy's armed forces to an Information-Age focus on changing the minds of the enemy's political decision makers" (Hammes, 2006:207). The attempt to win focuses on the use of all available net-works—political, economic, social, and military, rather than relying solely on defeating the enemy's military forces. A primary advantage of fourth generation warfare is that by relying on superior political will, when prop-erly used, it can defeat much superior military and economic power.

Fourth generation warfare includes much carryover from earlier trends. Generally, fourth generation warfare is "widely dispersed [and] largely undefined." There is greater dispersion on the battlefield, with increased importance of actions by small groups of combatants. A vivid illustration of this is the effect that 19 men had in the attack on the World Trade Center in New York. As we realized then, no element or part of US society, no matter where located, is off limits to being attacked. Concomitantly, there is a decreasing dependence on central-ized logistics, with the fighters having greater ability to live off the land and the enemy. There is more emphasis on maneuver. Masses of men or firepower become a disadvantage rather than an advantage, since they, or it, are easy to target. Small and nimble forces will continue to be at a premium. Finally, there is a goal of "collapsing the enemy internally rather than physically dominating him." Targets include the population's support for the war and the enemy's culture. Correct identification of the most important factors for targeting is very important. The distinction between the military and the civilian becomes increasingly blurred.

The effectiveness of a knowledgeable and well-executed attack can be illustrated by the conduct of the Iraqi insurgents in the fall and winter of 2003–04. They carefully targeted the organizations most vital to the Coalition Provisional Authority (CPA), including the police, the U.N., neutral embassies, and Shia clerics. "Each event was tactically sepa-rated by time and space, but each tied together operationally to attack America's strategic position in the country . . . with each attack designed to prevent a stable, democratic government from emerging" (Hammes,

2006:216). In many cases, a conventional campaign will be necessary for the final destruction of the enemy, but for most of the war the most effective means of furthering the cause will be those that are multifaceted and often very indirect. The use of media and even lobbying are often more important than military operations. In Somalia, the media both started the war—by publicizing the pictures of starving children—and ended it by showing the bodies of US soldiers being dragged through the streets.

There is a contradiction between the trends that have led to fourth generation warfare, where "each new generation has brought a major shift toward a battlefield of disorder," and the traditional stance of the military, which is a culture of order. That culture is largely a product of the first generation of warfare, but it is still an important part of the contemporary military: ranks, saluting, uniforms, drill, and so forth (Lind et al., 1989). This contradiction symbolizes the difficulties involved in shifting from traditional warfare to the more appropriate new approaches.[4]

There has been much comment on the long timelines connected with fourth generation warfare. The shift of US attention from Afghanistan in 2002–2004 in order to prepare and promote the war in Iraq illustrated the short American attention span as well as the lack of understanding of the type of war they were fighting. Instead of staying to subdue remaining insurgent capabilities and to rebuild the society to strengthen resistance to the Taliban's appeal, the Americans moved on to the next project and they are now paying the price with a renewed conflict in Afghanistan. In fourth generation warfare, constant vigilance is required.

Hammes portrays fourth generation warfare as an event that can be described in general terms, but can also take many incarnations depending on the nature of the leadership, the culture, and the conditions in the country or setting where it is conducted. Mao Zedong developed people's war that he used both against the Japanese and against the internal opposition, the Guomindang. Ho Chi Minh in Vietnam made further adaptations, relying heavily on political mechanisms to take over South Vietnam. Hammes also compares different versions of the intifada in Palestine at different times in history. One worked because it was essentially a movement from below, a second (the al Aqsa) didn't because it was inappropriately imposed from the top.

The concept of fourth generation war is a general one that must be applied with creativity. The key principle that must be respected is the need to win the support of the population, whatever the differences in strategies and tactics fitting each particular culture and situation. The dilemma is illustrated by the US actions in Iraq. The United States started out fighting a high-tech conventional war, but the anticoalition forces turned it into a low-tech, fourth generation fight. The United States did very well with the conventional war.[5] It first did very badly in the unconventional war, and then improved as the new approaches advocated by General Petraeus and others were implemented. These will be discussed in more details in Chapter 8. In spite of some successes, however, it remains to be seen whether the result will succeed. It may be that the odds against success in overthrowing the government and then rebuilding institutions were so bad that no strategy could have been wholly successful in uniting the country, even without US mistakes.

The optimism of the fourth generation advocates that their techniques can prevail in conflicts needs to be tempered by awareness of the wars discussed by Mary Kaldor. She has identified a new type of organized violence prevalent in the international system today. It blurs the distinction between war, organized crime, and large-scale violations of human rights. States, during the long development of variations in warfare through the centuries, have had a monopoly on the use of violence, but that monopoly is now being eroded with the privatization of violence. The capabilities of states previously meant that the military was able to provide security at home, but the world abroad may be very dangerous. Now this border has also broken down and the distinction between the domestic and international arenas has blurred. The new type of violence is perpetrated not only by states, but also by local paramilitary groups, international organizations, and foreign militaries. This violence, more persuasive but perhaps less extreme, represents a revolution in military affairs, but not in the usual sense in which that term is used. The revolution is not in technology, but in the social relations of warfare (Kaldor, 2001).

Kaldor agrees with fourth generation proponents that whereas the objective of traditional war was the capture of territory by military means, the new type of warfare aims at the political control of population. But control is based on identity politics, or a claim to power on the basis of a particular identity. The new warriors establish political control through allegiance to a label (Serb) rather than an idea (Marxism) and the implementation of the idea (Kaldor, 2001:6, 98). As opposed to the commonly cited objective of the Vietnam conflict, however, of "winning hearts and minds," the new warfare, as in Bosnia or Iraq, often uses techniques of destabilization, sowing fear and hatred to destroy those with different identities. It relies on mass killing, ethnic cleansing, and rendering an area uninhabitable. Kaldor's new war can be seen as a subcategory of fourth generation war, requiring the flexibility of fourth generation forces. Its reliance on destruction and identity make a successful counterinsurgency response more difficult, but possible, as Iraq has demonstrated.

The promoters of fourth generation war maintain only that the ability to fight this kind of war should be one tool that the United States needs to have available, and that such an approach will be required from time to time. Nobody believes that conventional forces or approaches should be abandoned entirely. Traditional adversaries such as China and Russia require that readiness for conventional warfare be maintained. But even preparation for conflict with traditional enemies, requires that concessions to fourth generation methods be made, in order to improve effectiveness of the US military in the wars requiring a counterinsurgency response.. Since no power wants to confront the United States on the conventional battlefield, even the type of war waged by China would require a more fourth generation approach. Cyber attacks, urban guerrilla warfare, and financial terrorism are techniques that China may see as appropriate, since they play to its strengths instead of its weaknesses (Hammes, 2006:257–60).

CHAPTER 2

AMERICAN POLICIES: ORIGINS AND OBJECTIVES

> There exists today an enormous divide between the values of the
> United States and those of many other parts of the world, reminiscent
> of some of the worst religious schisms in history.
>
> Leslie Gelb

Following independence and for 30 years thereafter, the foreign policy
preoccupation of the United States was protecting its shipping from pre-
dation by the British and the French. Weak militarily and lacking a navy
that could compete with European powers, far from following a policy
of voluntary isolation, the United States was involved in an endless effort
to find a formula whereby both France and Britain could be placated. In
1793 President Washington issued a neutrality proclamation declaring US
neutrality between the two powers. After numerous other negotiations and
agreements with Britain and France, an undeclared war with France, and
a war with the Barbary states, the War of 1812 with England provided
some resolution to the shipping problems, and the United States could
begin concentrating on continental expansion (Papp et al., 2004). For most
of the nineteenth century, the United States was occupied with continental
affairs, and as Henry Kissinger noted, for most of the first 150 years was
not integrated into the European balance of power system (Kissinger,
1994:20). Spain was weak and did not threaten the United States in
1898 when it declared war on Spain, seizing Cuba and the Philippines
in the process. The luxury of not being concerned with interference from
the more powerful states from Europe was to a great extent the result of the
informal but effective shield provided to the United States and its navy by
the British fleet and British diplomacy (Kennan, 1951:11). But the need to

reunite the union, the reaction to industrialization and the growing feeling of identity as a chosen people all matched the growing material power of the United States and created the imperial temptation that emerged in the war with Spain in 1898. According to one historian, militarist fantasy "runs like a red thread " from the Civil War to WWI, "surfacing in postwar desires to re-create conditions for heroic struggle, coalescing in the imperialist crusades of 1898, overreaching itself in the Great War and subsiding (temporarily) thereafter." These chosen Americans, said Senator Albert Beveridge, were henceforth to lead in the regeneration of the world. Theodore Roosevelt salivated for opportunities to expand US power overseas, and Woodrow Wilson was a master of melding principle and opportunity in foreign policy. After McKinley's assassination in September 1901, Roosevelt became president and continued the war in the Philippines, and the United States' active role in the rest of Asia. He also supported an active US role in Latin America with crises over Venezuela and the sponsorship of Panamanian independence. As the century began, the founders' emphasis on restraint in foreign policy had a less and less receptive audience (Lears, 2009). Roosevelt's realist policies and Wilson's idealistic aggressiveness greatly expanded the US role in the world. But in early twentieth century, the Americans showed that they were not yet fully ready for the leadership role that Roosevelt and Wilson and the country's newfound power bestowed on them (Nolan, 2006).

REALISM, IDEALISM, AND NEOCONSERVATISM

The balance of power system has long been controversial. Starting with the charge that there is no agreed definition of the term, opinions range from the belief that it is a figment of the imagination to those who believe it is an indispensable concept for understanding international politics (Waltz, 1979). The classical realists, such as Thucydides, Machiavelli, Kennan, and Hans Morgenthau held that in a system of anarchy lacking an effective central authority, the resulting struggle for power among the national units to ensure their survival would dominate all other concerns of nation-states. The result of this struggle for power would be determined by the material capabilities of the states and the skills and diplomacy of the leadership. The pursuit of interests defined as power displaces and predicts other more peripheral concerns. The ideology and morality of the statesmen, and the populace, including international law, is situational, that is, it is determined by the struggle for power and the needs of survival. The source of the struggle for power and the competitive nature of the system are, according to Morgenthau, human nature and the competitive drive for survival (Morgenthau, 1967).

Kenneth Waltz built his neorealist system on elements of classical realism, but he focused on the system level of international politics rather than the nation-state at the unit level (Waltz, 1979). He posited a group of units or states all struggling to survive in an anarchical system, resulting in an equilibrium or balance of power. The motivating force was not human nature, but the need for survival in a system where only self-help is available to ensure that survival. His theory is explained at the systemic level rather than at the state or individual level as in the case of Morgenthau's reductionist explanation. This neorealist emphasis on rationalism and parsimony, however, tends to slight unit-level factors, such as nationalist reactions to invasion, that have played a big role in the US difficulties in Iraq (Schmidt and Williams, 2008). Since all units seek to survive, they emulate those characteristics of other units that facilitate survival. All units therefore tend to resemble each other as each unit adapts the practices and characteristics that are favorable to survival.. Although neorealism's systemic focus is parsimonious as well as more conducive to theory building, its predictive capability as to the content of a state's foreign policy is probably inferior, since "much of the daily stuff of international relations is left to be accounted for by theories of foreign policy."

Offensive realists such as John Mearsheimer assume that the system leads states constantly to attempt to aggrandize and accumulate power (Mearsheimer, 2001). This question, whether states seek to maximize power or simply maintain the status quo in order to ensure their survival is one that Waltz is ambiguous on, and Morgenthau is usually seen as a power maximizer. Stephen Walt however, believes that the concept of the balance of power is too limiting. According to him, nations balance against threats, not just against power. "Threats, not power alone, are crucial." The most important aspect of the modification to focus on balance-of-threat is that the idea of threat allows the inclusion and calculation of opponents' intentions, not just capabilities. As Walt says, "States balance against the states that pose the greatest threat, and the latter need not be the most powerful states in the system" (Walt, 1987:vii, 263).

Neoclassical realism allows incorporation of unit-level explanations, in addition to systemic-level explanations, thereby enhancing understanding of foreign policy. Neoclassical realist theories are theories of foreign policy that treat the state as an intervening variable between the international system and foreign policy, eliminating the black-box treatment of the state in neorealism. The foreign policy executive is "Janus-faced," existing at the intersection of the international and the domestic. Threats can originate on either the systemic level or the domestic level. Neoclassical realism can account for how policy makers perceive data, which, as Jervis notes, is influenced not only by their cognitive structure and theories about other actors, but also by what they are concerned about at the time they receive the data. Misidentification of the enemy can lead to "inappropriate balancing," as occurred in the case of the United States vis-à-vis Iraq in 2003. Analysis at the state level allows the incorporation of additional data that improves understanding of foreign policy interventions (Rose, 1998; Lobell et al., 2009). Realism was once a doctrine stipulating that countries acted to balance against aggression in order to survive, while increasingly countries act in response to concrete incentives, because they gain more or lose less by taking certain actions. Countries, in time of danger, can choose strategies of waiting, balancing, or bandwagoning. The increasing availability of variable-sum games, as exemplified in the opportunity to join an institution, "induce[s] more cooperative responses . . . as balancing becomes less likely and less frequent" (Rosecrance, 2001).

It is a mistake, I believe, to suppose as one analyst has, that neoconservatism is closer to realism than to Wilsonian idealism (Rathbun, 2008). Both neoconservatists and Wilsonian liberal idealists tend to be more willing to use force than realists, in the pursuit of ideals that both schools believe other peoples and countries should have the privilege of enjoying, just as have Americans. Both Wilson and George W. Bush believed that there is a natural harmony of interest and belief between the United States and whichever country they happen to be intervening in at the moment. The Iraqis would welcome the United States with flowers, since both Americans and Iraqis realized that democracy is the preferable system, and both sets of peoples would welcome the overthrow of a gruesome tyrant like Saddam. Both groups believed that in the urgent circumstance of dealing with a Saddam, Goldwater's old slogan was appropriate and justified: extremism in the defense of liberty is no vice. The realist is more likely to show restraint in the use of force, unless there is a definite threat to the balance of power or a similar security menace. As Rathbun notes, neoconservatives draw on nationalism, while Wilsonian idealists are more likely to stress the ideal of democracy or liberation, but they both believe that the result of the intervention benefits both the United States and the target country, and possibly all mankind. Many of the basic tenets ascribed to the neoconservative worldview—a grand strategy of primacy, antipathy to the balance of power, a view of American omnipotence, and leadership as a prerequisite for an orderly and peaceful world—can also be found among the assumptions of the liberal idealists. Their common worldview is confirmed by the fact that, as noted in the chapter on Iraq, a sizeable number of liberals supported the neoconservative attack on Iraq. It is also well to remember that, contrary to the view that the neoconservatives are necessarily situated on the conservative end of the political spectrum, as Rathbun maintains, many of them started out as liberal democrats on domestic policy, and some still remain there. The main difference between the Wilsonians and the neoconservatives lies in the somewhat greater affinity of the former for respecting democratic processes and building institutions, and the proclivity of the latter for relying on power and resolve. In either case, the "sour skepticism" of the realists, who, in Krauthammer's words, offer "no vision beyond power," is incompatible with both outlooks. The neoconservatives "draw on the Wilsonian tradition of internationalism and universalism" (Schmidt and William, 2008; Rathbun, 2008). And whereas realists generally believe balancing is the inevitable result of the search for survival among nations, both the neoconservatives and the Wilsonians believe others will join their side, or bandwagon. In Wilsonian reasoning, this is because of the attraction of the ideal or institution to the target country, in the neoconservative view, because that country wants to be on the winning side. One commentary caught this commonality perfectly: "Wolfowitz and Richard Perle . . . the press often referred to as neoconservatives, but they might be more accurately called democratic imperialists." While many of Bush's advisers might more accurately have been tagged as assertive nationalists, after 9/11 the preferences of the neoconservatives carried the day (Daalder and Lindsay, 2003:46). According to Charles Krauthammer, National Security Advisor Rice, Vice President Cheney, Secretary of Defense Rumsfeld, and President Bush could be considered practitioners of neoconservatism (Schmidt and Williams, 2008). The Bush doctrine is a product of American exceptionalism. It is unique to the United States and was hatched in America, but it is also justified by foreign policy elites as an American offering that is a unique and beneficial happenstance, benefiting both the giver and the recipient.

STRATEGIES OF CONTAINMENT

Realist assumptions have driven but have not monopolized the shaping of cold war foreign policy after the end of WWII. The breakout of the cold war raised fears in the West about the security and stability of the status quo in light of the nature of the Soviet regime and the increasing divergence between Moscow and the American leadership. Whereas Roosevelt negotiated on the basis of both a degree of optimism about Soviet intentions concomitant with the necessity of reaching some kind of agreement on Eastern Europe and other issues, Truman was increasingly confronted with the growing obstinacy and deviant views of Moscow on the postwar order. These developments in turn stimulated the development of, in John Gaddis' words, "strategies of containment" that would have the objective of frustrating Soviet aggressiveness.

The original concept of containment came from George F. Kennan, a foreign service officer stationed in Moscow and author of the long telegram "The Sources of Soviet Conduct," and was later fleshed out with numerous Kennan speeches and memoranda. The uniqueness of Kennan's approach, in addition to a heavy emphasis on a political as opposed to a military approach to containment, was the selectivity in his choice of points at which the Soviets should be confronted.[1] He favored concentrating on "strong points," or those industrial areas where the West could strengthen "natural forces of resistance." In other words, selectivity of effort was the key. Promiscuous attention to peripheral areas should be avoided since it would sap the resources and effort that should be focused on vital points elsewhere. Kennan listed three criteria for choosing these points, criteria that would be too often disregarded in the coming decades: (1) Are there are any local forces of resistance worth strengthening? (2) What is the importance of the challenged areas to our own security? And (3) What are the probable costs of our action and their relation to the results to be achieved? It was indicative of the temper of the times that such a discriminatory approach was considered plausible in the late 1940s. The possibility that China might follow in Tito's footsteps was widely discussed at the State Department and at the embassy in Moscow. Secretary of State Dean Acheson told the senate foreign relations committee in March 1950 that the United States was concerned that "whoever runs China, even if the devil himself runs China, that he is an independent devil." Truman remarked favorably on the idea of recognizing communist China (Gaddis, 2005:39, 68, 100). In any case, the atmosphere changed radically with the outbreak of the Korean War and the promulgation of NSC-68 in 1950. NSC-68 approached containment with a more military orientation and less discrimination in the distribution of resources and the setting of priorities. In Gaddis' words, "nowhere did [NSC-68] set out the minimum requirements necessary to secure [the fundamental interests of balance of power, diversity, and freedom]. Instead it found in the simple presence of a Soviet threat sufficient cause to deem the interest threatened vital" (Gaddis, 2005:96).

Kennan supported Truman's response to Korea, although he was probably as surprised as most other policy makers by the attack. US policy makers were worried about either a Soviet nuclear attack on the United States, or an attack on Western Europe. They were not prepared for a Korea-like attack and had several times ruled Korea outside the US defense perimeter. Once the attack occurred, a case for a US security interest certainly could be made, for example, the vulnerability of Japan to a communist-occupied Korea. But the Truman administration mostly justified the war on the basis of traditional American values and principles rather than interests, law rather than power (Kissinger, 1994). What Kennan did not support was the first clear violation of the whole tenor of his containment policy, the decision to push north above the thirty-eighth parallel after the West's equilibrium had been regained following the shock of the entry of the Chinese into the war. Once the Chinese came into the war and U.N. troops had been pushed deep into the southern reaches of the peninsula, Kennan, in conjunction with Acheson and the rest of the government, resisted suggestions from both the Congress and some in the executive branch that entry into the war had been a mistake and the best path now was complete withdrawal. The attempt to extend the war to conquer the territory north of the thirty-eighth, not controlled *ante bellum*, however, proved to be a harbinger of the later expansion of containment policy with developments in Vietnam.

The restraint on such thinking should be Kennan's more straightforward and direct method for formulating policy, one based on defense priorities, not primarily on the availability of budget resources. Raising the first question in relation to Vietnam as early as the mid-1950, let alone 1963, would have highlighted serious doubts about the wisdom of intervention. There was not and had never been a government in South Vietnam that showed any promise of possessing a social base, governmental competence, or nationalist credentials that could serve as a focal point of resistance to the north or the insurgency movement in South Vietnam. US involvement in Vietnam was replacing the "strongpoint" policy with the "perimeter" policy.

The policy trends of the Vietnam period manifest another trait, already visible in American foreign policy, but one that would be driven to extremes during Vietnam. Credibility and reputation as criteria for formulating US foreign policy have long been important. Credibility was needed not only to deter potential aggressors, but to reassure friends as well. The discernment of credibility in a foreign policy lies in a cognitive process, and the finding of its presence or absence is necessarily subjective. But credibility has been an important basis for evaluating US foreign policy throughout the post-WWII period (McMahon, 1991). Its importance was magnified by the focus of the perimeter policy. When all geographical points are of equal importance and not differentiated by their intrinsic value to security, then one's credibility in defending all of them becomes the measure of resolve in foreign policy. There are no longer obvious criteria that mark certain points (western Europe) as clear priorities that will be defended. As Robert Jervis notes, "small issues will often loom large, not because of their intrinsic importance, but because they are taken as tests of resolve" (McMahon, 1991). This process of transformation of policy was well underway under Truman. His justification of intervention in Korea on world order criteria rather than national interests was accompanied by a change in Truman's rhetorical tone, shifting from the original more discriminatory approach up to 1948 to the more strident tone and comprehensive approach used thereafter, the better to rally public opinion behind the president (Macdonald, 1991). Eisenhower also relied heavily on the psychological value of showing resolve, and preserving reputation and credibility in formulating his policy of defending Quemoy and Matsu, to the point that Robert Bowie, director of state's policy planning bureau noted that stressing so heavily the value of defending islands lacking intrinsic security value threatened to discredit Eisenhower with his allies since the policy suggested he was reckless and lacked perspective on the relationship between the possible costs of the policy and the relatively minor security value of the islands (McMahon, 1991).[2]

Concern with credibility, which McMahon believes was magnified by both the advent of nuclear weapons and the bipolar nature of the international system, reached "obsessive heights in the case of Vietnam," overshadowing most other policy concerns. "I was as sure as a man could be that if we did not live up to our commitment in Southeast Asia and elsewhere," Johnson wrote in his memoirs, Moscow and Beijing "would move to exploit the disarray in the United States and in the alliances of the Free World." The point here is not that reputation or credibility is never important, although it has been shown to be less important than many imagine (Mercer, 1996). Rather, the importance of this psychological factor must be evaluated in each specific case and in the overall context of a foreign policy environment.

There was little direct military intervention under President Eisenhower. A short-term foray into Lebanon in 1958 came to little. Despite the extreme rhetoric of John Foster Dulles promising a rollback of communism, Eisenhower skillfully ensured that his administration restrained itself militarily to looking after major interests (Brown, 1994). He made sure that the United States did not commit more than material resources to the French cause in Indochina, and even those fell far short of the requests the French made prior to the defeat at Dien Bien Phu. Dulles' rhetoric did encourage hope of rollback in the east bloc, and some accused Dulles of giving false hope to the Hungarians in 1956 and encouraging unnecessary loss of human life. As Paul Nitze, Kennan's successor at policy planning at the State Department, realized, however, there were political advantages from rhetoric suggesting the creation of a better world, not just the mundane duties of repelling invasion. Eisenhower proved to be a master of combining sensible policy with politically salable pronouncements. Eisenhower himself stated that "there is no weapon too small, no arena too remote, to be ignored there is no free nation too humble to be forgotten."

A restrained military policy, continued support for Tito, and even sensitivity to the potential of Sino-Soviet differences, however, continued to be operable, despite the nationalistic and idealistic rhetoric of liberation and brinksmanship (Gaddis, 2005:128–29,166).[3]

Kennedy's negotiation of an atmospheric test ban treaty with the Russians in 1963 signaled a relaxation of the most extreme cold war tensions and laid the groundwork for more conciliatory relations that would develop into détente. Vietnam, however, loosened the restrictions that containment, as originally interpreted, had imposed. It represented the triumph of the principle of promiscuous intervention efforts aimed at protecting a weak country bordering China, the one country where, after Korea, almost nobody wanted to fight. Gaddis argues that it was Kennedy's policy of flexible response that put Vietnam on the agenda and allowed expansion of the principles of containment to include it. Flexible response was based on the theories of liberal economists that more economic resources were available, combined with the idea that the necessary military reaction to any given situation could be calculated and calibrated to provide the resources and response necessary to deal with the problem presented by the enemy. It represented a departure from the philosophy worked out by Eisenhower and John Foster Dulles that reliance on nuclear weapons for deterrence of the Soviet threat would allow more bang for the buck, thus allowing the containment of the Soviets without bankrupting the country. The advantage of this arrangement was, according to Gaddis, that it put limits on the resources available for defense, but it also reduced flexibility and narrowly dictated the nature of the "New Look" in defense strategy (Gaddis, 2005). This interpretation has merit, but it makes the policy maker a captive of the defense budget, or rather it implies that if he is released from the straitjacket of resource restraints there is no way of restraining policy and ensuring appropriate policy. The significance attached to Vietnam, exacerbated by idealistic sentiments and the personality of Lyndon Johnson, was "out of all proportion" to its strategic significance.

As a result of the disaster of Vietnam, an abrupt return to realism was engineered, ironically, by Richard Nixon, the president who in an earlier incarnation had been a fire-breathing anticommunist and facilitator of Joseph McCarthy's excesses. Nixon's turnabout was complete, however, as he opened relations with the People's Republic of China, reversing two decades of recognizing the Guomindang rather than the communists. This major revamping of American policy minimized ideology and catered to power, pitting Beijing against Moscow and introducing what Nixon and Kissinger conceived of as a five-way balance between China, the Soviet Union, the European Union, Japan, and the United States. Nixon eventually withdrew American forces from Vietnam, precipitating the fall of the

Saigon regime and a communist takeover, although some actions of the Nixon government, such as support for the overthrow of an elected Marxist government in Chile, failed to fit the amoral precepts of realism.

Carter and Reagan both restored the crusader flavor to American policy. Carter promoted human rights but reemphasized the realist agenda after the Soviet invasion of Afghanistan. Reagan instituted a new nationalist push in foreign policy, promoting aggressive policy against both the Soviet Union and numerous small and politically impotent countries such as Grenada and Nicaragua. Like Eisenhower, however, he had the good sense, with the exception of the bombing of US troops in Lebanon, to limit the militancy to rhetoric. Not only did he avoid significant direct interventions through two terms, his negotiations with Gorbachev paved the way for the end of the cold war, thus ending the bipolar system and preparing the way for a completely new international framework with a dominant United States.

STRATEGIES IN THE POST–COLD WAR WORLD

The collapse of the Soviet Union and the end of the bipolar international system had a major impact on the sole remaining superpower and important implications for its foreign policy. The United States became the dominant power in a unipolar system, although it did not exercise hegemony over other states in that system (Wilkinson, 1999). The stability of the system and how long it would persist were, and are, subjects of controversy (Kapstein and Mastanduno, 1999; Layne, 2009). Many realists, like Waltz, believe that inevitably other powers will balance against the United States (Waltz, 2000). Others believe American primacy will last indefinitely, as long as four decades (Bell, 1999; Kapstein and Mastanduno, 1999:Chapter 12). Controversy and disagreement also exist over the desirability of a unipolar system led by the United States, with positions sometimes changing over time. Compare, for instance, Huntington's early enthusiasm for American dominance with his later more restrained view (Huntington, 1993; 1999).

The end of the cold war led to significant new criticism of realism, not least for its inability to predict a major event such as the end of the cold war. Criticisms previously made against realism became more credible with new shifts in priorities and interests of states. The lessening of military tension among the great powers, the increased priority given to economic issues, and the increasing complexity of the international system seemed to validate Robert Keohane's earlier contention that states' perceptions of their interests and how their objectives should be pursued "depend not merely on national interests and the distribution of world power, but on the quantity, quality, and distribution of information" (Keohane, 1984:245). As the twentieth century melded into the twenty-first, it was obvious to many that both realism and, some said, liberalism needed to be supplemented with either mergers or new ideas. There were calls for moving beyond the confines of realism and liberalism with a "reconstructed theory" that integrates the "most relevant features" of both traditions, or, alternatively, construction of an "altogether different theoretical framework that transcends" both schools (Kegley, 1995:17; Brown, 1992).

One indicator of the questioning of realism was the end of the cold war, leading to charges that realism was ineffective in both predicting and explaining the cold war. One topic of contention, among many others, was whether the demise of the Soviet Union could best be explained by structural changes, declining Soviet capabilities and intense competition from the United States, or a more constructivist explanation focusing on the new thinking and new leadership represented by Gorbachev (Wohlforth, 1994–95; Lebow and Risse-Kappen, 1995). Of more importance, however, was what stance the United States should take toward the world now that the cold war had ended and the main opponent had disintegrated. For the first time in more than 50 years the United States was without a major opponent, but it was by far the largest great power economically and in conventional military capabilities. The cold war, which had been a staple of political debate, and often, partisan and ideological contention, had disappeared.

In a world where America enjoyed overwhelming power and was without a major opponent, it is not surprising that a broad range of advice was offered by scholars and officials regarding the preferred foreign policy for the United States. On the one hand were those advocating US "primacy" or maintenance of the unipolar system, what Chris Layne calls "preponderance." Such a preference would prolong the "unipolar moment," continuing close US involvement in traditional relationships or alliances in Europe, Asia, and the Middle East (Krauthammer, 1990–91). It sought to dissuade or at least delay a challenger from arising, and preserve close US political, economic, and military involvement around the world.

On the other end of the spectrum, some believed that the end of the cold war called for a sharp reduction in both US military involvement abroad and sharp reductions in defense spending. While the cold war was worth fighting, America's objectives were now best achieved by implementing a foreign policy of restraint. In an article entitled "Come Home, America," the authors stated that now that the cold war is over, "George McGovern is right" (Gholz et al., 1997). The authors foresaw a withdrawal from both Europe and Asia, leaving US allies to fend for themselves. This lessened responsibility would include withdrawal of a nuclear umbrella from allies. Encouraging responsibility for their own fate and security needs on the part of friends and allies would result in more cautious, responsible behavior. Layne's preferred strategy of "off-shore balancing" would involve a similar withdrawal of responsibility of support for friends and allies, except in the event of the rise of a hegemon that threatened American security and that would trigger US balancing against that power. This stance would recognize the lack of interdependence between the United States and the rest of the world. Extended deterrence would be discredited and there would be recognition that nuclear proliferation is inevitable.

Almost all foreign policy decisions are made in the context of both security and idealism, and the motivations, issues, and propaganda are all so intertwined as to make separation of the themes, causes, and consequences impossible. In the less constrained post–cold war world, however, the prevalence of the old "liberal internationalist" center that so often provided the pattern for cold war foreign policy appears to be a victim of the increasing polarization of American politics and to suggest a policy of selective engagement may be preferable to the older more robust form of involvement (Kupchan and Trubowitz, 2007). The Clinton administration, coming to power after the end of the cold war, by default put more emphasis on the developing world, away from the core of the industrialized/great power countries and back toward the periphery. Many scholars professed confusion about what administration priorities were after the cold war, others believed there was a great deal of continuity (Mastanduno, 1997). Clinton did little to disturb the basic outlines of alliance politics and relations with the developed world. The alliance with Japan was actually revised and strengthened, while NATO was expanded. But connected with the gravitation of policy emphasis toward the developing world was greater stress on idealism or liberal internationalism. There was more emphasis on economics and human rights, ethnic conflict, and international crime, but especially on engagement and the promotion of democracy in the developing world.

Clinton continued the occupation of Somalia, originally started by the George H. W. Bush administration as a humanitarian relief mission, intervened in Haiti, and later lamented the failure of the United States to intervene in Rwanda, where at least 800,000 died in a civil war. The Clinton administration's intervention in Bosnia followed four years of dithering and procrastination. Absent the Russian threat, there was doubt that a national security threat justified intervention. Moreover, public opinion was ambivalent and leery of any humanitarian intervention, still reflecting the influence of Vietnam. It was only a confluence of factors that led to action: a belated consensus developed between the United States and the Europeans on a plan to intervene and an agreement that something had to be done to end the violence and preserve NATO's credibility, domestic pressures on Clinton at home, the arming and military action of the Croats that showed the Serbs to be an ineffective force, and ill-timed Serbian attacks in Sarajevo, that set the stage for action. Once the decision to undertake serious military action was taken, it was a short distance to arriving at a military equilibrium that brought all sides to the negotiating table and a short period of intense negotiation with and pressure on the parties at the table that resulted in a settlement and ended the violence.

The George W. Bush administration came into office with a blandly orthodox realist agenda, lamenting the "foreign policy as social work" orientation of the Clinton people (Rice, 2000; Rathbun, 2008). Bush stressed the low-profile character of his policies by declaring a preference for a "humble" foreign policy that would respect friends and allies. The events of 9/11 overturned these intentions and ushered in one of the most assertive of US foreign policies in modern history, perhaps in all of American history. Bush's national security guidance suggested three areas where the new policy would be different. The United States would reserve the right to take action to (1) preempt the threat of attack from a foe, (2) it would reserve the right to take unilateral action without consultation with allies when necessary, and (3) it would work to prevent the emergence of a competitor in the international system. The Bush rhetoric contained numerous formulations suggesting a utopian perspective on international relations—a promise to rid the world of evil, and to maintain a "balance of power that favors freedom" (White House, 2002). Moreover, the spread of freedom was a central principle of the administration. As Bush said, "the defense of freedom requires the advance of freedom" (Joffe, 2006:55). The Bush administration in effect formulated a revolution in American foreign policy that alienated allies—both Germany and France opposed the intervention in Iraq—and the Arab world, led to ineptly handled interventions in both Afghanistan and Iraq that, nearly a decade later, have bogged the Americans down in two wars where the eventual outcome is uncertain.

One plausible explanation for the sudden increase in US offensives and intervention resulting in the Iraq intervention is the sudden improvement in the balance of forces in favor of the United States after the cold war, combined with the change in public opinion regarding an activist foreign policy following the shock of 9/11. Gideon Rose notes that the discrepancy between John Quincy Adam's admonition against the US going abroad "in search of monsters to destroy" as compared to the decision by Woodrow Wilson to take the United States into WWI, despite the absence of a demonstrable threat to the United States, can be explained by the change in the relative power of the United States (Rose, 1998). But this explanation is less probable than it first appears. While Clinton signed the Iraq

Liberation Act, there is no evidence he intended to implement it. As will be argued below, the impetus for the war in Iraq came from Bush and the neoconservative advisors he employed.

AMERICAN EXCEPTIONALISM AND THE NATIONAL STYLE

It would be a mistake to imagine that American foreign policy behavior can be deduced solely from hardheaded calculations of military security. An examination of American rhetoric and the justifications given for US interventions suggest that idealism played a large role in justifying, rationalizing, and motivating American intervention. American exceptionalism may refer to a style of leadership as well as ideas, but it is the content of the ideas about the United States and its policies that are most influential. American idealism, American beliefs about their exceptional role in the world, does not always translate directly into policy, metamorphosing directly from the values of a policy maker. Rather it suffuses the environment, turning up to influence events in unexpected ways. Perhaps the most common mode of influence is its use by decision makers to mobilize and influence public opinion. Or, conversely, it may push elites in directions they were previously hesitant to go. When security issues are claimed as motivation for an intervention, liberal ideals may well play a back-up role in policy formulation, but the line between them is fuzzy and ever shifting. The shape of the role ideals play is often amorphous, but as Weisberg, Kissinger, and others have noted, it is hard to conduct US foreign policy without the overlay of idealism.

Most official pronouncements on US interventions conflate realist concerns and moral and idealistic positions. During the interventions in Vietnam and Iraq, in particular, both security objectives and moral goals were claimed, often in the same paragraph if not in the same sentence. A particularly flamboyant example during the 1991 Gulf War justified the war as a means of stopping aggression, but also added the moral judgment that Saddam Hussein was the equivalent of Hitler, thereby justifying action against him. This melding of foreign policy objectives fits particularly well with neoconservative pronouncements since their philosophy explicitly melds a strong nationalism and commitment to American institutions such as democracy with national security objectives (Rathbun, 2008).[4] Robert Kagan has shown that American meliorism and aggressiveness was not something that appeared only after the civil war, as some have suggested. Contrary to the myths of isolationism and notwithstanding the supposedly restrained policies advocated by Washington, Jefferson, or Franklin, Americans from the beginning were "territorial imperialists," and this tendency was especially pronounced regarding the Indians (Kagan,

2006; McDougall, 1997). Arthur Schlesinger believed that in the United States debates over foreign policy respond to an old argument between experiment and destiny. The founders adhered to a historical, empirical approach to the world, but as the nation became stronger and more secure, Americans occasionally veered off toward theology, ideology, and a susceptibility to the dogma of American destiny. There is much truth to this interpretation; nonetheless it is true that from the beginning the founding fathers grounded the declaration of independence in the assumption that the nation and its citizens were endowed with natural rights grounded in natural law. This assumption provided credibility for the expansion of ideas about national destiny as the nation matured and indulged romantic speculation, the notion that there is a "reality behind that which we can see, a world of truths that can't be inferred from observation or reason (Schlesinger, 1986:51; Fogarty, 2009:51). The concept of American exceptionalism, or more precisely, a new interpretation of American exceptionalism, played an important part in this change. Henry Kissinger, possibly because of his own European background, has perceptively noted the central place in American foreign policy thinking of Woodrow Wilson's ideas of self-determination, democracy, peace, and escape from the mundane bargaining and adjustments of power politics. Critics have attacked Wilson's critiques and conclusions for three generations, yet, during all this time Wilson's principles "have remained the bedrock" of US foreign policy thinking (Kissinger, 1994:52). Wilsonian ideals permeate US rhetoric and US behavior. As noted above, it becomes difficult to mobilize the American populace for any significant foreign policy action without the use of this language. As G. K. Chesterton said, America is "the only nation in the world that is founded on a creed," a creed set forth in the Declaration of Independence (Lipset, 1996:31). The unifying factor is the unique experience and location, the absence of a feudal history and geographical isolation from Europe because of the Atlantic Ocean, and the universal acceptance of a liberal outlook as a result of that experience (Lipset, 1996; Hartz, 1955). Many powerful nations and empires have demonstrated a belief that they have an obligation to improve the world according to their own values. But America stands out as one country where this tendency has been particularly noticeable (Brands, 1998). Americans, receiving their foreign policy guidance from their ideals and not from history, do not realize how difficult it is to shed the "burning garment" of history that clings to them (Hoffmann, 1968a:363). These liberal values, asserting that the same ethical principles that apply to individual behavior are also obligatory in international conduct, are revolutionary and unsettling beyond what most Americans, taking these values for granted, imagine (Kissinger, 1994:22). Americans have tremendous pride and confidence in their culture and social system. In the mid-1990s, 75 percent of Americans said they were proud to be Americans, while only 54 percent in Britain, 20 percent in West Germany, and 35 percent in France answered affirmatively. Among youth, 98 percent of Americans reported being proud of their nationality, compared to 58 percent for Britain, 65 percent for Germany, and 80 percent in France. A 2002 report on a survey of travel abroad in the past 5 years indicated that only 22 percent of Americans had done so, compared to 66 percent of Canadians, 73 percent of Britons, 60 percent of French, and 77 percent of Germans. It also reported that only 26 percent of Americans said they were following foreign news closely and 45 percent said international events did not affect them (Pei, 2003).[5]

Americans consistently stand out as more religious than people in other developed countries. Americans are "utopian moralists who press hard to institutionalize virtue, to destroy evil people, and eliminate wicked institutions and practices." Surveys measuring whether moral values are absolute or relative showed that Americans, agreeing with the Bush quote below, believe they are absolute by much larger numbers than Europeans or the Japanese. Those believing in absolute as opposed to circumstantial morality in the United States, 50 percent, contrasted with 19 percent expressing the same belief in Sweden. (Lipset, 1996:51, 60–64). This confidence that they understand morality and have the duty to promote it, necessarily forces leaders to justify conflict and wars abroad in moralistic terms, which means that such causes, once started, have a tendency to develop a momentum of their own, are hard to stop, and make it difficult to negotiate compromises.[6] There is a long line of "foreign contagions that washed up on the shores of liberty," of which abolition was one of the first. From the first days of existence in the new world, "Europe was the source of corruption—of heresy, tyranny, immorality. The city on a hill had lit a beacon for Europe; but the incorrigible old world kept threatening to extinguish the American experiment" (Morone, 2003:185).

While it was Theodore Roosevelt who advocated "muscular diplomacy" and insisted it was "America's duty to make its influence felt globally," it was Woodrow Wilson who cloaked that new muscular foreign policy in the ideals of American exceptionalism, an innovation that has outlasted Roosevelt's influence and become the bedrock of America's position in the world (Kissinger, 1994). Wilson insisted that nations should follow principles of the highest moral order, and he expressed his views in the most direct way. For Wilson, "truth was truth and justice, justice; and there was no need to modify their expression to suit any man" (George and George, 1964:232). The keystone of Wilsonianism has been described as "democratic government built on strong foundations of national self-determination" (Ikenberry et al., 2009:97). Although Wilson insisted that true Americans should think

of themselves and behave as individuals, yet he was contemptuous of acting in favor of self-interest in international relations. The United States, he
insisted, was founded for the benefit of humanity. As he told the daughters
of the American Revolution in 1916:

> No other nation was ever born into this world with the purpose of serv-
> ing the rest of the world just as much as it served itself. . . . And the only
> excuse that America can ever have for the assertion of physical force is
> that she asserts it in behalf of the interest of humanity. . . . When America
> ceases to be unselfish, she will cease to be America. . . . We are the cham-
> pions of the rights of mankind. . . .
>
> Robinson and West, 1917:315–16, 329

Perhaps it was this sort of utterance that de Tocqueville had in mind
when he lamented that among the Americans "one cannot imagine a
more disagreeable and talkative patriotism. It fatigues even whose [*sic*—
those] who honor it" (de Tocqueville, 2002:585). Wilson could speak for
Americans because there was an unusual agreement on values, and on
America's role in the world. Even in the 1960s, a time of relative divisiveness and rancor, a Canadian scholar visiting the United States found an
emphasis on national consensus, a national myth that was "invest [ed]
with all the moral and emotional appeal of a religious symbol." And this
in a country with arbitrary frontiers and a bewildering mixture of race
and creed (Lipset, 1996:290–92). But, we should also remember that in
all the major wars the Americans have been involved in, with the partial
exception of WWII, there has been substantial opposition and dissent.

Wilson's high ideals did not deter him, however, from foreign policy
actions that mere mortals   might mistake for the mundane pursuit of
a national interest. After his government had shelled and captured the
Mexican city of Veracruz following the arrest of some American soldiers
in Mexico, for which the Mexican government had offered an apology,
Wilson justified the action by citing the "high doctrine of the Virginia bill
of rights," that a government is instituted for the protection and benefit
of the people, nation, or community. If a government behaves contrary
to these purposes, Wilson said, then a majority of the community has a
right to "reform, alter or abolish it." Stated Wilson, we have "unhesitat-
ingly applied that heroic principle to the case of Mexico, and now hope-
fully await the rebirth of the troubled Republic" (Robinson and West,
1917:296).[7] In fairness to Wilson, according to a leading authority on him,
John Wilson Cooper, he came to regret the US use of force to help democrats in the Mexican civil war and to believe that outside force should not
be used to direct a country's internal processes (Ikenberry et al., 2009:93).

Is America's foreign policy truly exceptional or is exceptionalism a myth used to justify the foreign policy objectives and the use of force? Both are true. America is exceptional. No European country enjoys its historical isolation behind an ocean, the absence of a feudal history, and the consequent class structure. The result is an optimism and a de-emphasis on class conflict that encourages a classically liberal orientation toward the world domestically, and, at least until September 11, 2001, a sense of invulnerability in foreign affairs.[8] This optimistic liberalism encourages a belief that the gap between America's interests and those of the rest of the world is minimal.

Woodrow Wilson's elegant pronouncements were made 90 years ago, but his sentiments are still reflected in the rhetoric of American presidents. In his address at 2002 graduation at the United States military academy at West Point, George W. Bush, as have many presidents preceding or following him, made it plain that he viewed the world in the terms of American moralism and idealism. He sees a very close correspondence between the American definition of morality and the world's definition of it, and he believes the United States should lead the charge against evil. Just as Christian missionaries carried the gospel to far-flung parts of the world, so should the American government promote American ideals.[9]

> Some worry that it is somehow undiplomatic or impolite to speak the language of right and wrong. I disagree. Different circumstances require different methods, but not different moralities. Moral truth is the same in every culture, in every time, and in every place. Targeting innocent civilians for murder is always and everywhere wrong. Brutality against women is always and everywhere wrong. There can be no neutrality between justice and cruelty, between the innocent and the guilty. We are in a conflict between good and evil, and America will call evil by its name. By confronting evil and lawless regimes, we do not create a problem, we reveal a problem. And we will lead the world in opposing it (Bush, 2002a).[10]

These sentiments, and the nationalism they represent, evoked a positive response from the American public. It was only after the war in Iraq turned sour that public support suffered. This nationalist culture, and not only public ignorance, explains how the Bush administration "could transfer the anger Americans felt after 9/11 to targets which had nothing to do with that attack . . . " (Lieven, 2004:90).[11]

But on balance, idealism plays a substantial role in motivating US policy, sometimes in framing the context, sometimes in motivating more direct action. Kissinger has noted that Americans take their values so much for granted that they fail to realize how radical they appear to the rest of the world. And Robert Kagan adds: "Americans are creators of turmoil." They are seen by the Europeans as the Greeks saw the Athenians, as "incapable of either living a quiet life themselves or of allowing anyone else to do so" (Kagan, 2009). Americans are incapable of saving the world, but at the same time they can't leave it alone (Brands, 1998: 50). At the time of writing, as the competition for the 2012 Republican presidential campaign gets underway, the concept of exceptionalism has become a standard currency of the Republican contenders, hoping to profit from the electorate's view that America is exceptional, despite the battering of the US image after two costly wars and a severe economic recession (Tumulty, 2010).

It is misleading, however, to imply that US foreign policy is inevitably one that promotes change and revolutionizes societies. Racism, a key to understanding American society pre–civil war, was a conservative force in foreign policy that suggested, at best, that the United States' racial differences were inevitable and irredeemable. As Brian Fogarty points out, the United States was the first society to enshrine racism with an elaborate system of laws justifying discrimination on racial grounds (Fogarty, 2009:123). Racial discrimination was a "sine qua non if expansion was to be reconciled with liberty." If Indians had the same status as whites—if they were not discriminated against—then how could their lands be taken? To ask, in the mid-nineteenth century, whether American law, agriculture and commerce, technology, religion, and culture were superior to those of primitive aborigines would have "certified someone as mad. Was the United States superior to Mexico? The question itself would have met with hilarity" (McDougall, 1997:88).[12]

Theodore Roosevelt, Henry Cabot Lodge, and Senator Albert J. Beveridge all held racist views that legitimated, if not required, imperialist expansion (Weston, 1998). Racism was not the motive for expansion—since the Americans were just as willing to target other whites as they were willing to target Indians and Mexicans—for instance the Canadians, and Americans' own countrymen in the civil war (McDougal, 1997:87–89). But the Indians, the Chinese, and the Afro-Americans bore the brunt of racist policies and attitudes. The Asian part of WWII against the Japanese was routinely portrayed in press and on Capitol Hill as a race war. The use of derogatory slurs such as gooks and slopes in Vietnam was only the most obvious sign of continuing racial differentiation. According to one American analyst on Vietnam, "American concepts do not always fit the Oriental mind." While this assertion probably confuses culture and race, the lack of precision is disturbing. More perplexing, because of the sheer naiveté and lack of understanding of communist organizational principles, was the comment of one US official that in reacting to "internal, covert dangers" the North Vietnamese look out for themselves and "as orientals do not naturally band together to face a common danger" (FRUS, 1/19/62; 5/11/62). The careless use of "free fire zones," indiscriminant bombing and use of napalm, execution of prisoners, and massacres of civilians as at My Lai are the stuff of war, but were widely perceived as reflecting actions that would not have been taken against Europeans. Edward Said's work on representations of "the Orient" details how Western images of those in lands outside the Western industrialized world fixed them in a perceived position of inferiority that the West then proceeded to institutionalize, not least in the systems of colonialism. In this view, the outlying regions of the world had no significant life, history, or culture and no "independence or integrity worth representing without the West" (Said, 1978, 1993:xix).

INDIVIDUAL LEADERS, ETHNOCENTRISM, AND NATIONALISM

In addition to security issues and culture and ideology, another factor determining American foreign policy and decisions to intervene is the particular leader or individual who is in power in Washington. The emphasis of this study is on the content of policy and it makes no attempt to authoritatively explicate psychological factors or individual administrative styles of specific presidents and their effect on intervention. Still, it may be useful to briefly review some basic concepts that are relevant to the performance of individual presidents. The personalities, leadership styles, and individual perspectives on the world undoubtedly affect the policy emanating from any one administration.

Attempts by political scientists to construct systematic methods of explaining policy and government behavior have downplayed the role of individuals and concentrated on the international system as one level of action, and the policy of particular national governments as a second. But it is clear that throughout history and still today the idiosyncrasies of individuals, on a third level are also very important. As one study of the role of individuals put it, "had it not been for the idiosyncrasies of one man and one woman, European history would look very, very different" (Byman and Pollack, 2001:107). Although authoritarian rulers may most clearly reflect the influence of the individual since they have the greatest leeway to influence events given their relatively unlimited power within their own political system (Byman and Pollack, 2001), the US president is also very powerful in the democratic American system, especially in foreign policy. Modern presidents have an extraordinary impact on reality, because of the importance of centralized decision making, the extension of government to many areas of the life of the ordinary citizen, and structural amplification, or the use of advanced technology and communication that enables the president to carry out and influence administration of policies in a way that was not previously possible (Renshon, 1998:42–43). Robert Jervis argued that in the post–cold war world policy makers have even more influence than during the cold war, and must make more value trade-offs. The bipolarity of the cold war world and the presence of nuclear weapons made it, for all its danger, "essentially quite simple." The international environment then was "relatively compelling," and leaders could afford to be hedgehogs, whereas in the present world they must be foxes. The reference here is to Isaiah Berlin's essay suggesting that some leaders, like a fox, know many things, but the hedgehog knows one big thing (Jervis, 1994; Berlin, 1993:3). This view has merit, but US policy makers have often had much leeway for intervention under a variety of system structures. Even in the case of the cold war bipolar system, they have had the potential for imposing great costs on both the target of intervention as well as on the domestic sponsors at home in the United States, as Vietnam demonstrated.

The two leaders in these cases who most clearly and obviously put their unique imprint on their foreign policies were Lyndon Johnson and George W. Bush. These two presidents stand out because there is evidence that both had unusual personal beliefs or personalities, or both, and second, it is difficult to explain their actions without recourse to these categories. Bill Clinton's behavior in Bosnia, while perhaps reflecting his lack of interest in foreign affairs and chaotic decision-making process, can best be explained by the political realities: there were no immediate and pressing vital interests at stake, and at the time there was perceived to be a great deal of risk involved an involvement that might come to resemble the problems incurred in Somalia. Considering that George H. W. Bush declared upfront that he had no intention of getting involved in Bosnia, it is not surprising that it took Clinton four years to take significant action. President McKinley's decision also followed a trajectory that has become familiar to students of the presidency. He, and to a great extent, the nation, was perplexed about how to handle the Philippines, which they had suddenly and somewhat astonishingly acquired. He basically took the route of least resistance—followed public opinion—and opted to take control of the islands without really realizing the resistance he would meet. Johnson's motives, on the other hand, are still debated and his objectives found to be uncertain. Was it his ideological beliefs that motivated him to prosecute the war in Vietnam? Or his concern about electoral politics? Or the need to uphold the Kennedy legacy? Whatever it was, he took great risk in the face of much evidence that the war could not be won. His personality seems crucial to a full understanding of his statements and actions. In the case of Bush, we are even further from an explanation of his decision to invade

Iraq. Even considering his personality and beliefs, there are differences in interpretation of the significance of his seemingly rather narrow religious and cultural beliefs. It is puzzling what motivated him in the face of so much uncertainty about events inside Iraq and what US interests might be. In such circumstances, these attributes of his beliefs and personality clearly have to be discussed.

Perhaps significantly, both of these presidents came to office with more experience and interest in domestic than foreign affairs. Neither had traveled much. Even more damning, neither president showed much curiosity or interest in learning about foreign cultures or processes, and both showed a lack of flexibility and imagination when dealing with alternatives to the policies they ultimately became stuck with. Johnson's insistence on persisting in a deeper and deeper involvement in Vietnam in spite of a stream of staffers resigning, and amidst predictions that the war could not be "won," suggest the reaction of a rigid personality. Johnson was judged by some advisors to be interested only in the "bottom line," not the explanations and discussions that inform one about why a particular decision is preferable. His ethnocentrism showed when he once indicated his discomfort with foreigners saying only half-jokingly that "foreigners are not like the people I am used to" (Logevall, 1999:78–79).

He could not understand how Ho Chi Minh could pass up his generous offer to sponsor economic development with a TVA-type project in Vietnam in exchange for an end to the war. The intensity of the nationalism that motivated Ho—indeed the nationalist basis of the whole conflict—escaped him, since he viewed the conflict mainly in ideological terms.[13] Johnson had a tendency to personalize all issues and to conflate attacks on his policy with attacks on him personally. In so doing, it has been argued, he diminished his ability to render objective judgment on Vietnam issues and to "retain the necessary level of detachment." Further, many have noted that Johnson had a strong element of *machismo* in his worldview. He distinguished between the weak men and the strong; the strong were the doers who made things happen, who were tough and refused to back down. The weak were the "skeptics, who set around contemplating, talking, criticizing." Johnson was haunted by the fear that he would "be judged insufficiently manly for the job, that he would lack courage when the chips were down." This personal insecurity reinforced his intolerance for dissent. He early on was "incredulous" to learn that some people opposed his policy of fully supporting South Vietnam during the cold war. He believed that this was un-American (Logevall, 1999:389–95). None felt this intolerance, in the form of shunning, more than Vice President Humphrey who had dared to suggest criticisms of his president's policy. Presidential scholar Fred I. Greenstein, in comparing

Eisenhower and Johnson, found that Eisenhower had superior cognitive skills; he was able to cut through to the nub of the matter after a complex discussion. Further, he expected people to give their opinions, even if they contradicted his. And his aides did. Eisenhower put a premium on having a formal advisory system. Johnson, who lacked knowledge of foreign affairs and contacts abroad and therefore was in need of reliable analysis, had an advisory system that was a shambles (Greenstein and Burke, 1989:262–66, 293–95). None of the leaders studied in these cases were more susceptible to ethnocentrism than Lyndon Johnson and George W. Bush, and none were more in need of a clear-eyed vision for setting strategy. As Ken Booth put it, "Trying to see the world as others see it, and thereby predict their behaviour, is the central creative act in the business of strategy: this may be seriously distorted by ethnocentrism which involves seeing the other's world as we see it ourselves" (Booth, 1979:104). These presidents' policies all too often reflected the world as Americans saw it themselves.

There has been much debate over whether or not President Kennedy would or would not have responded to events in Vietnam in the same way that Lyndon Johnson did. Some have argued either that Kennedy would not have intervened with combat troops or that if he intervened he would have shown more flexibility and imagination in managing the conflict (Blight et al., 2009; Logevall, 1999; Garofano, 2002; Rosenburg, 1986). One supporting bit of evidence is that in comparing speeches and quotes on Vietnam from the two presidents, it is clear that Kennedy was more aware of and considered more carefully the developing split between China and the Soviet Union in his description of and references to the situation in the communist world (Pentagon Papers, 1971b:809, 813, 815). He appeared interested in the phenomenon as one of political philosophy, whereas Johnson showed no interest in the split at all. McNamara and Rusk, however, did appear to see Beijing as the bigger threat in Southeast Asia (Pentagon Papers, 1979:697, 714). Vietnam is an instance where a statesman's peculiar beliefs and personal style influenced the way he provided leadership and worked against what is perceived to be the interest of the government or the nation. This issue is discussed in more detail in Chapter 5.

In the case of George W. Bush, his decision to invade Iraq was based on erroneous and "cherry picked" information, questionable assumptions, and policy implementation by subordinates badly split on the issues, and on the basis of grossly inadequate planning. Reading George W. Bush's speeches on Iraq brings to mind an image of a president who believes that all foreigners have a little American zipped up inside them just waiting to pop out at the right time, perhaps just when the US military arrives to liberate them. If the United States intervenes in their country to settle some defect or problem, American policies, institutions, and values will make them happy, because we all share common values. After all, people all over the world share the same goals, preferences, and morals. Bush and Secretary of State Rice routinely criticized those who "condescended" to foreigners by suggesting they may not want or be ready for an American-style democracy, or that a preparation period may be necessary before a society adopts formal democracy. This issue is certainly a matter of debate, but to ignore the evidence and proclaim it a truism that democracy can flourish everywhere, even if transplanted by force, is certainly a questionable argument. Bush is also a born-again Christian, and he has made statements that suggest he had a special God-given mission as president to carry out his policies. This combination of his ideological crusade for democracy and his statements about God and religion give his presidency a missionary cast that many found disturbing, and suspected it plays a major role in putting blinders on the way he perceived the world. This subject is further discussed in the chapter on Iraq.

One political operative maintains that "[u]ltimately, most presidential campaigns are about character, broadly defined" (Susan Estrich quoted in Renshon, 1998:46). If what voters want is representative of what is important in a leader, then perhaps character, personality, and temperament are more important in choosing officials than their policy positions. John Foster Dulles, who had a surfeit of that peculiar American belief in the "moral excellences" of which the United States was thought by him to be possessed, was criticized by Walter Lippmann who believed that Dulles was "too noble" about American ideals and "never humble at all" about "our human, our very human, failures and faults." According to Lippmann, this alienated and outraged "those who are by national interest our friends and allies" (Craig and George, 1990:276). On the other hand, George H. W. Bush received high marks from one analyst as a president who guided the United States through a sensitive period as the cold war was winding down and helped produce a stable result conducive to US interests. He was "consistently the master of his own brief," and his personal engagement in the policy "preempted bureaucratic warfare" resulted in functional and coherent policy. Bush himself claimed to be a practical man and his personal self-assurance and extensive foreign affairs experience resulted in an administration that was pragmatic, transparent, and relatively free of jealousies and suspicions, "human frailties [that] are the norm in Washington" (Rodman, 2009:182). His main failure, perhaps, was alienation of his political base, in part because his pragmatic style and policies alienated a Republican Party that preferred a more flashy and ideological leader. People may differ on the evaluation of various leaders, but there seems no doubt that the choice of leader is important and makes a significant difference in the policy and processes that result from a given presidency. Finally, whether an intervention is efficiently and well administered and implemented has an important impact on how well the intervention succeeds. But beyond that, it may also influence whether the project is undertaken to begin with. If the government has an inadequate understanding of what is involved in an intervention, or an inadequate plan, it may take excessive risks that it would not have taken had there been a precise understanding of the risks involved in intervening.

While making decisions and then implementing them usually are interrelated and cannot be completely separated, the latter often receives much less attention than the first. As two scholars on implementation contend, a decision may be clear and centralized in terms of its declaratory purposes, but quite decentralized "in terms of its requirement for action" (Smith and Clarke, 1985). The way in which a decision is prepared and made, however, may be quite important in determining how well it is implemented. As we will see, the much remarked ineptitude in implementing the Iraq War was in no small measure related to the haphazard nature of the George W. Bush administration's initial decisions to start the war. The Eisenhower administration, however, provided striking counterexamples of decisions that were very well thought through and paved the way for smooth implementation. Meena Bose remarks on Eisenhower's many statements emphasizing the importance of organization. Other modern presidents "do not come close to matching his carefully designed advisory systems in domestic and foreign affairs" (Bose, 2006:31–32). President Kennedy is given credit for setting up procedures to derive the best possible information and a variety of opinions and preferences when dealing with the Cuban missile crisis. Kennedy put a priority on orderly and thorough decision making in the missile crisis, since the knowledge that the Soviets were installing missiles in Cuba came suddenly and required a quick decision to deal with the issue before the missiles became operational. He was also acutely aware of the need to defend his decisions in order to maintain his political viability. George H. W. Bush, because of his direct and active engagement in policy making and implementation, helped ensure that policy was coherent and consistently implemented (Rodman, 2009).

Eisenhower, deciding what the US stance should be in the case of the Hungarian uprising in 1956, had the advantage of having already considered and decided his administration's stance on John Foster Dulles' "roll back" policy. General Goodpaster links Eisenhower's response to the 1956 uprising to the results of the Solarium study done earlier on policy toward the communist bloc. The decision to abandon the liberation policy had been taken at that time (Glad and Kitts, 2006). At the time of the uprising, therefore, Eisenhower had the advantage of being familiar with the basic issues involved and having already chosen a general policy for application to such situations. He had the luxury of being able to limit direct consideration of the issue to himself and a few close advisors and to concentrate on providing readily available arguments to support his decision, arguments the experts had already looked at, in order to generate support among as broad a group of politicians and staff as possible. Fred Greenstein suggests that Eisenhower knew how to play the game of "preventive politics" (Bose, 2006). He was determined to avoid war with the Soviets, and to create support for his policies within the administration. He moved skillfully to keep the issue off the agenda—or at least delay consideration until it was too late—of the NSC and the U.N. General Assembly. Especially evocative of his ability to grasp the overall picture, and in direct contrast to the preparation for the Iraq War, was his statement: "What would we do with Russia if we should win a global war?"

CHOOSING TO INTERVENE

The balance of power and balance of threat concepts discussed above are good starting points for assessing security risks and needs. But it is necessary to move from the high level of generality represented by balance of power or balance of threat to the specifics of historical events in order to present a meaningful representation of the security situation and to specify which unique security threats might justify undertaking military intervention. Situations of all sorts may represent some sort of threat or power challenge and therefore fall under these general rubrics. Outright military action, declaratory threats, cooperation of one power with another US adversary against the United States, supplying key goods or weapons to an adversary, including nuclear proliferation, embargoing essentials (such as oil), the existence of a failed state and the possible harboring of dangerous nonstate actors, or the need to deprive an adversary of influence in a given country and many other possible actions could be perceived as security issues.[14] Obviously the threat of terrorists is now a high priority for many countries, as is dealing with the failed states that often provide a breeding ground for terrorist activity. As stated above, Richard Rosecrance suggests that increasingly, because of greater opportunities for cooperation, and especially for joining institutions, more opportunities exist for a state to pursue its interests. Therefore the range of reactions to danger increases and a greater variety of responses are available to minimize costs and optimize benefits. One scholar suggests that increasingly for US foreign policy, threats or dangers, often posed by so-called rogue states, are a matter of a lack of shared values as much as a discrepancy in perceived power capabilities (O'Reilly, 2007:298). Their variant outlooks can be viewed as a threat to the (US-led) international order and the institutions it represents. This suggests that threats are increasingly subjectively defined, may be indirect, and that their nature is diverse (Buzan, 1991; Zartman, 2005). Stanley Hoffmann goes so far as to argue that the "distinction between values and interests is largely fallacious" (Hoffmann, 1996). Realist categories and metrics are a good place to start in determining security interests, but they may need qualification or extension. The crucial requirement is that there be a full and sophisticated discussion of the pros and cons of intervention.

The tools of analysis discussed above are therefore of use in explaining US intervention in the cases discussed in this book, but also controversial. With the exception of Afghanistan in 2001, it is difficult if not impossible to make a case that in traditional military terms any of the states in question were close to equaling the power of the United States, or indeed, presented a convincing threat to it. In all of the cases except Bosnia, however, the decision makers believed there were security issues at stake. In the case of Vietnam, the Kennedy and, especially, the Johnson administration saw the loss of Vietnam as a significant threat. In the case of Iraq, the George W. Bush administration believed it presented a threat. On the other hand, if one measures power by the ability to prevail in a conflict, then the US advantage tends to disappear. Especially in the case of Vietnam, the outcome of the conflict would indicate the relative weakness of the United States.[15] Rather than pursue those issues further here, they will be dealt with in the specific sections where the arguments that were directly applicable to each case can be discussed in detail.

Military interventions can be quite costly for the intervening power. It is the most drastic and potentially most costly way of exercising influence. The United States has relations with numerous countries and non-state actors around the world. There are many ways of wielding influence in these relationships, including declarations, negotiation and diplomacy, economic means, and threats of military action. Military intervention usually signals that other means have not worked and therefore resort is being made to the potentially most costly type of intervention. It is possible that at least some other means that have not been tried are simply not appropriate. It is also possible in some cases that military action is less costly or more appropriate than other means and therefore justifies the potentially high cost. But any prudent decision maker would want to be quite certain that intervention is necessary, serves a worthwhile goal, and is the best approach, before committing troops.

Costs can be in the form of material, lives, international prestige and power, and domestic instability. In the case of an intervention, costs can be covered by one of two payers, either the intervening country or the target country. The focus in this study is on the intervening country, the United States. In many cases, however, because of differing technological capabilities, the costs to the target country are even greater than to the intervening country. The goal sought, the means used, and the costs of the resulting war will be discussed in each specific country case.[16]

CHAPTER 3

COUNTERINSURGENCY AND US ADAPTATION TO FOURTH GENERATION WAR

> Great progress has been made on the ground by our civilians and our military, who have learned to work together and have adapted in innovative ways to meet these challenges. But for every ingenious adaptation we see in the field, we should ask ourselves—what institutional failure were they trying to overcome? What tools did we fail to provide them?
>
> Ambassador Eric S. Edelman
> US Undersecretary of Defense for Policy

What is often called the American style of war presumes a superiority of material and is based on a strategy of attrition rather than maneuver. It is "war in the administrative manner, a la Eisenhower rather than Patton, where the important command decisions are in fact logistic decisions." It eschews relational action, or "action guided by a careful study of the enemy and *his* way of doing things."[1] Maneuver warfare, when practiced by an opponent, "allows the enemy to dictate" one's force structure and tactics (Luttwak, 1985). As we note later in this chapter, much of American history has found the United States grappling with highly unconventional war, but the failure has been in not developing an appropriate response to that kind of war.

World War II reinforced the American commitment to the "annihilatory approach" to war. Subsisting off a mobilized nation that went all out to maximize industrial production and ration materials and foodstuffs, the Americans, from a protected homeland, made the most of their superiority in materials and technical advancement to produce the equipment and munitions that, in the end, overwhelmed the enemy and led to complete surrender. This success was reinforced as well by the Korean experience, which would have been a much shorter war if the mistaken decision to advance beyond the thirty-eighth parallel, thus practically inviting the Chinese to come in, had not been made. The United States had a tradition of fighting low-intensity war prior to WWII, even though the two world wars more closely fit the norm of large-scale and massive use of force. Very little of the experience of low-intensity war survived in the institutional memory of the army after WWII (Lock-Pullan, 2006). Military leaders grew more risk adverse. They were reluctant to learn from other militaries, and, at least until the past few years, the US military looked much as it did after WWII. In a "love match between firepower and mobility," skills for irregular warfare eroded. The US military can spend more on defense than everyone else and still not have the strategy or the weapons it needs for present and future wars, as we learned to our chagrin in both Afghanistan and Iraq (Arquilla, 2008:31).

This old frame of reference, the traditional war of attrition, no longer suffices in a world where fourth generation warfare is the norm. The environment has changed; the response must also change. As Murray Weidenbaum, an economic advisor to President Reagan said, the post–cold war world is one of "small wars and big defense." He was concerned over how a defense establishment suited to great wars and superpower competition would fare in a world of brushfire wars and irregular conflict (Arquilla, 2008: 229). The purpose here is not to give a definitive treatment or commentary on counterinsurgency, or to suggest a "recipe" for US military actions. What is required varies with each conflict and the requirements must be assembled based on the facts on the ground. As one analyst put it, "It takes time and effort and considerable trial and error before the counter-insurgent mobilizes the right set of instruments for an effective strategy" (Hashim, 2006:xx–xxi). Counterterrorist warfare requires different objectives and methods, but if the objective is to stabilize a society, counterinsurgency is what will be needed. Counterinsurgency is opposing an insurgency by orienting all action around supporting a movement and a government that can out-compete the insurgency in gaining the people's loyalty. This is done by providing services, treating the populace well, and being seen as a just movement with nationalist credentials. The two steps in fighting a counterinsurgency war are: first, adapting such a strategy, and second, successfully carrying it out. I hope to draw a sharp contrast with pre-Iraq methods of warfare and suggest why changes were and still are necessary. I also want to convey a sense of how the thinking about the mode of warfare in the United States has evolved since WWII.

A crucial part of warfare under modern conditions is the maintenance of public support. The United States cannot limit itself to short conventional wars and still maintain its present imperial obligations. Further, the public must have confidence that the strategy and tactics used by one's military make sense. Based on the Vietnam experience, it is no wonder the public is turned off by the wasteful and tactical excess. Public support must be earned, but what is observed by officers and citizens often does little to enhance enthusiasm. Based on the Vietnam experience, Luttwak describes how military operations appeared to the uninitiated

> heavyweight fighter bombers converging to bomb a few flimsy huts, the air cavalry helicopters sweeping a patch of tall grass with a million dollars' worth of ammunition. Some observers could recognize tactical poverty in the very abundance with which the ordnance was used; others could detect the lack of any one clear-cut strategy in the generosity with which each service and branch was granted a role in the war; others still were simply disgusted by the wasteful disproportion between efforts and results.
>
> Luttwak, 1985:196–97

And for the regular soldier, for a weapon the United States provides the precision tolerance of an M-16, which requires high standards of cleanliness. A magazine-fed light machine gun that is more difficult to jam would be more useful in the conditions in which many counterinsurgents are likely to fight (Simon, 1997).

HISTORICAL EXPERIENCE WITH UNCONVENTIONAL WAR

Irregular warfare has played an important role in US history. Principles of insurgency and irregular tactics were honed in the French and Indian wars. General Washington effectively used ruthless measures of dwelling and crop destruction against the Iroquois to break up their military alliance with the British. And while many of the winning battles in these wars were fought along "classic linear European lines," they furnished much experience that was liberally applied to successful outcomes in the Revolutionary War (Tierney, 2006:5). The revolutionary experience was a wildly successful assault of the underdog against Goliath, and insurgency tactics and strategy play no little role in that conflict as the Americans tried to avoid head-on conflicts with superior firepower. The patriots harassed the British troops and chose their battles carefully. One particularly famous irregular was Francis Marion. A teetotaler and Huguenot, he commanded a ragtag band of irregulars, young boys and slaves. His force became skilled in night and dawn raids against the British. He was agile and innovative. His men rode on horseback, but fought on foot, employing tactics like posting pickets up in trees, using whistles, and covering bridges with blankets to muffle the horses' footsteps. Nor were the insurgent tactics limited only to the conflict between the Americans and the British. With roughly one-third of the population pro-revolution and one-third loyal to the crown, internecine conflict was rife as fellow Americans often took on a more villainous status than the British—witness the vitriol reserved for Benedict Arnold. Mob action and terror against traitors in the midst were only a natural outcome of the revolutionary situation. Unfortunately most Americans know little of this history because of the "stubborn incapacity of the American political culture to appreciate the dimensions of this type of conflict." This classic defensive use of irregular tactics, so common to countries all over the world when they are threatened by outside forces, has always been unappreciated in the United States, which has "overwhelmingly regarded guerrilla war as dishonorable and has associated one of the guerrillas' main tactics, terrorism, as the worst human scourge," despite its use and application throughout history. Thus, much of American political culture is ahistorical since this experience with irregular war has been "buried by the experience of great-power wars" (Tierney, 2006:5). The strength and overwhelming firepower we possessed for so much of our history has shielded us from the necessity of using it and the ability to appreciate the battlefield methods of the underdog.

In the second Seminole war in Florida (1835–42), a classic insurgency that forced the United States to adopt unconventional tactics and cost it dearly, as well as in numerous Indian wars in western United States, unconventional tactics were of necessity and often successfully used, but the tendency within the army was to regard each mission as an irrelevance. A former civil war general, Major General George C. Crook, a Civil War veteran with extensive experience among Indian tribes was skilled in using counterinsurgency against Indians, particularly the Navajo, as did Colonel Nelson A. Miles against the Sioux and Cheyenne in Montana during 1876–77. But this imagination in counterinsurgency was not generalized throughout the army, nor was it "generalized into official doctrines. By and large the United States still fought most of the Indian wars with troops using the regularized tactics that were the natural lessons derived from most American battlefield victories (Tierney, 2006:95). Professionally, the army was oriented toward Europe. It studied conventional warfare, and each Indian campaign was seen as "a tiresome temporary irritant" (Beckett, 1988:109). These neglected opportunities to institutionalize unconventional military approaches ended up costing the Americans dearly, especially in recent decades. According to one analyst, "*Without exception*, there is not a single case from U.S. history in which an infantry, either by doctrine, equipment, or tactics, was prepared at the outset to fight an insurrection when faced with such a challenge" (Tierney, 2006:2). In Mexico, in Kansas, where US troops fought the confederate raider William Quantrill and his murderous compatriots terrorizing the Kansas-Missouri border, fighting Agusto Sandino in Nicaragua during an eight-year struggle there, and in Panama and Haiti, the United States experienced and carried out various combinations of diplomacy, conventional military force, and irregular operations (Tierney, 2006).

The US involvement in irregular war continued up through WWII, the period of America's peak performance as a world leader when it derived the maximum advantage of its industrial might and weapons of mass destruction. The United States fought effective campaigns of unconventional warfare against the Japanese in the Asian-Pacific theatre, as portrayed, for instance, in the movie *The Bridge on the River Kwai*. These were small-scale, and some were the result of improvised strategies "devised by a handful of adventurous soldiers," others were coordinated from Washington by the head of the Office of Strategic Services (OSS), "Wild Bill" Donovan. One OSS guerrilla unit operating behind the lines in Burma (4 Americans and 200 Burmese), kept a whole Japanese regiment of 3,000 men "marching and countermarching over the mountains far away from the front lines." McArthur refused to allow the OSS to operate in the Philippines, but individual American officers organized groups of Filipinos who carried out scores of uprisings. Tellingly, the innovative OSS, the first organization dedicated to unconventional war, was hated by the regular military and was abolished soon after the war (Tierney, 2006:211–13).

The discrepancy in military capabilities with the British forced the continental army to adapt guerrilla tactics. Since then, however, "concentration on the 'conventional' at the exclusion of the 'irregular' has characterized the US military." Following the civil war, there was a "focus on large-scale warfare and military engineering while dismissing the frontier, counterguerrilla, and peacekeeping operations of the time as skirmishes and police work" (Ucko, 2009:26). The study of counterinsurgency in the army virtually ceased after 1916 if not before. Although the marines, by virtue of the kinds of missions they undertook, maintained more emphasis on irregular war, Beckett has argued that "neither army nor marines were suited temperamentally to counter-insurgency both from long standing American cultural attitudes and their own professional ethos." Both had more important roles to play. Prior to Vietnam, American intervention often required the techniques of counterinsurgency, but when they were not available and Americans were not prepared to practice them, the United States muddled through.

INSTITUTIONALIZING COUNTERINSURGENCY:
VIETNAM—IRAQ—AFGHANISTAN

Vietnam was unique to the American experience in that for the first time since the American revolutionary war the conventional techniques and those irregular tactics that happened to be close at hand were not sufficient to carry the day. What the United States confronted for the first time in Southeast Asia was a new kind of ideological and highly organized fourth generation warfare movement in a new and nationalistic postcolonial age. It was a change in international politics that was qualitatively different from the experience in the Philippines and intensified the perils of intervention. It would not disappear as an aberration, but would continue to haunt US foreign policy for decades to come.

It was a shock and a jolting experience for the nation and the military to find that American ingenuity was inadequate to win a war that had appeared to many to be a sure victory. President Kennedy anticipated the unique situation confronting the United States in Vietnam, the new norms of the postcolonial world. The Vietnamese were highly motivated by a nationalist and egalitarian ideology and intent on uniting their country. Kennedy himself had noted the inability to differentiate between combatants and civilians, the close link between the guerrillas and the people.[2] Because the Vietnamese were highly motivated and highly *organized*, short of destroying the entire country, it was difficult to counter the communist movement by conventional military strategy. Realizing this unique, new environment and referencing speeches by Nikita Khrushchev on wars of national liberation in the third world, Kennedy spoke of a "monolithic and ruthless conspiracy that relies primarily on covert means for expanding its sphere of influence—infiltration rather than invasion [and] on guerrillas by night instead of armies by day." He was concerned over "troubles with communists in Laos and Vietnam, ideological doubts regarding African decolonization, and unfinished business in Cuba—where efforts were underway to slap down the first successful communist revolution in America's 'backyard'" (Ucko, 2009:30–31). The military did take steps in the 1960s, and later after the Vietnam War, in the 1980s when Kennedy's apprehensions had been proven well founded, to improve counterinsurgency skills and knowledge. Kennedy issued several national security action memorandums, one requesting that the secretary of defense put emphasis on the development of counterguerrilla forces and another establishing a high-level interagency committee—special group—especially concerned with counterinsurgency. There were revisions to manuals to include sections on counterinsurgency. The point is that all this activity, even though originating with the president, had very little positive impact on the operations in Vietnam (Ucko, 2009; Krepinevich, 1986). During the whole conflict, in spite of much talk of implementing counterinsurgency doctrine and a new emphasis on that aspect after Creighton Abrams replaced Westmoreland as the general in command in Vietnam, only the civil operations and revolutionary development support (CORDS) program and the combined action platoon (CAP) programs were ever successful in actually developing counterinsurgency strategies, and both were of minimal importance in the overall conflict (Ucko, 2009:28).

An even better indicator of the ineffectiveness of Kennedy's attempt to develop counterinsurgency capabilities is what happened after the failure of the Vietnam conflict in the 1980s. The 1980s were hailed by some as having "ushered in a new counterinsurgency era." A center for low-intensity conflict was established, the army started developing light infantry divisions more suitable for such conflict, a study on low-intensity conflict was conducted and Secretary of Defense Weinberger sponsored a conference on counterinsurgency at National Defense University in 1986. But when the wars of the early 2000s appeared on the scene, the United States was as usual, unprepared to grapple with the unconventional demands they made.

The debacle of Vietnam was not easy for the US Army to deal with. According to one observer, the "scars of Vietnam . . . were too deep to develop low-intensity conflict without the Army having first redeveloped its core identity, and confidence in the support from the nation." *On Strategy*, a book explaining the Vietnam defeat as due to the reluctance of the US political leaders to take on the North Vietnamese with, essentially, conventional war, was very influential with the military in the aftermath of Vietnam and generally accepted as the official version of the war. The explanation fit nicely with conventional notions of how the US military should operate. Chief of Staff Creighton W. Abrams authorized a war college strategic assessment that concluded that there would be no more Vietnams, no more infantry-dominated land wars in the third world. The only region where the army had a legitimate and politically acceptable role was in NATO defense against the Soviet Union. As one observer remarked, one could easily get the impression that the defense establishment does not recognize low-intensity conflict as a legitimate form of conflict (Summers, 1982; Linn, 2007:195, 197, 213). The experience in Vietnam was the United States' psychological equivalent of WWI for Britain and France, a devastating blow to the world as it was previously known. It was easier to forget what was learned there and revert to the traditional view as a reference for the future (Lock-Pullan, 2006). The 1991 Gulf War revived US morale, but it also "bred arrogance, complacency and the habit of using established patterns to solve military problems" (Linn, 2007:221).[3]

The post–cold war aftermath of Vietnam has now been superceded by the travails of Iraq and Afghanistan. Right in line with past experience, when confronted with the need for counterinsurgency in these two countries, the Pentagon was unprepared. Rumsfeld first denied that an insurgent situation existed in Iraq; this was followed by a long period during which both the civilian and military leadership seemed clueless as to how to deal with the situation. As the situation deteriorated, ethnic strife developed into civil war, minor military fracases metamorphed into widespread chaos, and living conditions shifted from stable to a state pervaded by intense fear, culminating in the high casualties of 2007. For the most part, the DoD leadership opposed the "application of counterinsurgency methods" in Iraq. The change in strategy, it turns out, was "driven by the White House and forced on the Pentagon." In his survey of counterinsurgency in the current era, David Ucko notes that all too often the Iraqi situation was cast as an exception to the rule, unlikely to ever occur again. Three reasons were adduced for this: (1) the political circumstances prior to the war were so peculiar, (2) the international isolation of the United States so inauspicious, and (3) the initial occupation of Iraq so bungled that it was thought unlikely a similar situation would ever occur. At best, therefore, Ucko asserts, "the learning of counterinsurgency was understood as an Iraq exit strategy, after which time the topic would lose relevance. More often the learning of counterinsurgency was dismissed as an unimaginative attempt to 'prepare to fight the last war,' a fallacy typical of military institutions undergoing change." The changes adopted in Iraq in 2007 did not enjoy support among the Pentagon's top brass. If important segments of the leadership were resistant to the need for change resulting from the shock of the deteriorating Iraqi situation, one wonders what might bring the institutionalized change that is required. The civilian leadership, driven by the imperative of sinking political support, was able to team up with a faction of the military that was imaginative, capable, and willing to transform the situation in Iraq.

In Afghanistan, an innovative blend of use of an Afghan proxy force combined with selected bombing and use of special forces troops resulted in a routing of the Taliban and other insurgents and a state of relative stability. Instead of guarding this state of affairs and preventing the development of conditions that would allow revival of the insurgency, the Bush administration shifted focus and priorities to Iraq, thus allowing a revival of the radical insurgency. In Afghanistan, too, however, there is substantial evidence that the strategy now being followed is one of genuine counterinsurgency in principal. To read General McChrystal's report on the situation there is to marvel at the very different voice in which the US military speaks now, both in Iraq and in Afghanistan, when compared to the language they and the civilian leadership used only a few years ago (McChrystal, 2009). There is no doubt that for the first time in US history, the strategy on which the United States has been reliant in two major wars is one based on the general principles of counterinsurgency. Unfortunately, in Afghanistan the United States is also saddled with an ally that is not a reliable supplier of the competent and effective government needed to win a counterinsurgency conflict. This shortcoming encourages over-reliance on military tactics as compensation for inadequate government, and leads to problems like the killing of civilians. Further, as Secretary of Defense Robert Gates has said, the hard, tough lessons of Iraq and Afghanistan that allowed the military to "pull Iraq back from the brink of chaos in 2007 must be "not merely 'observed' but truly 'learned'" (Gates, 2011).

If he were a betting theorist, analyst Colin Gray writes, he would wager that those prophets and executives seeking to transform the American way of war will find their attempts shaped, reshaped, and possibly hindered by a persistent adherence to the assumptions and values of the past (Gray, 2005:36).[4] Ucko notes that even the British army, despite its historically successful use of counterinsurgency, still finds it difficult to institutionalize its use, necessitating "quick adaptation on the ground with each new engagement."[5] DoD is a highly conformist organization, and the real test will be whether the revolutionary achievements of Petraeus and others will earn a place in the future priorities at the Pentagon, or whether they will be shuttled off on a dead end as has been the case in the past (Ucko, 2009:181).

PART II

CASE STUDIES

CHAPTER 4

THE PHILIPPINES— 1898–1902

> Every nation, and especially every strong nation, must sometimes be conscious of an impulse to rush into difficulties that do not concern it, except in a highly imaginary way.
>
> Walter Q. Gresham, Secretary of State in Grover Cleveland's second term

This chapter will discuss three questions relating to our analysis of the United States' intervention in the Philippines in 1898. The first discussion is that of American participation in the Spanish-American War, the second is the US involvement in and takeover of the Philippines, and the third is the US conduct of the war against the Philippine Republic and the taking of the Philippine Islands as a US colony.

From the end of the American Civil War through the nineteenth century was a period of unprecedented growth in America's economy, and its emergence as a potential power in the international system was spectacular. As one scholar puts it, the United States seemed to have all the economic advantages that some of the other powers possessed in part, but it had none of the disadvantages. During this period, US production of wheat increased by 256 percent, coal by 800 percent, and miles of railway track in operation by 567 percent. By 1914 the United States had by far the largest national income and also the largest per capita income in the world (Kennedy, 1987:242–43). By 1898 western expansion over the American continent was complete and the frontier had disappeared. The increasing ability of the United States to compete with the Europeans militarily plus the popularity of imperialism as a way of life led to a reexamination of America's role in the world.

The War of 1898 did not start out as an effort to annex colonies. During the war and even after the war was over but before a final settlement had been agreed upon, there was a great deal of confusion and indecision among those responsible for setting policy and prosecuting the war as to the exact war aims and the American attitude toward territorial acquisition. US public opinion at the time on the Philippines and the war in general could be described as a confused jumble of ignorance, jingoism, and protestant piety (Boot, 2002: 105). A mix of hyperbole and megalomania comprised several accounts of thinking at the time; one of the presidents supposed nocturnal anguish over what to do about the Philippines[1] and the second an account of the mindset of the president's emissary to the Philippines, William Howard Taft.[2]

But the fate of the Philippines was not something that would be decided solely by the actions of outside major powers. Just as in Cuba, there was a thriving rebellion against reactionary Spanish rule, beginning in August 1896, a rebellion led by Emilio Aguinaldo and his *katipunan* (Society of the Sons of the People). This was a revolutionary organization but one that was established and led primarily by moderately educated representatives of Manila's urban middle sector and municipal elite (Cullinone, 2003:332). It drew its support primarily from the propertied classes and had only limited luck mobilizing the average Filipino. Aguinaldo signed an agreement with the Spanish, received a payment of 400,000 Mexican pesos and promises of reform, and went into exile in late 1897, only to be discovered by the Americans and brought back to the Philippines in May 1898 in the hope that he would be of use to them in the war against Spain (Smith, 1994; Boudreau, 2003). On June 12 he proclaimed the existence of the Republic of the Philippines, hoping to head off American efforts to establish control and sovereignty over the islands.

The British diplomat and historian James Bryce marveled in the autumn of 1898, "Six months ago you no more thought of annexing the Philippine Isles and Porto Rico than you think of annexing Spitzbergen today" (Kinzer, 2006:80). Why exactly the United States went to war with Spain in 1898 and why the United States got involved in Philippine issues in which it had previously displayed little interest is a question on which different perspectives exist. Messianic ideas and the reigning fad of colonialism, economic pressures and the need to consolidate the US position in Asia, and a crisis in national self-confidence and a war that was largely the product of mass emotions in the United States all have their supporters as explanations for the war (May, 1968; LaFeber, 1998; Dallek, 1983). The Spanish practiced severe repression in Cuba, which infuriated a large number of Americans. Promised reforms were not forthcoming. It is important to remember that Spanish abuse of Cubans was not something that had just commenced, but was an American grievance for the last quarter of the century. The Americans had threatened to go to war with Spain in 1873, over the capture and execution of the crew of the *Virginius*, a ship involved in promoting Cuban rebellion against Spanish "barbarism." The mood of the country was one of anger and discontent reflecting a general dissatisfaction because of a series of depressions and the general discomfiting and alienation of people by the large scale and impersonality resulting from a rapidly industrializing United States. This discontent and alienation was projected unto the retrograde Spanish and their empire in Cuba. The war "served as an outlet for expressing aggressive impulses while presenting itself, quite truthfully, as an idealistic and humanitarian crusade" (Hofstadter, 1964:161). But as Robert Kagan points out, the United States was led into war not by bellicose "jingoes," but by "a moderate, cautious, mainstream Republican," representing a "broad cross section of Americans" and supporting a cause that was "undertaken primarily, though not exclusively for humanitarian purposes" (Kagan, 2006). The battleship Maine was sent to Havana to protect American nationals if necessary, and it was the explosion that racked the Maine that angered the public, although the explosion was determined by a recent study to have been a rather commonly occurring coal bin accident rather than a Spanish conspiracy deserving of retaliation.

McKinley was a serious statesman who abhorred violence and war, but in the end the outcry in the country over conditions in Cuba, the steadily deteriorating relations with Spain, and the catalyst of the Maine pushed him into war.[3] McKinley's precondition for a settlement with Spain was independence for Cuba. When he was convinced that there was no chance of that coming about, he sent a war message to Congress on April 11, 1898. Historian David Trask stated that if McKinley had "capitulated to the jingoes," there was good reason. In April, McKinley and other proponents of peace made up a "lonely and debilitated remnant indeed. If ever there was a 'popular war'—one forced upon a reluctant leadership by the people—it was the war of 1898" (Trask, 1981:56).

And what of the Philippines? When we went to war with Spain in April, "virtually no one in the United States had any notion of acquiring an Asiatic empire" (Halle, 1985:2). At no time, writes Louis Halle, did the principal actors at the time, including the president, consider the long-term implications of the decisions that they were making in order to deal with the immediate military circumstances. Prewar planning did not anticipate major territorial acquisitions (Trask, 1981). Ironically, the one acquisition for which the battle plans were most complete was the acquisition most people least expected, to end up with them as a colony. Theodore Roosevelt, the assistant secretary of the navy, was a proponent and advocate of war with Spain. Roosevelt included these plans in his recommendations to

Secretary of the Navy Long with his contingency plans for war with Spain. But he went further. When Long took a day off from work, Roosevelt took the liberty of sending a cablegram to Dewey instructing him that in case of war, it would be his duty to "see that the Spanish squadron does not leave the Asiatic coast, and then offensive operations in Philippines."

Dewey confronted the Spanish fleet in Manila bay and thoroughly defeated it on May 1. The Americans in the Philippines were under strict instructions not to coordinate their activities with Aguinaldo and the Republic of the Philippines after it was proclaimed in June. Still in the process of deciding the disposition of the islands, Washington wanted a free hand to make any decision it deemed appropriate. The Filipinos controlled much of the main island, Luzon, and they initially acquiesced willingly in the American landing, apparently believing that their own forces would be able to cooperate with the Americans in capturing Manila. As it became clear that the Americans had their own agenda and they had no intention of coordinating their plans and operations with Aguinaldo and the Filipinos, relations between the Americans and the insurgents grew "rapidly worse." Only gradually did the United States absorb the fact that the revolt of the insurgents against Spain, begun years before the Americans even started to think about the Philippines, was "truly a revolt for independence and not one for reform" (Grunder and Livezey, 1951:22, 52; Smith, 1994).

US SECURITY ISSUES

All of this is not unrelated to the key question that is a major part of the analysis of all these case studies: Was US security involved in the decision to intervene? In the most obvious and direct sense, the question is easy to answer. The American desire to oust Spain from Cuba and end the practices there that had long perturbed the United States and its citizens had nothing to do with the security of the United States, even though one objective in starting the war was certainly to create a more stable environment for economic activity in and with Cuba. Not even the most feverish of the war proponents (and there were many) suggested that there was any serious military security threat to the United States. As one modern Filipino author put it, "Spain was a country receding into the past, the United States loomed in the future" (Mojares, 1999:208). Backward looking, unprepared for military conflict, and simultaneously unwilling to face reality and to compromise on its situation in Cuba sufficiently to head off a crisis, the Madrid government suffered a further setback when a new and inflexible Conservative Party government came to power in 1895.[4] The American concern from the beginning was the inhumane nature of Spanish rule in

Cuba and concern with stability and the economic situation, an American messianic impulse nurtured by the "yellow press."[5]

The Americans got more than they bargained for. Because of the initial involvement in the Philippines, relieving Spain of its authority there, the United States was now faced with some decisions of its own, particularly because of its refusal to share the responsibility for defeating the Spanish in the islands with Aguinaldo and his movement.[6] Racist sentiments appeared on both sides of the foreign policy continuum, the interventionists believing with William Taft that the "little brown brothers" (Wolff, 1961) were incapable of governing themselves. But even the pronouncements of the anti-imperialists offend our modern sensibilities; they argued that the Americans should not try to absorb people who were "racially incapable of self-government" (Hofstadter, 1964:172).[7]

Making this assumption rather drastically decreased the number of alternatives for disposing of the islands. Since Spanish authority was collapsing, if the insurgents could not govern themselves, then the United States was faced with a choice of either walking away, and letting the Filipinos fend for themselves the best they could, or devising some form of American rule or protectorate to govern the islands until they were able to govern themselves. The Americans had brought on themselves a dilemma. The Spanish-American War was, as we would say today, post-Iraq, an "optional" war. There was no real threat to the United States from either Cuba or Spain and there was no military reason why the Americans should have attacked either. The opponents of the war, in fact, argued that it worsened US national security. It would break the "nation's ocean belt of security" by making American interests and possessions vulnerable to attack or intimidation by others. It would increase US vulnerability in three ways: by putting the United States in competition for empire with European powers, by encouraging new European encroachments in the Caribbean because it undermined the Monroe Doctrine pledge "that the United States would stay out of the affairs of the Old World in return for European restraint in the New," and it would align the United States too closely with British interests (Beisner, 1968).

But the American Congress, the populace, and the press were ready for a war, and President McKinley was not up to holding back the tide. Opinion in the United States was deeply divided on the war from the very first, as public opinion has been on many US wars. Theodore Roosevelt, Senator Albert Beveridge, and others were firmly in the proimperialist camp. William Allen White echoed Kipling, saying "[i]t is the Anglo-Saxon's manifest destiny to go forth as a world conqueror. He will take possession of the islands of the sea . . . this is what fate holds for the chosen people." White was representative of many of his countrymen when he said he was bound to two idols, "Whitman, the great democrat, and Kipling, the imperialist" (Halle, 1985:17; Hofstadter, 1964:158). Former President Grover Cleveland, William Jennings Bryan, Mark Twain, and Andrew Carnegie were among a diverse group of anti-imperialists, and strenuously opposed much of US policy. Senator Gray, a member of the peace commission, believed that there was no place for "colonial administration or government of subject people in the American system" (Grunder and Livezey, 1951:33). This was thoughtful but, alas, unheeded. Others shifted their positions, favoring the war but not the taking of colonies, or vice versa.

McKinley, in the matter of the war and its implications, displayed a kind of flexibility that gave the maximum play to public opinion. He was not really in favor of the war with Spain, until public pressure made it difficult to resist. As to the Philippines, as McKinley himself explained, at the beginning of the war he had opposed adding anything to the national domain. Over time, however, he came to the realization that the consequences of not annexing land would be detrimental. At that point he was still against taking the Philippines, but he again realized the problems involved, and decided it would be preferable to take a coaling station. He then settled on taking Luzon, and finally came to conclude that taking control of the whole of the Philippines was the preferable course of action. One factor reputed to have been important to the decision on the Philippines was a speaking tour the president made in the Mid-west during October of 1898. On this tour, McKinley frequently broached the possibility of keeping the Philippines. To large crowds McKinley stressed that the United States went into the war for humanitarian reasons and now must do its "duty" to those people who had been liberated from Spanish despotism. For this idea he invariably found an enthusiastic response. The religious press was almost uniformly in favor of a US takeover of the islands. One crisp assessment of McKinley is that he "was a party man, a follower and not a leader" (Trask, 1981; Smith, 1994:198; Grunder and Livezey, 1951:31).

But were there real alternatives? The prevailing sentiment, as we have seen, rejected the possibility of granting self-government, and the *New York Times* stated that giving the islands back to Spain was out of the question. The one military security concern was the possibility of another great power grabbing the Philippines if the United States departed. Britain, France, Russia, Germany, and Japan were all candidates; with the latter two being the most frequently mentioned possibilities. Germany had ships in Manila Bay when Dewey first arrived, and the United States had sparred with Germany over the Marianas, Wake Island, and Samoa. It was normal behavior for great powers to send warships to a trouble spot, but the size of the German fleet was suspicious, as was their practice of going in and out of the harbor without signaling their intentions. And

Table 4.1   US-Philippines war statistics

US intervention force (peak nos.)	US casualties	Philippine casualties
70,000	4,234	16–20,000 military 200,000 civilians (est.)

Sources: Welch, 1979: May, 1983.

Germany had attempted to elicit British cooperation against the United States, and we later learned, did have aspirations in the Philippines. Dewey later indicated regret over not destroying the German ships at Manila when he had a chance (Trask, 1981; Smith, 1994; Halle, 1985).

A completely unprotected Philippines might have been opened up to possession by another power. Lacking a proper defense, susceptible to a German takeover, and vulnerable to being used as a base for attacks on American shipping in the Pacific, there were all kinds of vulnerabilities for the islands as well as for the United States. It would have been hard to explain to the American public how the government could justify pulling out and leaving the islands alone after the fanfare and hyperbole accompanying the war against Spain. If the war against Spain was for humanitarian purposes, how could leaving this sort of unfinished business in East Asia be tolerated? It would have undercut the initial justification for the war as well as worsening the US strategic position. Philippine vulnerability to German or Japanese control would in effect be substituting a hapless and ineffective Spain for a vigorous and aggressive Germany that might threaten American interests in Asia.

Given the importance of ensuring the autonomy of the Philippines from interference from any great power that would potentially be hostile to both US and Filipino interests, were there other ways to treat the Filipinos and the insurgency that would develop from American insistence on dominating the transition away from Spanish rule? Undoubtedly there were.

TAKING A COLONY: REAPING INSURGENT WARFARE

The intention of the civilian and military leadership was to finish the job of deposing the Spanish in the Philippines and leaving quickly. But the way the takeover and occupation was handled virtually ensured that this would not be possible. From the beginning the United States operated unilaterally and demanded that the Filipinos recognize the military occupation and authority of the United States. There is little evidence that McKinley promised independence, just as there is little evidence Aguinaldo expected anything else. But the Americans held the upper hand. They were responsible for the final defeat of the Spanish and the Americans easily held Manila. While the Filipinos had deposed the Spanish in much of the territory of the islands and by default still controlled it, at this time, what counted for completing the saga of the Spanish-American conflict was control of Manila. The final treaty, signed in December 1898, ceded the Philippines to the United States and mandated a payment of $20 million to Spain. Ratification of the treaty by the Senate passed by a vote of 57-27, one vote more than the required two-thirds majority. Fighting between the Americans and Filipinos broke out on February 4, 1899, two days before ratification by the Senate. Fighting continued on a large scale for over two years, with intermittent skirmishes until 1904 (Grunder and Livezey, 1951).

It is hard not to believe that inclusion of the Aguinaldo forces in the temporary occupation and some sort of effort to reach an agreement with the Filipinos on the ultimate disposition of the islands would have led to a very different result. The United States could have taken control and assumed sovereignty of the islands but still made clear its intention to grant independence by a specific date. An alternative course of action could have left the islands under the temporary international protection of the Americans, but by mutual agreement the Filipinos would have exercised self-government. This alternative, a limited and temporary protectorate, was suggested by the Filipinos before the outbreak of hostilities. In a talk with Aguinaldo, a high American officer asked him what he expected the United States to do. "To furnish the navy, while the Filipinos held all the country and administered civil offices with its own people," Aguinaldo replied (Wolff, 1961:148; Welch, 1979:8; Karnow, 1989:135). Either one of these arrangements might have avoided the military clash that followed the end of the war with Spain, but the negotiators seriously considered neither. One US argument was that leaving the Philippines as a protectorate of the United States would have entailed all the responsibilities and costs, but none of the benefits of taking the islands as a colony. If the major part of the coming military conflict could have been avoided, however, it would have been a major advantage for both sides. A core problem was that almost nobody among those likely to be influential in making the decision on the American side seemed to believe the Philippines were ready to govern themselves. Said Senator Albert Beveridge, "The opposition tells us we ought not to rule a people without their consent. I answer, the rule of liberty, that all just governments derive their authority from the consent of the governed, applies only to those who are capable of self-government" (Wolff, 1961:157).[8] The people in the Philippines glimpsed an opportunity—the decline and defeat of their colonial ruler—and they attempted to take advantage of it to end their colonial experience.[9] Perhaps because they were ahead of their time, they were not able to emerge victorious in the first round of their struggle with the Americans.[10]

WEAKNESSES OF THE PHILIPPINE REPUBLIC

Few low-intensity wars or guerrilla struggles have been successfully repressed in the modern period. The most famous is the ethnic Chinese guerrilla movement led by the Communist Party of Malaysia in the 1950s. A second example is the struggle against American rule in the Philippines, although that particular war resembled guerrilla warfare more in its later stages—after November 1899—than in the earlier phases. This example is particularly intriguing since compared to their oppressors the Philippine insurgents appeared to have many advantages. They were the inhabitants of the islands, already having driven the Spanish from positions of authority in the parts of the country where most of the struggle with the Americans took place. Further, the Filipinos were fighting against strangers only recently arrived and with very little knowledge of the country. Many accounts have assumed that the United States clearly had superior forces, but Glenn A. May has shown that the forces were more evenly matched than often assumed. The US troop presence in the Philippines existed in a considerably higher ratio to the overall population numbers in Vietnam than in the Philippines—and thus more favorable to the United States in Vietnam, while the ratio of troops between the two sides was roughly the same in both countries.

Further, comparing the weapons used on both sides in the two wars shows that the Filipinos had superior rifles at the onset of the conflict, since the Americans were using obsolete Springfield rifles, a .45 caliber breech-loading weapon. These were later replaced by Krag-Jorgensens, the equal of the Mausers used by the Filipinos. In Vietnam, by contrast, the Americans had a distinct advantage in weaponry. There were other American advantages in the Philippines, artillery, the use of cavalry, and control of the sea. Differences in weaponry and the use of cavalry diminished in importance when the mode of warfare shifted to guerrilla tactics in late 1899 (May, 1983:356–59).

There were social factors, however, that were more important in explaining the outcome of the war. Aguinaldo, from the beginning, did not attempt to mobilize the lower ranks of society. The *katipunan* always recruited from the upper reaches of society and had little appeal to the ordinary peasant. The *ilustrado* often sided with the Americans, although some did join Aguinaldo's *katipunan*. But quite unlike the National Liberation

Front and the North Vietnamese forces who built their organizations on redistribution and through appeals to peasants, especially poor peasants, Aguinaldo showed little interest in such a strategy, and failed to offer "genuine change" to the Filipino masses. The Luzon town of Ilagan, capital of Isabela province, provides one example of the lack of inclusiveness in Aguinaldo's Republic. Out of a population of nearly 14,000, only 73 citizens were qualified to vote. The regional elections held in 1898 for the most part ratified the status quo. Ilagan elected Dimas Guzman, a "skilled survivor" who had been rewarded by the Spanish and was later elected to the Philippine legislature organized by the Americans (Karnow, 1989: 186). Aguinaldo made deals favorable to vested interests and showed little interest in the pressing economic problems of the peasants and the poor. Tax relief, or restitution of lands seized by the Spanish, was not a cause that engaged Aguinaldo. Instead of distributing lands confiscated from the Spanish monastic order, in Laguna he kept the estates for himself and his friends, on the pretext that they were now government custodians. Some peasants joined messianic sects that opposed Aguinaldo (Karnow, 1989).

Not only was "virtually every ranking officer" in the Filipino army a member of the political-economic elite, but men of that type also provided most of the supplies and food that the army needed. These men were both wealthy and well educated and in many cases had served as officials under the Spanish. One analyst reports "[a]n overwhelming majority of the peasants were essentially indifferent to the conflict. They tried to remain on good terms with both sides, and, as best they could, they avoided involvement and simply cultivated their crops." Many peasants did fight against the Americans, but much of this behavior may be better explained by patron-client behavior where they were serving in units commanded by their landlords (May, 1983:365–67). His revolution, in short, was a political revolution, not an economic one. Aguinaldo was a nationalist who fought for independence from Spain and wanted to prevent the reassertion of colonial control by the Americans, but he limited the potential of his movement when he refused to appeal to the lower rungs of society and combine his nationalism with social and economic change.

The Filipino cause was also hurt by the ethnic tension in the country. The Philippines was not a tightly unified entity, and it enjoyed its distinctiveness as a polity primarily because of the Spanish-defined colonial area. The Muslim south was quite separate from the other islands, and had never really been integrated into the rest of the archipelago. The Tagalogs, in Luzon, provided most of the leadership and the backbone of the insurgency against the Spanish, and later the Americans, and for this they were often resented. Other ethnic groups had a lesser degree of commitment to the Republic. Lacking a uniform, written language and culture, the archipelago lacked a unifying theme. Personal and regional antagonism was such that participants drew knives and revolvers at councils of war (Linn, 2000:17).

One important reason for the defeat of the Philippine Republic was Aguinaldo's failure to adopt a more effective military strategy. As one observer puts it, after losing a conventional war with the Spaniards from August 1896 to November 1897, Aguinaldo adopted virtually the same approach in his war with the Americans. Only in November 1899, after his crack units had been destroyed, did Aguinaldo decide to resort to guerrilla tactics. Neither Aguinaldo nor Antonio Luna, Aguinaldo's principal field commander, was a professional military man, and neither had served in the field before the war with Spain. Aguinaldo appears to have viewed guerrilla warfare as a tactic of last resort, to be adapted after he had lost his conventional forces.

AMERICAN ADAPTATION TO THE PHILIPPINE CONFLICT

Adjusting to the tropical climate in the Philippines the Americans naturally found difficult. Rain, heat, disease, and topographical difficulties afflicted any army on the march. One march by General Samuel Young and his 1,100-men cavalry brigade in northern Luzon became famous in the records of Philippine service. Young commented that nothing in his four decades of active service had prepared him for the "tropical deluges, mud and water, the swimming, bridging and rafting of innumerable streams," most of which were unmarked on the map. Another problem was a shortage of supplies. As has been the case in all recent wars, the American soldiers were high maintenance; maintaining the logistical train was a major task in itself. Luna, not having yet caught on to this and assuming that the Americans were living off the land, often ordered destruction of villages given up to the enemy, a practice that condemned many noncombatant Filipinos to poverty and hunger (Linn, 2000:99).

As soon as possible the Americans set up a structure of local government to provide administration, enhance control, and provide information. They soon became aware, however, that the role played by Philippine officials could be as much of an asset to the other side as to themselves. A report by Lt. William Johnston in May 1900 provided the first news that the insurgents were actively at work organizing and that the Filipino officials of the towns were "playing a double role." In at least two northern provinces, Ilocos Norte and La Union, many municipal governments were shown to "be heavily influenced, if not controlled, by the revolutionaries. In some cases, the very people the army depended on to assert American authority were clandestinely working for the enemy" (Linn, 1989:49).

As one soldier put it, "after leaving the scene of combat they conceal their weapons and appear as innocent amigos" (Linn, 1989: 133).

After November 1899 when Aguinaldo dissolved his conventional forces and told the soldiers to go home and create guerrilla movements, the Americans became frustrated by the unconventional nature of the war. Major General Elwell S. Otis, commander of ground forces in the Philippines told both his subordinates and the American people, in a harbinger of attitudes in the military during and after Vietnam, that "war in the proper meaning had ceased to exist . . . The revolutionaries no longer sought military victory; henceforth they would wear the Americans down, relying on disease, terrain, and frustration to demoralize the soldiers." This type of frustration, in turn, distorted American strategy. For much of the war, the American was "a blind giant" and had little facility for gathering intelligence. The Americans could not have a spy and scouting system because they were so much bigger and so much lighter than the Filipinos, who spoke an "unpublished dog language." On the other hand, their adversary seemed to have no intelligence system but yet they knew everything, and had limitless ways of notifying the countryside when the American troops went out on patrol. (Linn, 1988:5, 8–9).

The Americans adapted to the infuriating guerrilla tactics the Filipinos eventually developed. Problems in attaining intelligence, in taking revenge for surprises and catastrophes and the duplicity of those Filipinos working both sides of the conflict sometimes led to frustration being taken out on the Filipinos with the widespread destruction of crops, the killing of prisoners and suspects, the intensifying of racist attitudes and the use of torture. At the same time, both the civilian and the military leadership realized that without the support of the populace, the war could not be won, and that support would not be generated solely from military action. The effort to win militarily was therefore supplemented, as we have seen, by efforts to provide stable government, social services, and education and to present a more positive view of the Americans. Combining these two contradictory approaches is never easy, and the troops worked with a distinct handicap because of their condescension toward Philippine culture and society. "Even the most highly motivated and best intentioned sought to make over the Filipinos into little brown Americans." The Americans lacked empathy for "indigenous traditions" and "failed to detect the Filipinos' passionate, and often semi-mystical desire for independence," and their contempt for the new colonial occupiers. The Americans perceived events and interpreted them in this narrow ethnocentric framework. They underestimated the appeal of Aguinaldo and the power of the "revolutionary forces in the provinces" (Linn, 1988:7).

As an American captain put it, "This business of fighting and civilizing and educating at the same time doesn't mix very well. Peace is needed first" (Linn, 1989: 128). But even during the war the Americans completed an impressive amount of humanitarian work, reform, and provision of services that was of value to and undoubtedly impressed the local population. Especially in the area of education, services and facilities were provided that were effective and much appreciated by individual Filipinos.[11] Likewise, in disease eradication, sanitation, roads and building construction, and agricultural reforms, many useful things were done. All too often, however, such efforts were marred by, even (or especially) among the highest level of officers and civilians, a "penchant for racist remarks and repressive solutions . . . All too often, American reforms either ignored local customs or they were pursued with more self-righteousness than tact." In an order prohibiting cock fighting and gambling, an order that incidentally destroyed major sources of revenue, General Young alleged that the "prevalence of these vices has been a serious hindrance to the mental, moral and material development of the Filipino people and their continuance will in the future prevent them from having a place among the people of modern civilization" (Linn, 1989:34–36).

But the problem with winning hearts and minds was not limited to the tendency to spout such pedantry. The dilemma goes to the heart of the task of waging guerrilla warfare, and it is one that we meet numerous times in later American wars. Facing attacks by guerrillas that cut communication wires, sabotage equipment or stage surprise attacks and then disappear, melding into the population, commanders are forced to devise responses. All too often those responses included burning and destroying villages and communities where the offense was carried out, or over an even wide area, destruction of rice and other foodstuffs or agricultural crops, thus threatening famine and starvation. The war in the Philippines made famous the "water cure," where the victim was forced to imbibe water until his stomach protruded, at which time the executor pressed against the area and forced the prisoner to expel the water, so the whole process could be begun again.

Infamous instances of abuse of prisoners and enemy personnel included General J. Franklin Bell's activities in the first military district as the war came to an end. Bell was known as someone who was "willing and able to escalate the war to a level that the revolutionary leaders found intolerable." Once they surrendered, however, he was "able to reconcile them to American rule." He was complemented by one civilian on his passion for education and his concern for the general welfare of the people." But he was also known for his controversial introduction of "concentration areas" where civilians were herded into "protected zones" with stiff penalties for being in the wrong place. Brian Linn writes that they were effective as a counterinsurgency technique, but that the cost in human suffering was "unquestionably high." The practice shocked many Americans (Linn, 1989:154–55). In the province of Batanga in southern Luzon, 11,000 died in Bell's concentration camps from a combination of disease, poor sanitation, malnutrition, and other health problems (Boot, 2002:124).

Equally famous was another general, Jacob H. Smith, better known as "Hell-Roaring Jake," for the streams of invective he directed at his subordinates. Asked to deal with the aftermath of a surprise attack on American troops on the island of Samar, he told a subordinate, a Major Waller, that he wanted to see the interior of Samar turned into a "howling wilderness." He declared, "I want no prisoners. I wish you to kill and burn, the more you kill and the more you burn the better you will please me . . . I want all persons killed who are capable of bearing arms." Pressed by Waller on what the age limit should be for executing this order, he replied, "Ten years." Waller, in a subsequent campaign was charged with murder for executing without trial 11 of his porters accused of attacking an officer. His trial turned into a duel for survival between Smith and Waller, with Waller recounting the whole story of the orders he was given. Waller was acquitted of murder, but his career was harmed while Hell-Roaring Jake was forced into retirement (Boot, 2002:120–22).

The racism rampant in this era, the lack of US experience with a guerrilla enemy and the tropical conditions in the Philippines all contributed a vicious edge to the effort in the Philippines. However deplorable the objective of repressing a people fighting for self-government, nonetheless, the military effort in the islands was surprisingly effective, especially when compared with more recent efforts at promoting this synthesis of military and political approaches. One general in particular exemplified the ability to adapt to low-intensity war during the Philippine ordeal and to synthesize effective military action with a simultaneous effort to win the loyalty of the populace. He may serve as one of the more impressive examples of flexibility and innovation in US strategy. "Fighting Fred" Funston was arguably the most famous general to come out of the war. He was best known for successfully carrying out a daring plan that captured Aguinaldo in March 1901. According to Brian Linn, as revolutionary terrorism grew, Funston

> evolved from an advocate of harsh and rather indiscriminate repression into a humane and sympathetic commander who made increasing efforts to ensure that military consequences fell upon the guerrillas and their active supporters [as opposed to the ordinary civilians].[12]

He believed that effective military operations were compatible with conciliating the population and he attempted to insure that the two efforts went together. The evolution of his tactics can be seen in his response to the cutting of wires. In early 1900, his policy was to arrest a village headman, burn down houses around the area where the cuts occurred, and if the cuts continued, burn a whole village and hint at even more drastic measures. A year later, he had decided that three wire cuts a month did not amount to much in time of war. Further, he believed that it was improbable that the culprits would remain in the village and that there was no point in burning down barrios since the destructive act, in all probability, was done by people from elsewhere, and that it was futile to chase down two or three people. His tolerance paid off in San Antonio, where a guerrilla who demanded that the people tear up wire was seized by the townspeople and delivered to the Americans.

The tradition of low-intensity warfare in the American army got a substantial boost in the War of 1898. The Americans learned to use the tools of counterinsurgency in the context of a formal ongoing war. And they learned to respect and relate to the indigenous population in spite of the racist atmosphere and the lack of understanding among Americans of preindustrial cultures. They learned to understand that Filipinos behaved like people everywhere and Funston, for instance, designed policies that correctly predicted the on-the-ground situation and the likely response to his policies. Later, the Americans promoted democratic institutions and eventual independence with fewer of the repressive policies and delays that characterized other colonial powers.

THE PHILIPPINE LEGACY

President McKinley believed that the Filipinos were unfit to govern themselves but assured the world: "We hold the Philippines for the benefit of the Filipinos" (Ekbladh, 2010:20). But that most incorrigible of American imperialists, Theodore Roosevelt, had second thoughts about the decision to retain the Philippines. "While I have never varied in my feeling that we had to hold the Philippines," he wrote in 1901, "I have varied very much in my feelings whether we were to be considered fortunate or unfortunate in having to hold them" (Green, 2007:71). Roosevelt was not unusual. After only a few years, many Americans began to have misgivings about whether the acquisition of empire, in the form of the Philippines, was worth the trouble."[13] And it is clear that the United States could have protected its national security without taking over the Philippines. The acquisition was bereft of careful analysis of that aspect of US interests.

The results of the American intervention for the Philippines and the Filipino people were a mixture of benefits and costs with both positive and negative consequences. The American legacy in education and tutoring in democracy, as well as development of infrastructure and service provides evidence for an affirmative view. Evidence of the positive nature of American rule was the fact that between 1906 and 1941 there was only one large-scale revolutionary outbreak, and that was directed against Filipino political and economic leaders more than Americans. "Damn the Americans," said Manual Quezon, a leader of the nationalist party and chief tactician of independence, "why don't they tyrannize us more?" (Thomson, 1981:118–20). As time went on, many Americans lost interest in the Philippines, making the islands less than an urgent concern. Only one official congressional committee ever investigated the Philippines and this occurred after the decision to free the islands had already been made (Grunder and Livezey, 1951:180). At the same time, the largest lingering problem in the Philippines, the continued stratification of the society and domination of the economy and the political system by an outmoded and unimaginative elite, is in part the result of American rule. It augmented and reinforced the approach of the leaders of the Philippine Republic—to avoid any policies leading to land reform, redistribution, or enhanced economic competition. It is surely no accident that high degrees of inequality are also found in US society. The Philippines is still paying the price for that historical bias as even current governments resist badly needed radical reform.

A final lesson from the US intervention in the Philippines is another one that will reappear in connection with future interventions. The initial part of the intervention, the defeat of the Spanish, was the easy part. Subduing the Filipinos was the unanticipated and more difficult second act of the intervention. The United States had neither foreseen nor prepared for such a possibility. The acquisition of the Philippines fits Louis J. Halle's comment that "[h]istory is full of incidents in which nations have competed for the possession of liabilities that look like assets" (1985:22).

CHAPTER 5

VIETNAM—1945–1973

> Anticommunism will remain a useless tool in our hands as long as the
> problem of nationalism remains unsolved.
>
> General Philippe Leclerc
> Commander of French Forces in Indochina, 1945–47

Vietnam has a unique culture particularly attentive toward foreign
threats. That culture has been formed by thousands of years of living
beside China, first the Chinese Empire and now a more modernized
China. This geographical fate has instilled in the Vietnamese an acute
sensitivity toward the disasters their country can face because of China's
superior size and strength. Twice in more than two millennia China has
dominated Vietnam, once for a period of a thousand years between 111
BCE and 934 CE. Many Vietnamese stories of Chinese cruelty exist, and
when the Chinese briefly occupied North Vietnam for a few months after
WWII, the oft-told stories were reconfirmed, since the Chinese pillaged,
stole, cheated, and removed from the country anything that was portable
and valuable (Honey, 1963:1–3; McAlister, 1971).

The Vietnamese are uniquely aware that small nations like Vietnam
must be ever vigilant to maintain their survival. Henry Kissinger quotes
Nguyen Van Thieu speaking on why South Vietnam rejected the agreement to end the war negotiated by Kissinger and Le Duc Tho in 1972.
A giant country like the United States, Thieu said, can afford to make
mistakes. The loss of Vietnam is of little consequence to the United
States. But for Vietnam, what is at stake is survival (Waltz, 1979:194–5).
It is this situation, facing potential obliteration in the face of the power
of overwhelming neighbors that has formed the attitudes of Vietnamese
in international relations. A Vietnamese psychologist told the journalist
Stanley Karnow that "[e]ven the lowliest peasant is deeply nationalistic,
and in times of war, the sentiment can border on xenophobia" (Karnow,

1997:22). But Vietnamese fears have not been stoked only by the Chinese. For nearly a century, the Vietnamese people resisted French domination, which intensified as the last half of the nineteenth century wore on. In 1946, when Ho Chi Minh had to justify to his fellow citizens a controversial deal with the French enabling the ejection of the nationalist Chinese army from northern Vietnam, he expressed himself in language immediately understood by those familiar with Vietnamese history: "Better to sniff a bit of French shit briefly than eat Chinese shit for the rest of our lives." When you are faced with a choice between two evils, he was saying, you choose the lesser evil of the two and live with it in order to deal with the worse situation. The Chinese would always be there beside Vietnam. The French would eventually leave. But it was this environment of constant threat that led Ho to say that it was patriotism and not communism that originally inspired him (Karnow, 1997:112, 134). Irregular or guerrilla warfare was something that the Vietnamese learned long before the Americans showed up in Indochina. They were simply continuing a long tradition of using unorthodox strategies, not, like the Americans, being confronted with something they were unprepared for.

THE EARLY YEARS: THE FRENCH AND THE UNITED STATES IN INDOCHINA

But it was the French attempt to reimpose colonial rule after WWII that had the most relevance for the Americans in Vietnam. Although the United States, and Roosevelt in particular, was against the reintroduction of colonialism in Southeast Asia after the defeat of the Japanese, the United States ended up abetting as much as opposing the events that allowed the French to return to Indochina. Losing faith in French willingness to work out any kind of compromise, the Vietnamese under Ho Chi Minh determined they had no alternative but to resist the French if they hoped to gain independence.

The Indochinese Communist Party had been founded by Ho about 1930, but in 1941, Ho, back in Vietnam after a 30-year absence, founded the Viet Nam Independence League, known as the Vietminh. A broad alliance of organizations, of which the party theoretically was only one, this change reflected an important shift in strategy away from a class revolution against feudalism to a nationalist revolution against imperialism, uniting as broad a front of allies as possible to secure national independence. By 1945, the Vietminh had a web of 5,000 activists all across Vietnam (Karnow, 1997; McAlister, 1971). Bao Dai, the "playboy emperor" who had led a pro-Japanese puppet regime in Indochina, after he had responded to the Vietminh request to resign as emperor, described the atmosphere in Vietnam in a warning he transmitted to General de Gaulle:

> You would understand better if you could see what is happening here, if you could feel this yearning for independence that is in everyone's heart, and which no human force can any longer restrain. Should you reestablish a French administration here, it will not be obeyed. Every village will be a nest of resistance, each former collaborator an enemy, and your officials and colonists will themselves seek to leave this atmosphere, which will choke them.
>
> Karnow, 1997:163

Bao Dai was no radical, but the French and their allies, alas, were not listening. Ho had many times expressed his hope that he would receive assistance from the United States and he clearly differentiated between the United States and the other powers that had colonies in Southeast Asia. Ho's expressed dedication to primarily nationalist rather than communist goals, his antipathy to French rule and his unwillingness to countenance French dominance in Indochina was not dissimilar to the American perspective, but American priorities were increasingly anticommunist, and there was no place for Ho in that strategy (Arnold, 1991).

The communist victory in China in 1949 and the outbreak of the Korean War in the spring of 1950 increased American interest in opposing the Vietnamese communists. These developments had resulted in the United States reversing an earlier decision and interposing the American fleet in the Strait of Taiwan to ensure China did not take over nationalist Taiwan, thus prolonging the Chinese civil war. US leaders were now very concerned about Indochina, and saw it as one of the most vulnerable areas to communist aggressors, especially once the Chinese had come into the war in Korea. The United States began an aid program to assist the French effort, increasingly handicapped by exhaustion after the war and by inefficiency. This aid, which began with only $10 million in 1950, had escalated to $1063 millions or 78 percent of the cost of the war in 1954 (Pentagon Papers, 1971a:76–77). The United States in turn endorsed the French Navarre plan, which promised to win the war against the Vietminh.

But US reservations about the French ability to make progress in Indochina without meeting the demands of the Vietminh that the three countries of French Indochina, Vietnam, Cambodia, and Laos, be given independence, turned out to be justified. The turning point came in the spring of 1954 when the French suffered decisive defeat at Dien Bien Phu, a valley along the Laotian border west of Hanoi in northern Vietnam. Dien Bien Phu stands as a symbol not only of French ineptitude in the former Indochina, but literally of their ignorance of the mentality of the resistance and the methods they would use to win.[1]

Table 5.1 US-Vietnam war statistics

Country	GNP/GDP (bn $)	Pop (million)	Total armed force	Defense expend. (mil. $)	Intervention forces (peak nos.)	US casualties	Vietnamese casualties
Communist Vietnam (1963)		17	522,500 [a]	500			2 million [b]
US (1963)	676	189	2,815,000	52,500	536,000	58,209 [c]	

Sources: World Bank Atlas; The Military Balance (London: IISS); *Strategic Survey* (London: IISS); Hannah Fischer, *American War and Military Operations Casualties: Lists and Statistics* (Washington, DC: Congressional Research Service) http://www.history.navy.mil/library/online/american%20war%20casualty.htm#intro, accessed 12/06/08; S. Mintz, "Learn About the Vietnam War" and "Background," *Digital History,* http://www.digitalhistory.uh.edu/modules/vietnam/index.cfm, accessed 12,06/08; *Statistical Abstract of the United States 1966* (Washington, DC: US Dept of Commerce, 1966).

[a] 1964 – includes VC in Laos and South Vietnam
[b] Estimate. Some estimates go as high as three million.
[c] November 1955-May 1975

Eisenhower refused direct intervention by the United States chiefly on the grounds that it would risk general war with China—this message was relayed by Soviet Foreign Minister Molotov—something the United States was extremely sensitive to following the Korea involvement. Further, the president believed that if the Americans intervened to support France, the stigma of colonialism now adhering to France would, in the eyes of many Asiatic people, be passed to the United States. Eisenhower questioned whether US leaders would be effective under the conditions in which it would intervene. "[T]here are plenty of people in Asia," he said, "and we can train them to fight well. I don't see any reason for American ground troops to be committed" (Arnold, 1991:197–98).

A conference held at Geneva that summer resulted in the issuance of a final declaration on July 21, which formalized the outcome. The French and the United States had hoped to use a victory at Dien Bien Phu to bolster their negotiating position at Geneva, but the results obviously had the opposite effect.[2] The final agreement noted the understanding between the parties on the ending of hostilities, provided for independent states of Laos and Cambodia to be free of foreign alliances, and to hold elections in 1955. It prohibited the introduction into Vietnam of foreign troops or military personnel or arms and ammunition, recognized a provisional military demarcation line across Vietnam, but also provided for the holding of a free election throughout Vietnam in July 1956, under the supervision of an international supervisory commission provided for by the agreement. The elections were never held, reflecting the gulf in perspective between the two sides.

US Security Interests and Objectives in the Former French Indochina

The problem facing policy makers in the 1950s as the French relinquished their role in French Indochina was to define any threat to US interests in the Southeast Asian area, suggest how the threat could be countered, and what the costs, in people, material, and dollars would be. Finally, a cost-benefit analysis of whether the objectives could be accomplished within the boundaries of the acceptable cost would need to be made.

A February 1950 National Security Council (NSC) report 64 under President Truman's administration stated that

> [i]t is important to United States security interests that all practicable measures be taken to prevent further communist expansion in Southeast Asia. Indochina is a key area of Southeast Asia and is under immediate threat. The neighboring countries of Thailand and Burma could be expected to fall under Communist domination if Indochina were controlled by

a Communist-dominated government. The balance of Southeast Asia would then be in grave hazard.

Pentagon Papers, 1971a:83

This quote encapsulates many of the assumptions that dominated US policy in Southeast Asia from the Truman administration through to the end of the war in Vietnam. In the post-WWII world, and following the takeover of China by the communists in 1949, the virtually monolithic communist bloc, governed by expansionist-minded rulers intent on spreading their ideology and form of government, was perceived as a real threat to Southeast Asia. This fear of the influence of the bloc was heightened by an active independence movement headed by the Vietminh and Ho Chi Minh, explicitly aimed first at expelling the French from the area and then uniting Vietnam. Unless this challenge was met by the West, it was assumed, the Sino-Soviet bloc would be encouraged to undertake aggressive policies that, while starting with French Indochina, would have an impact on the surrounding area, and much of the developed world. How accurate were these assumptions? Using standard "balance of power" or "balance of threat" concepts to measure the severity of a nation's security deficiencies, it would be hard to get too concerned about the impact of the loss of a country like Vietnam, which Lyndon Johnson called a "raggedy-ass fourth-rate country" (Jones, 2001:356; Table 5.2). But it was assumed that the communist bloc (Russia and China and their allies) was a powerful coherent group that threatened US interests.

THE DOMINO THEORY

Beliefs about the importance of dominoes in international politics depend on the assumption that there are "tight connections between threats to the periphery and to the hard core of an empire." They rest on the "expectation that a defeat or retreat on one issue or in one area of the world is likely to produce . . . further demands on the state by its adversaries and defections from its allies." These beliefs were not new or unique in the US relationship with Vietnam, but are as old as Thucydides, and have been cited to predict the fate or the potential fate of colonial contests in Africa and Asia, the result of conflicts leading up to the world wars, the outcome of US actions in Berlin during the cold war, and the consequences of not acting in Korea (Jervis, 1991).

Ironically, as Jervis points out, the domino theory is the rare instance when the statesmen subscribing to it think in the long term rather than following the usual tendency for political leaders to focus on short-term issues. It is also noteworthy that the theory assumes that the country that is the suspected "domino" will bandwagon, that is, it will ally itself with the stronger side, rather than balance against the strongest and most threatening state. Bandwagoning occurred on the axis side in WWII, but it is contrary to most realist theories of international politics, which predict that weak countries will balance against the stronger side. Bandwagoning, in contrast, requires joining the stronger side (Jervis, 1991:3, 22, 27; Schweller, 1998:65–70). A row of falling dominos reflects a winning and increasingly powerful coalition.[3]

Thinking in terms of falling dominos began in the US government at least as early as 1949. It also coincided with French thinking about the strategic importance of Indochina, especially as represented by the French high commissioner and commander in chief of the French union forces in Indochina, General de Lattre de Tassigny and his flamboyant ideas (FRUS, 9/20/51). As the communist takeover of China neared, in June of that year the NSC concluded that "[t]he extension of communist authority in China represents a grievous political defeat for us. . . . If Southeast Asia is also swept by communist authority we shall have suffered a major political rout the repercussions of which will be felt throughout the rest of the world, especially in the Middle East and in a then critically exposed Australia." From that time through the end of the Vietnam War, the decibel level of threatened catastrophe if the dominos were not stopped from top-pling seemed to know few limits. The shrillest predictions of threatened negative consequences from disregarding the necessity to join the battle in Southeast Asia emanated from the Kennedy and Johnson administrations, to include even the loss of Japan and India, the precipitation of nuclear war and the necessity of withdrawing to "Fortress America" (Slater, 1993–94). According to NSC 124/2 [June 1952], the loss of any Southeast Asian country to communist control as a result of overt or covert Chinese aggression would have "critical psychological, political and economic consequences." The loss of "any single country would probably lead to relatively swift submission to or an alignment with communism by the remaining countries of the group." When it was decision time, anticom-munism trumped anticolonialism. In US eyes, the French insistence on trying to preserve their empire looked foolish and self-defeating, but in view of the threat from the communist bloc, Truman and Eisenhower felt they had no alternative but to provide assistance.

An essential component of any domino theory is an enemy that will facilitate the overturn of the domino. There was a pervasive attempt throughout the war to denigrate and downplay any idea that the war was one stemming from legitimate grievances among the population of South Vietnam. The National Liberation Front (NLF) was seen largely as a pawn of outside forces, particularly the North Vietnamese. The US presence was predicated on the idea that the war was one of aggression, which the United States had intervened to stop. But who was the aggressor? During the French phase of the war and through the late 1950s, the focus was on the Soviet Union, the Sino-Soviet bloc or "international communism," although during this period there was also much talk of a potential Chinese invasion. As awareness of the existence of the Sino-Soviet dispute developed during the 1960s, emphasis shifted to focusing on China, "Asian communism," or North Vietnam (Slater, 1993–94:193). North Vietnam became increasingly implicated as the enemy in the 1960s as US involvement increased dramatically (Kail, 1973), and throughout the conflict it was viewed as a tool of one or both of the larger communist powers.

Equal amounts of confusion existed over the method by which the enemy threatened the sovereignty of South Vietnam. Overt aggression was always a fear and the sending of men and materials across the border from the North became important in the late 1960s and 1970s, but for the earlier period of the war it was acknowledged that the war was waged by subversion (externally sponsored revolution) and accommodation. During the later stages of the war the danger of promulgation by inspiration or emulation became part of the US argument. The idea was that the United States would lose credibility and prestige if it allowed dominos to fall. In the late 1960s much of the US case for remaining in Vietnam rested on this need to maintain credibility, as the critics zeroed in on the lack of a US intrinsic security interest in preserving South Vietnam. As argued above, this focus on credibility and reputation for meeting potential threats has always been an important part of US foreign policy, and as the war progressed this emphasis became a larger and larger part of the justification for remaining in Indochina and continuing the war.

It is a weakness of the discussions of US foreign policy that there is often too much reliance on abstractions and not enough specificity or even definition of terms. The concept of the domino theory exemplifies this problem. The general assertions were often accepted at face value, without trying to puzzle out the specifics of how the process of falling dominoes might work. Area specialists and foreign policy generalists often differ in emphasis, with the area specialists stressing the specific situation and the intrinsic strategic value of a country, and generalists applying a more global geopolitical perspective where all events are tightly connected. Those with the last perspective argued in London in 1917, for instance, that the British must suppress the rebellion in Ireland if they were to have any hope of ruling India (Jervis, 1991:26–27). In Vietnam, those most influential in the policy process were generalists, of whom the most extreme example was W. W. Rostow, who flatly refused to listen to "particularistic" briefings on countries like Vietnam or China and would send the briefer away as irrelevant (Kattenburg, 1980:80, 170–71). Questions such as how would the process proceed; would it be mechanical and automatic, one fallen domino and the others would automatically fall; or would it depend on the culture of the country, the ideology, the level of institutionalization, the quality of leadership, and so forth were not dealt with.[4] Would cross-border aid and assistance from a domino to a potential domino hasten the process of falling dominoes, or would the process be stimulated primarily by the psychological impact of the fall of contiguous or surrounding countries? Over how long a time would this process play out? Would the time frame be the same for all countries or would it vary from country to country? What effect would this development of falling dominoes have on the communist bloc? Would all countries comply with the party line from Moscow? Or would some be more independent than others? Would national quarrels develop within regions, or would the common ideology overcome nationalist tendencies? Simply to list the questions raised in the process of trying to precisely define the term indicates the primitive and limited nature of the concept.[5] One CIA National Intelligence Estimate (NIE) in March 1951 did suggest that in the absence of a Chinese conquest of the area—a constant concern in the early and mid-1950s—it was unlikely that the Vietminh would attempt to conquer Burma or Thailand in 1951. But, the report went on, the two countries would be subjected to increasing subversion and intimidation, which in the absence of increased aid and countermeasures might lead to the overthrow of the noncommunist governments (FRUS, 3/20/51). Even this amount of detail in the analysis was exceptional. One can only conclude that the paucity of factual material and supporting evidence reflects a lack of intelligence, a lack of curiosity or imagination, or all three. The domino theory was an assumption. It was not an assertion backed by or even argued with empirical evidence.

It can be argued that the domino theory is best analyzed as rhetoric, or possibly as a psychological mechanism on which the speaker projects his personal grievances (Kail, 1973). Perhaps even the speaker didn't take his verbiage literally, but used the phraseology for public relations purposes. But a critic evaluating justifications for the war has little choice but to take seriously the suggested rationale the policy maker has proposed. It is worth quoting Lyndon Johnson's view on Southeast Asia, even after he had retired from office, suggesting his views were indeed deeply felt. As he went on walks over the Texas hill country or spent sleepless nights, he claimed, he thought about what would happen "to our nation and to the world if we did not act with courage and stamina—if we let South Vietnam fall to Hanoi."

[F]rom all the evidence available to me it seemed likely that all of Southeast Asia would pass under Communist control, slowly or quickly, but inevitably, at least down to Singapore but almost certainly to Djakarta. I realize that some Americans believe they have, through talking with one another, repealed the domino theory. In 1965 there was no indication in

Asia, or from Asians, that this was so. On both sides of the line between Communist and non-Communist Asia the struggle for Vietnam and Laos was regarded as a struggle for the fate of Southeast Asia. The evidence before me as President confirmed the previous assessments of President Eisenhower and of President Kennedy.

Johnson, 1971:151

In the case of Vietnam, the theory first confronted problems with the fall of Dien Bien Phu in 1954, ending the French presence in Indochina. Since the establishment of North Vietnam, after the defeat of the French, represented the fall of the first domino to communism, would the next step be the fall of the South, as the concept would predict? Dulles decided that all was not necessarily lost, that things could be done to prevent further communist gains even after the "loss" of North Vietnam. The result of this thinking was the organization of SEATO (Southeast Asia Treaty Organization), a defense pact including both Western and Asian powers to save other potential "dominoes" (Pentagon Papers, 1971a:87, 106–7). As F. M. Kail put it, "what had previously been advertised as an irreversible disaster became a problem of manageable proportions." But during the war, the domino theory survived, if sometimes not in its purest form, then in derivative formulations such as "the crumbling process," or speaking of South Vietnam as "the cork in the bottle," or "the key" to a larger area. It continued to appear in unmistakable form well into the 1960s, sometimes coupled with broader terms such as a potential "test case" or the Munich analogy (Arnold, 1991; Kail, 1973:86–91).

ACHIEVING STABLE, POPULAR, AND EFFECTIVE GOVERNMENT

Was it feasible for the United States to take the kind of action that would prevent a domino from falling, at an acceptable cost? What was the first order of business to accomplish the objective of preventing the loss of South Vietnam? Vietnam from the late 1940s on was going through a time of revolutionary change, in which a communist nationalist movement was competing with, first, a French-sponsored colonial government, and following Dien Bien Phu, an American-sponsored government—one led from 1955–63 by President Ngo Dinh Diem. American discussion of the situation in Indochina makes it very clear that there was a great deal of concern about whether this government could gain the loyalty of the populace as a legitimate representative of the Vietnamese people. This question persisted from the first involvement there through to the end of American involvement, even after the coup d'etat that deposed Diem in 1963. American sources reiterated over and over again that the main problem was creating an environment in which a stable and legitimate government with nationalist credentials could function and meet the needs of the Vietnamese people (FRUS, 6/29/51; 1/3/55; 1/4/62; 1/16/62). A second question was whether the government would be able to take the necessary actions to resist the gains of the communists and to command the loyalty and motivation of the Vietnamese soldier. Would the army of the Republic of Vietnam (ARVN) fight as well as that of North Vietnam or the NLF? Almost always, the answer to both questions was no. One report from the minister in Saigon to the secretary of state in early 1951 noted there was nobody in the government capable of providing popular inspiration or enlisting public enthusiasm. The majority was suspected of being pro-French or subservient to French interests. There was no clear answer to the political and social propaganda of the Viet Minh (FRUS, 2/24/51; 1/3/55; 1/4/62). As one observer noted, in Vietnam, very often the American judgment was that the Diem government (and those that followed it) could not be reformed. But, instead of changing the policy and US objectives in Vietnam to conform with that assumption, the decision was repeatedly made to try harder.[6] Many Westerners (French as well as Americans) did not fully absorb the importance of reform and amelioration of the lot of the peasants, the backbone of Vietnamese society. If the South Vietnamese government was to prevail, it had to be able to compete with the communist-sponsored alternative. The hawkish journalist Joseph Alsop, a friend of President Kennedy, did understand.

> It was difficult for me, as it is for any Westerner, to conceive of a Communist government's genuinely "serving the people." I could hardly imagine a Communist government that was also a popular government and almost a democratic government. But this was just the sort of government the palm-hut state was while the struggle with the French continued. The Viet Minh could not possibly have carried on the resistance for one year, let alone nine years, without the people's strong, untied support.
>
> Pentagon Papers, 1971a: 308

Diem was undoubtedly a nationalist and anti-French, but his governing style was to give his own need to prevent challenges to his power priority over programs that would gain the support of the populace (FRUS, 1/4/62; 1/11/62). In the end, this approach gained him neither. The list of Diem's shortcomings was long. While his communist counterpart government carried out land reform and continually demonstrated its commitment to the nationalism and ideological creed it claimed to adhere to, the Diem government fell short by almost all criteria. Diem's government enacted a land reform law, but it was extremely moderate, and in any case was never fully implemented. The Pentagon Papers report that even when fully implemented, it would never have positively affected more than 20 percent of the peasantry. As it was implemented, it provided land to only about 10 percent of the peasantry. Land tended to go to Diem's core supporters, northerners, catholics, and refugees, and considerable corruption was involved. According to Bernard Fall, even after Diem's land reform, 2 percent of landowners controlled 45 percent of the land, and 15 percent controlled 75 percent (Pentagon Papers, 1971a:309). If, as a State Department Bureau of Intelligence and Research report maintained, the struggle for South Vietnam is "essentially a battle for control of the villages," then the prospects for winning that struggle were not good (FRUS, 2/2/62). Diem was a "fervent reactionary," intent on founding a new family dynasty in a country where most thinking people believed that dynasties were anachronisms.[7]

The fate of the civic action teams in the mid-1950s is a telling reflection of the problems faced by Diem and the fate of many of the programs that were attempted under him. The American Colonel Edward Landsdale, who was fresh from devising a program in the Philippines to end the Hukbalahaps rebellion there, relates the circumstances and results of the civic action program. Based on the French experience in Vietnam as well as American experience in the Philippines, the idea was to recruit a group of 1,400–1,800 of the urban elite, who would live in the countryside and provide expertise, carry out diverse kinds of development activity, beginning with surveys of the physical needs of the villagers and including the building of maternity hospitals, schools, information halls, repairing and enlarging local roads, digging wells and irrigation canals, teaching general school as well as personal and public hygiene, distributing medicine, and so forth. A promising idea to have a group of personnel out working among the people, in simple dress—the same black calico of farmers and laborers—getting their hands dirty, came in 1955 from an official, Kieu Cong Cung, sponsored by Defense Minister Minh. The Vietnamese functionaries were aghast "since they cherished their desk work in Saigon and their dignified white-collar authority." They fought hard against the idea, and it took Diem's personal intervention to get a pilot Civic Action program started. Provincial authorities originally refused to recognize civic action personnel as government officials because of their dress. The work of the civic action teams, says Lansdale, was at the same grass-roots level as that of communist workers, and it was effective. It was so effective that they became the target of political attacks and even murders. Diem ordered the teams to start working with the army commands in what were essentially combat zones. The civic action teams proved effective enough that they were expanded to all provinces in South Vietnam, but the next developments were less promising. The cadres became preoccupied with Diem's anticommunist campaign, and their operations were attacked by the bureaucratic agencies in Saigon unwilling to let the civic action teams carry their programs to the villages. In 1957 Kieu Cong Cung died and the programs were absorbed into other organizations (Pentagon Papers, 1971a: 306–08).

Diem's weaknesses in political and social leadership, not surprisingly, were also reflected in the conduct of his soldiers and the consequent military fortunes. Stories of the ARVN's reluctance to fight, and especially their refusal to fight well were legion during the war. They did not like night patrols, thus giving the enemy a substantial period of time when they were not vulnerable. When out in the field and close to confronting the enemy, ARVN personnel would often give themselves away with a cough or the snap of a bolt on a weapon, warning the enemy that they were coming. They were alleged to have a sense of inferiority toward the enemy.

Stories abound about the mishandling of personnel and maladroit decision making in Saigon. Captain Minh was a dashing and energetic ARVN officer who had a special touch for relating to the people in his district. David Elliott, who conducted field research in the villages, states that he was not unique among ARVN officers, but his type was rare. His common sense, his accessibility, his tactical sense were "a model" of what the Saigon government required to win the war. Saigon, however, not only did not support "its most capable and aggressive officials" but often turned on them because they were perceived as a threat to less effective officers, or corruption, or both. In Minh's case, an incident from years previously, a charge for which he had been tried once and been found innocent, was revived, in this case involving an incident in which he had led a group accused of killing civilians. Since this was an old case in a war in which such things were common, it was assumed that the party had probably arranged for surrogates to revive the case to get rid of an effective and popular officer. In a final twist to the plot, and a tribute to the American advisory presence, leading citizens of Vinh Kim (the district town) petitioned President Johnson to extend the term of the American subsector advisor, a Major Wilcox. "Sentiment, or even a desire to do a more effective job," the chronicler of this incident notes, "could not prevail over military bureaucracy, however, and Wilcox, too departed." (Elliott, 2007:272–73).

John Paul Vann was an American who served first in Vietnam as a member of the military, and later returned as a civilian engaged in development work. According to his biographer, Neil Sheehan, Vann knew nothing of Vietnamese culture when he came to Vietnam, and he believed the fact that the French had been defeated in Indochina was irrelevant. The Americans were not colonizers as the French had been (Sheehan, 1988:42–43; FRUS,

6/7/56). In this way, he was typical of the Americans who went to Vietnam and can be seen as symbolic of the American effort there. But he was not typical in that he developed strong ideas about how the war should be fought, he saw the problems that were inherent in the Vietnamese effort, and he set out energetically to correct them. Part of his plan to reverse the losing course and turn the war around involved Vietnamese Colonel Huynh Van Cao, 34 years old in the summer of 1962 and the commander of a division. Vann had worked with and flattered Cao by praising his efforts, and was convinced that he was generally in sympathy with Vann's vision of a more rigorous approach to the war, and that with a little cajoling and admonition they could work together to improve the performance of the ARVN. Vann thought they could "get this thing organized and run it just like an American outfit."

Vann knew where a battalion of guerrillas was located near My Tho, devised a plan to eradicate the communists, and gained Cao's assent to implement it. When the plan was executed, one group of guerrillas was surprised and eliminated, but others were fleeing and it was time to implement the later stages of the plan. Vann was infuriated that Cao refused to commit the necessary troops to close the trap on the communists as had been arranged. The commander of the regiment responsible for the first skirmish did not want to share "his big victory" with another regiment, and Cao, as division commander, refused to overrule him. The commanders in Saigon saw nothing wrong with the way Cao had behaved, rewarded him, and Diem was reportedly considering promoting Cao. Sheehan diagnoses the ARVN as having an "institutionalized unwillingness to fight" (Sheehan, 1988:49–91). Diem had an inability to relate to and motivate the peasantry, and the lack of commitment and discipline in the ARVN, much of which could be traced to Diem's paranoia about a possible coup and consequent attempts to buy loyalty among commanders, were major problems. His obsessive anticommunism obscured long-term problems— such as Buddhist dissent and disputes with other sects—and was a major problem for the US government from 1955 until Diem's overthrow in 1963. After that the problems continued but with less stability than during the Diem days, as one government rapidly replaced another.

In 1954 a CIA NIE stated that the analysts believed that the communists would "without violating the armistice to the extent of launching an armed invasion to the south or west, pursue their objectives by political, psychological and paramilitary means," will "consolidate control over North Vietnam with little difficulty," and "will pursue a moderate program, which together with its strong military posture, will be calculated to make that regime appeal to the nationalist feelings of the Vietnamese population generally" (United States, 1971:691–92).

The CIA was very pessimistic about the establishment of a "strong regime" in South Vietnam. In April 1955 it said that it would be extremely difficult for a [South] Vietnamese government to "make progress toward developing a strong, stable, anti-Communist government capable of resolving the basic social, economic, and political problems of Vietnam, the special problems arising from the Geneva Agreement and capable of meeting the long-range challenge of the Communists" (Pentagon Papers, 1971a:266). As early as 1954, the NIE had predicted that if the elections scheduled by the Geneva agreements were held in 1956, the "Viet Minh will almost certainly win." In his memoirs, published in 1963, former President Eisenhower concurred with this view (Eisenhower, 1963:337–38).

But within a matter of weeks after the 1955 warning the United States firmly and finally committed itself to full support of Ngo Dinh Diem, "accepted his refusal to comply with the political settlement of Geneva, and acceded to withdrawal of French military power and political influence from South Vietnam." The next NIE on Vietnam published in 1959 had a similar tone, expressing doubts about the ability of the government to provide stability and avoid repression. US policy still remained firmly behind the Diem government (Pentagon Papers, 1971a:266–67). The numerous reservations about US policy had not affected official optimism. An interdepartmental task force report sent to the president in April 1961 estimated that in early 1960 there had been 4,400 hardcore communists in South Vietnam, while in April 1961 that number had expanded to 12,000. The percentage of the country presumed to be under some degree of communist control was 58 percent. South Vietnam, the report intoned, "is nearing the decisive phase in its battle for survival" (United States, 1971:44). By November, the president's most senior advisers warned that the chances were against "preventing the fall of South Viet-Nam by any measures short of the introduction of U.S. forces on a substantial scale" (Goldstein, 2008:60).

Clark Clifford, who in 1965 counseled President Johnson against involvement in the war and later replaced Robert McNamara as secretary of defense, said, "From the beginning . . . we were constrained by the fact that our South Vietnamese allies were corrupt, inefficient, and poorly motivated. This was critical: in the final analysis, American objectives in Vietnam depended more on the capabilities of our allies in Saigon than on our own efforts. And the more we did for them, the more dependent and ineffectual they became" (Record, 1998:178), the more the large-scale American presence in the country "presents a potential source of offense to Vietnamese sensibilities." While the general Vietnamese attitude toward the United States is friendly, "extreme nationalism and concomitant anti-western feeling are not far below the surface" (FRUS, 6/4/58). At that time the war was being lost, and this led to the introduction of substantial numbers of US fighting forces in 1965 to try another way to stem the tide. One commentator put it bluntly: "There is ample evidence that revolutionary forces would have taken over control of the South in 1965 had it not been for the introduction of U.S. combat troops [in March 1965]" (Duiker, 1994:374).

The government of South Vietnam "directly reflects the personal characteristics and philosophy of President Diem," wrote one perceptive Defense Department analyst in early 1962. Diem's aloof paternalism, dedication, and courage; his inability to delegate authority or compromise; and his illusions of omnipotence stemming from his past luck in going against advice and winning result in a government that is authoritarian and overcentralized and not popular. It is inefficient and corrupt, but not by the standards of Southeast Asia. In normal times, it might suffice. But these are not normal times—they are revolutionary times. Lyndon Johnson said it is too much to ask young and underdeveloped countries to carry out economic and democratic political development while they are also resisting communist violence, all at the same time. We could assist with all three tasks, but the "*main objective at present was to help them resist those using force against them*" (emphasis added, Johnson, 1971:44). This emphasis on the military always characterized American policy in Vietnam, and Diem's policy, and with disastrous results (FRUS, 12/7/59; 5/26/59; 11/17/58). Johnson rightly realized that the demands made upon the South Vietnamese government might have exceeded its capacity. His disastrous solution, therefore, was to give priority to the military and postpone social/political reform till later.

DEVELOPMENT OF THE SINO-SOVIET DISPUTE

The development of the Sino-Soviet dispute was a major event in the international system. The chief enemy of the United States, one pole in a bipolar system, was substantially weakened once the Chinese refused to give obeisance to the Soviets as the leader and authority of the communist movement. This was not so much because of Chinese power—China was relatively weak—but because it vastly weakened the authority and mystic of the Soviet Union and the solidarity of the communist bloc. From then on, no state could be considered an automatic ally of any communist country, since there was no center or ultimate authority and the disposition of each individual state was decided by itself, given its own circumstances. The potential for communist states or even the United States playing one communist power off against another was greatly increased. In his pathbreaking work, Donald Zagoria pointed out that as early as September 1956 Mao was reported to be siding with Eastern

European countries in their struggle against Moscow, thereby weakening Moscow's authority and aiding in putting distance between them and Moscow (Zagoria, 1962:55–56).[8] The assumptions that lay behind the Korean War of a monolithic communist bloc, including the idea that Stalin had sanctioned and supported the invasion by the North, could no longer be so easily assumed in Vietnam as the conflict continued. In a literal sense, the dispute did not change much. Yugoslavia had already split off from the bloc and gone its own way. It helped that it did not have a border with the Soviets, but the development of a conflict between the Soviets and China made such similar developments elsewhere much more likely. Now, not only was it "legitimate" to have an independent position in international politics, it was mandatory, since the bloc was split in two and each communist country must decide to whom it was loyal and what its position on the dispute was. In the new situation, "diversity threatens unity." "Communism will gain from polycentrism in that local Communist parties, in adapting themselves to local conditions and sentiments, will be better able to gain the genuine support of their own peoples" (Zagoria, 1962:398–99).

A second consequence of the development of the conflict for the situation in Vietnam was the potential dispersal of power. By the late 1950s the dispute was quite significant although it was neither acknowledged publicly by either the Soviets or the Chinese nor was it well-known among other nations. In the 1960s, however, the accelerating developments and their significance could no longer be missed. By 1963 the Soviets and the Chinese were openly trading charges and insults. It was clear that this phenomenon was important and was here to stay, although opinions differed greatly on how wide the breach between Moscow and Beijing would grow (Zagoria, 1962). This development obviously had enormous significance for the situation in Vietnam and for American policy there. During the 1950s, when the dispute was unknown or sub rosa, it was sensible to assume that North Vietnamese activities aimed at subverting or taking over South Vietnam or other countries had the support of either China, or the Soviets, or most probably, both. North Vietnam expansionist activities therefore represented an extension of communist bloc power and could represent a real challenge to the West. As the 1960s wore on, however, these assumptions became irrelevant and outmoded.[9] Given the lessened intensity of the linkage between North Vietnam and both the Soviet Union and the Chinese, the United States could exploit policies that would exacerbate the friction between Vietnam and each of the communist powers, and promote those policies that would pull North Vietnamese policies toward those favorable to US interests.[10] To the extent this effort was successful, North Vietnam would become a nonproblem for the Americans. Because of its small size and weak status, an eventual conquest of South Vietnam would not threaten US interests. Even more, the closer it could be drawn into the US orbit, the bigger problem it would be for China and the Soviet Union.

If the United States was really primarily concerned about the foreign policy threat of China in Asia because of its size and potential capabilities, then in light of the Sino-Soviet dispute it made little sense to follow a policy aimed at destroying and demoralizing Vietnam. It would have been the wiser policy to support Vietnam in its tacit declaration of autonomy from China. The Sino-Soviet dispute, in other words, increased the chance of an Asian Tito. The United States should have supported that development, rather than punish a potentially deviant small country and drive it to embrace its erstwhile communist allies. This was essentially the argument made by Hans Morgenthau. China is the hereditary enemy of Vietnam. Ho Chi Minh came to power by leading an indigenous revolution, and is a natural candidate to be an Asian Tito.

> How adversely would a Titoist Ho Chi Minh, governing all of Vietnam, affect the interests of the United States? The answer can only be: not at all. One can even maintain the proposition that, far from affecting adversely the interests of the Untied States, it would be in the interest of the United States if the western periphery of China were ringed by a chain of independent states.

Morgenthau is arguing that it should not have been US policy to contain all Asian communist countries, but rather the main concern should be Chinese power and the extent to which that affects US interests. Morgenthau did not believe one significantly diminished Chinese power by militarily attacking Vietnam, any more than the Chinese could contain the power of the United States in the Western Hemisphere by arming Costa Rica and Nicaragua (Morgenthau, 1965:63, 68).[11] A more promising approach would have been to appeal to nationalism. The Sino-Soviet dispute laid that nationalist content bare for all to see. "In all Communist states, the ally of the West is nationalism" (Zagoria, 1962:401). Why did US policy makers have so much trouble recognizing this?

The Pentagon Papers provide documentation showing that Kennedy gave more consideration to the dispute and had more awareness of its implications than Johnson. In March 1962 at the University of California, Kennedy talked of "profound divisions within the Communist world . . . divisions which have already shattered the image of communism as a universal system guaranteed to abolish all social and international conflicts." The long view, he intoned, shows that "the revolution of national independence is a fundamental fact of our era." And diversity and independence represent the very essence of the US vision of the future. And in his annual message to the Congress in January 1963, Kennedy spoke cautiously of "the comfort we can take from the increasing strains and tensions within the Communist bloc." While cautioning that the dispute is about means and not ends, and "a strain is not a fracture," he nonetheless concluded that the forces of diversity are at work inside the communist camp and "the historical force of nationalism" is a formidable force (Pentagon Papers, 1971b:808, 815). Perusal of documents produced under President Johnson, however, shows they provided a rationale for the war for him and his staff for 1964 and the first half of 1965. None of the statements showed any significant awareness of the dispute or its significance regarding the Vietnam problem (Pentagon Papers, 1979). In spite of Johnson's repeated attempts to cloak his handling of the war with the Kennedy mantle, in this case his views seemed to differ substantially from the former president's. As late as June 1964, Secretary of Defense MacNamara was referring to the "Sino-Soviet bloc" that threatens "potential military aggression from without" and "attempted subversion from within" (Pentagon Papers, 1979: 7171).[12] On the other hand, there is evidence that lower levels of officialdom were very aware of the implications of the dispute. There was a healthy tradition in US diplomacy of officials, starting with Truman's secretary of state, Dean Acheson, noting the potential for separating the Soviets and the Chinese and advocating policies to accomplish that. On May 17, 1951, an NSC meeting stated current objectives were to "[d]etach China as an effective ally of the USSR and support the development of an independent China," and "stimulate differences between the Peiping and Moscow regimes." Unfortunately these broad goals were contradicted by further admonitions to keep China out of the U.N. and otherwise antagonize it, hardly the way to approach intensification of the Sino-Soviet dispute (FRUS, 5/17/51; Gaddis, 2005). This tradition of thinking in terms of separated communist powers was substantially curtailed by the McCarthyite atmosphere in the 1950s and State Department purges of China hands. An NIE of May 14, 1957, notes the probable disappointment of North Vietnam over the inadequacy of support it has received from the Soviets and the Chinese toward uniting the country under northern rule (FRUS, 5/14/57). In early 1962, Philip Bridgham in International Security Affairs in the Pentagon prepared a paper in which he argued that in 1960–61, the North Vietnamese achieved a "new status of independence and influence in the Communist bloc" and that they have every reason to "persist in their chosen role of mediator and neutral in the deepening conflict between the Soviet Union and China" (FRUS, 2/6/62).

Leslie Gelb and Richard Betts, in their well-known contention that "the system worked" regarding decisions taken on Vietnam, argue that post-mortems that criticize the Kennedy administration for thinking in terms of a monolithic communist bloc are not persuasive because spokesmen for "informed opinion" also thought that way (Gelb and Betts, 1979:71). This logic is indeed jarring. The US government has, and had for decades, a very expensive intelligence service whose job it was to discern trends in international affairs and inform policy makers of them so that they can act on this information. Officials should not need the help of "informed opinion" to discover these issues.

In fact, the CIA was studying the Sino-Soviet dispute, since Zagoria's study itself had originated in the CIA. Although late in discussing it publicly, the organization was well aware of the dispute by 1961, discussed it privately, and by 1962 it had become an increasingly important theme in intelligence reports. But the policy community in particular was unsure of the policy implications, and it continued to publish contradictory information (United States, 1971:291–94). The isolation of official Washington, seemingly still given to the "old myths," as J. William Fulbright had it, had not yet caught up to the "new realities" (Fulbright, 1966). This situation did not constitute a felicitous environment for the determination of what US security interests were.

It should not be imagined, however, that the rest of the country was as clueless about developments in Southeast Asia as were Washington policy makers. Teach-ins on the war took place and books against the war highlighting the dispute appeared. Until resignations started (presidential aide McGeorge Bundy, February 1966; George Ball, September 1966; Bill Moyers, early 1967; Secretary of Defense Robert McNamara, February 1968) one would have thought there was little or no communication between the dissenters in the country and the officials who made policy.

THE INTELLECTUAL ISOLATION OF US POLICY MAKERS

Midway through their stimulating book on Vietnam, Gelb and Betts, discussing the "reasoned faith" on the importance of not losing Vietnam held by the men in the upper echelons of American policy making, make the insightful statement that "[t]hese men were locked into their perspectives." No foreign policy review by the officials involved would change the situation, only a stimulus from outside, an intrusion of the domestic political process, could affect the situation (Gelb and Bettts, 1979: 200). Of course that intrusion of domestic political forces did come, but belatedly. It came belatedly because American society too, except for an articulate minority, was locked into an outlook, or at least an intuitive belief, that corresponded roughly to the worldview of the foreign-policy-making elite. It was this parochial shared outlook that is the key to understanding the Vietnam debacle. As Gelb and Betts say, Vietnam was not "an aberration of the decisionmaking system, but a logical culmination of the principles that leaders brought with them into it" (Gelb and Betts, 1979:2). They made decisions reflecting policy that followed from their underlying assumptions, and that had resulted from the normal bargaining and to and fro of the democratic decision-making process. What was missing from this calculation was consideration of what was likely to happen over the long term when the substantial evidence of the ineffectiveness of US policy merged with the American people's impatience with casualties and a war that was clearly not being won.

Homegrown critics of the war were not lacking. Especially by mid-decade cogent criticism was audible. Hans Morgenthau's critique of the policy came out in 1965, presenting a realist perspective and making explicit the implications of the Sino-Soviet conflict.[13] Other critics were to follow shortly, including Walter Lippmann, George Kennan, Arthur Schlesinger, and others. Some in-house critics of the war existed in the administration. Best known was George Ball, who had already resigned in frustration by late 1966. And former Undersecretary of State Chester Bowles, another dissenter, had been removed from his post.

But the best indicator of the isolation of the United States on the issue of Vietnam was its difficulty in finding allies and similar perspectives among countries abroad. In July 1964, for example, the State Department urged allied governments, both in Europe and Asia, to provide greater material and rhetorical support for the war and to publicly distance themselves from the French position on the war crafted by de Gaulle, which Johnson was finding increasingly nettlesome. "I am gravely disappointed," the president wrote, "by the inadequacy of the actions by our friends and allies in response to our request that they share the burden of the free world responsibility in Vietnam." Given that the United States then had 16,000 "advisers" on the ground in Vietnam, the president thought the allied contribution, especially that of the larger countries, should be hundreds of men each, not mere dozens. West Germany, Britain, the Netherlands, Denmark, and Italy had already ruled out even a small military presence in South Vietnam (Logevall, 1999:178–79). Only a few Asian countries, Thailand, the Philippines, Australia, New Zealand and the Republic of Korea eventually made signifi-cant contributions. Korea sent two fighting infantry divisions to Vietnam and suffered heavy casualties there (Logevall, 1999:178–79; Kattenburg, 1980:218–20).

Among the most impassioned and articulate of the critics was Charles de Gaulle, who not only made his criticism known, but presented his own plan for dealing with the situation in former French Indochina. France, which had liquidated its Indochina responsibilities, had developed the habit of involuntarily liquidating colonial possessions. De Gaulle himself had overseen the withdrawal from Algeria and the granting of its status as an independent country. Following on Dien Bien Phu, the humiliating defeat in Vietnam, the war in Algeria seemed to suggest that the French were slow learners, since that was also a mismanaged war that dragged on too long, soured the country on the cause, and led to defeat. So the French and de Gaulle were not without experience regarding the situation the Americans were facing in Vietnam.[14]

In May of 1961 de Gaulle met with the newly inaugurated President Kennedy, and de Gaulle gave his opinion on the US dilemma in Vietnam. "You will find," de Gaulle told him, "that intervention in this area will be an endless entanglement. Once a nation has been aroused, no foreign power, however strong, can impose its will upon it." The more you become involved out there against communism, the more the communists will appear as the champions of national independence, de Gaulle warned. You will sink step by step into a quagmire no matter how much you spend in men and money (de Gaulle, 1971:256). There was plenty of mutual suspicion on both sides of the US-French divide. The Americans saw France, and particularly de Gaulle, pursuing only its own egotistical ends at the expense of broader Western goals. American officials found traces of *Schadenfreude* in French criticism and they were deeply hurt by it. The French saw the Americans as naïve and intent on implementing their version of policy at the expense of the Europeans, and particularly the French. They thought the American leadership with its gung ho approach to Vietnam sounded like the French premiers of the 1950s. Kennedy said de Gaulle should be listened to,[15] and George Ball met with him in 1964 and found they had similar views on the war, but as the war escalated and French criticism went public Johnson became increasingly paranoid about de Gaulle's criticism and the likely impact of it.[16]

Gelb and Betts argue the system worked because the process worked, even if the substance of the policy failed. One must distinguish between substance and process. But did the *process* work? Perhaps all the decision points were touched and each legitimate decision-making institution had its say in making individual decisions on Vietnam. But the key is that US decision makers, just as the rest of the country, were not able to transcend the cultural assumptions and perspectives to which they were captive. The rest of the world disagreed with the Americans on Vietnam. They did not subscribe to American objectives in Vietnam nor did they believe the objectives were obtainable; but those facts had little impact on American thinking. It took Richard Nixon's trip to Beijing to finally destroy the 1950s perception of the monolithic communist bloc that had survived beyond its time.[17]

BEYOND SECURITY INTERESTS

The focus here has been on US security interests in Vietnam. But there were other factors propelling the United States toward prosecuting the war in Vietnam. Messianic idealism pervades the rhetoric on Vietnam and is tightly commingled with security proclamations. Americans and many American policy makers believed they were doing good deeds in Vietnam separate from and independent of any US security concerns. When Colin Powell first went to Vietnam as a 25-year old, a Major General gave them a pep talk the day after their arrival on why they had come to Vietnam. "To stop the spread of Marxism; to help the South Vietnamese save their country from a communist takeover. That was the finest thing we could do for our families, our country, and freedom-loving people everywhere. I was fired up all over again" (Powell, 1995:77–79). Powell became considerably more cynical as his time in the country extended, but there is no reason to doubt these feelings were genuine, as were those of plenty of more senior people. Writer Guenter Lewy, who also fought in Vietnam, speaks of the "moral impulse which played a significant part on the original decision to help protect the independence of South Vietnam" (Lewy, 1978:441).

Norman Podhoretz, still a strong defender of the war, wrote that the United States went into Vietnam not for the sake of its own direct interests but "for the sake of an ideal." We were trying to save South Vietnam from the evils of communism (Podhoretz, 1983:197). Some would say these utterances are simply the appeals used by the leadership to rally the population to fight the war. No doubt it was that, but it was more. From the top of the society to the bottom these kinds of sentiments were common. They permeated the atmosphere. In many cases discussion of the war included both elements of national security concerns and moral aspirations, in many cases all entangled with one another. The speaker never stopped to think about how to separate them, or indeed, wouldn't have been able to do so even if asked. Just as in the Philippine War in 1898, the jingoism, or the moral statements—each individual can make her choice of words—were rampant. But in Vietnam, many believed passionately that there was a strong case to be made for national security concerns as well.

One doesn't have to have read a lot of official pronouncements on the Vietnam War to know that the distinction between security and values was maintained more in the breach than in the observance. Without doubt the importance of the moral element as an ingredient tended to justify greater costs in the war, in terms of both soldiers and civilians, than could have been done on purely security grounds. Here Kissinger's belief that one cannot conduct foreign policy in America without paying proper deference to moral issues is most relevant. The increased confusion that results from conflating the two issues is the price that must be paid for conducting foreign policy, or at least unpopular foreign policy.

HOW THE WAR WAS PROSECUTED

We have seen that the social, political, and economic situation in South Vietnam should have been an important factor in the decision whether or not to go to war. Perhaps nothing better illustrates the delusions inherent in the thinking that went into the Vietnam War than an interview given in 1964 in which the former chief American military adviser in South Vietnam from 1955–1960, General Samuel T. Williams, admitted that his first priority had been to "organize the armed forces to repel an invasion coming down from the Communist North" (Wohlstetter, 1968). A common preconception, especially during the 1950s, was the expectation of an invasion from China. Once the decision was made to support the Vietnamese, and ultimately to commit American troops, then it was again necessary to consider the totality of Vietnamese society when deciding how to fight the war. It was the failure to give sufficient attention to the unique situation in Vietnam and adjust the battlefield strategy and tactics sufficiently that resulted in the magnitude of the defeat. What the outcome of the war would have been using another approach is hypothetical and we cannot know the answer to that question. It is clear, however, that the American propensity to view the Vietnamese conflict through the perspective of other conflicts, in which the United States has excelled, had a detrimental effect on the prosecution of this one. The American armed forces "contributed to their own defeat in Vietnam by fighting the war they wanted to fight rather than the one at hand." US civilian and military officials were ignorant of Vietnam's "martial history and culture" and believed there was "little if anything to be learned by studying the French defeat in Indochina" (Record, 1998:xix–xxiii).[18] Unlike the British in Malaya, the US army was not a "learning institution." Having an interest in counterinsurgency was hardly a way to further one's career. In one infamous case, a briefing that Lt. Colonel John Paul Vann had scheduled with the chair of the joint chiefs Maxwell Taylor on the disastrous battle of Ap Bac was cancelled in July of 1963 when Kennedy's special assistant for counterinsurgency obtained a copy of Vann's briefing and decided he did not want Vann's dissent on the record. After one instance in which the ARVN was thoroughly defeated in the autumn of 1964, one US military spokesman made a statement that it was "our fervent hope" that the communists would "stick their neck out with about six battalions around here some day and try to hold something." At that time, he said, "they've had it." The VC, he went on to say, are excellent at ambushes, but that is a coward's way of fighting the war (Nagl, 2005:xxii, 135, 139–42). This is a frequent reaction to confronting the need to adapt to the exigencies of guerrilla warfare. Rather than recognize the situation for what it is—and getting educated about what is going on around you—the tendency is to criticize the guerrilla for following what is the classic guerrilla technique for dealing with a stronger force. That technique does not include showing up with a half-dozen battalions to serve as cannon fodder for the other side. The spokesman would not only have a long wait for the desired situation to materialize, but in the meantime the opportunity to take the adaptive steps to fight the guerrillas on their own terms will have disappeared.

The communists suffered criticism and self-criticism, and in the process honed their tactics and increased their effectiveness against the ARVN and the Americans. Their *raison d'etre* was to encourage flexibility and enhance their approach to the point of maximum effectiveness against the enemy by studying failures and disasters and learning all they could from them. "The record . . . shows that though the revolutionaries were often knocked down, they were never knocked out. They seemed to find ways of recovering from every setback by devising new approaches when old tactics faltered, from the French period right through to the end" (Elliott, 2007:8). This kind of flexibility on the enemy's side mandates the same adaptability on the other side. While the ARVN and the United States became better at adapting to the tactics of the communists after General Creighton Abrams took over Westmoreland's position, leading the effort in Vietnam by putting more emphasis on meeting peasant needs and controlling fire-power, the effort was too little, too late. All along, Robert Thompson notes, there had been plenty of young Americans with insightful criticism of the war and plenty of alternatives to suggest, but there was no channel for this kind of dialogue and consequently there was little impact on the conduct of the war (Nagl, 2005:199–200). On the other hand, had all these factors determining the situation and dictating the kind of war that needed to be fought been more carefully considered at the beginning, there might have been a decision to avoid getting involved militarily at all.

The first Vietnam crisis culminating in Dien Bien Phu, was not one of "military exigency . . . [r]ather the crisis centered on the failure of the West to respond to the broad spectrum of challenges underlying a popular surge of nationalistic, anti-imperialist sentiment that had been evident and powerful in Indochina since 1945" (Gurtov, 1967,161–62). But what does it mean to respond to a surge of nationalist and anti-imperialist sentiment?

It goes beyond the literal elimination of the foreigner and the institution of local rule. Implicit in the charge of imperialism is the idea that rule by the foreigner is bad, and elimination of the imperialist invader will result in an improvement of government and the citizen's—the peasant's—livelihood. The mechanism of rule will become more "democratic" in the broad sense, that is, it will better reflect the will of the peasant. Thus, Gurtov lists the following grievances that had been experienced from the end of WWII: inadequacy of land reform; gaps separating the Saigon leaders from the peasantry; corruption and inefficiency of a powerless native elite; instability of the currency; inequities in the legal system; press controls; inability to provide security for peasant villages and absence of a counterappeal to communist propaganda. To this one can add the simple reality of the foreign presence. "It was the foreign intervention in Vietnam and the division of the country imposed from outside that created a receptive audience for the simple nationalist message" (Elliott, 2007:xxi). It was the combustible mix of nationalist appeals and hopes for a better future that constituted the motivational tool the communists used, and that the South Vietnamese side lacked (FRUS, 5/26/59; 3/23/62).[19]

An extensive and highly regarded study by Jeffrey Race throws additional light on the dynamics of the communist movement and the factors that led to their success and the American withdrawal from Vietnam. He studied Long An province, lying south and west of Saigon, and created in 1957. Drawing on documents and extensive interviews with cadres, government officials, and peasants he was able to analyze extensively the plans, programs, and mind-set of people on both sides of the conflict. The results suggest the political underpinning of the organization and military capability that made life difficult for the government side and the American military.

According to Race, the failure of the [South Vietnamese] government "[was] a conceptual one." The government was defensive when it should have been proactive. It was centrally oriented when it should have been community- or participation-centered, and it favored the status quo when it should have favored change that would benefit the lower levels of the social structure. The result was a lack of appeal for the government side that gave the peasant little reason to support the government or to contribute to its political and military activities in the countryside. The revolutionary side, on the other hand, was able to motivate the peasant and compel him to take risks, even the risk of death, when forced to choose between the two sides (Race, 1972).

The party's movement was political; it had definite objectives that had some appeal to the people in the villages, allowing mobilization of the villagers. Not the least of these were objectives of a redistributional nature, which the government ignored, assuming the countryside was basically happy. Passiveness equates with consent, was the assumption among officials representing South Vietnam. Words such as "class," "conflict," and "contradiction" or their non-Marxist equivalents were not part of the vocabulary of the Saigon government. Officials were oblivious to the land problem, and often in denial that the other side had distributed land. The balance of forces in a political sense was not a part of the frame of reference of government personnel. Lacking any predisposition toward redistribution and with unconvincing nationalist credentials, the government lacked objectives or a program to mobilize for action. The government presence, therefore, was limited to administrative tasks, the very perspective that the party, when exhorting its cadre, warned against. The government's administrative effectiveness, moreover, was not high. A low level of competence characterized the government apparatus in tax collection or preparation of an accident report, for instance.

The party was therefore proactive, while the government was defensive, and the former was for change, while the latter was pro status quo. The government assumed contentment and resistance to the revolutionary movement on the part of the peasant; the party fermented the revolution by assuming the peasants wanted less inequality and a larger role in political decisions. Further, the party's political and administrative focus was on the local level, the village and the hamlet. The government's was on the province and the district level. Higher government officials viewed the village heads as errand boys for carrying out decisions arrived at by higher ups, whereas the party empowered lower village-level officials with authority on issues important to the peasants, such as taxation, justice, military recruitment, and land.

But if nationalism and anticolonialism were collective slogans, the party made sure they were defined and implemented in a way that benefited the individual. Redistribution of land and recruitment of lower-class individuals to political positions gave these peasants a stake in taking action to ensure that communist-controlled area did not revert to government rule. The communist view of human action is that it is determined by interest. The cadres aimed at creating a plan of action that would allow the peasant to connect his interest with a long-term change in the social situation. Race's perspective is thus in line with that of James C. Scott, who believed that the issues of exploitation and rebellion cannot be explained just in terms of calories and income, but are rather the question of peasant conceptions of justice, of rights and obligations, and of reciprocity (Scott, 1976).

Of much interest is the observation that the principles outlined here seemed to work when employed in other than revolutionary settings and by groups other than the communists. Race notes that Luong Hua, a catholic village, which in the whole province best *resisted* revolutionary pressures, was the "one which most closely resembled in form the approach which the party itself had employed in developing its strength." By 1965, Luong Hua was miles from the nearest government outpost and accessible only by air. Yet despite heavy pressure, local officials remained at their posts and the village remained in the government camp (Race, 1972:186–87). Luong Hua was the exception that proved the rule. The party had a purpose and a direction that allowed it to mobilize its followers and advance toward the goal, in this case, the takeover of South Vietnam. The catholics of Luong Hua had a mission of maintaining autonomy and independence in the face of communist pressure. But South Vietnam as a whole was never able to develop the sense of purpose and solidarity to provide the necessary bulwark against the revolutionary movement. On the contrary, it was the government's weakness and lack of communication with the villages that allowed the revolutionary movement to proceed. If all of the south had displayed the solidarity and purpose of the catholics of Luong Hua, the war might well have had a different ending. But the reality was that the government played its assigned role, that of a centralized, corrupt, and bureaucratic behemoth that was only minimally responsive to the problems of the countryside, and it allowed the revolution to progress.

But the military strategy was also wrong. Komer contrasts the "mixed counterinsurgency strategy which U.S. and GVN policy called for from the outset, and the overwhelmingly conventional and militarized nature of our actual response." Instead of matching our military and our strategy there to the unique circumstances of Vietnam, we "fought the enemy our way," because we lacked the "incentive and the . . . capability to do otherwise" (Komer, 1972:vi–vii).[20] As discussed in Chapter 1, the central characteristic of counterinsurgency is "the reliance on population for active support or a least passive acquiescence" (Long, 2006:15). According to Komer, the US's costly search-and-destroy or attrition strategy had tremendous costs and tragic side effects. American leaders did not make a real effort to come to grips with these key social and political problems. Instead, most often the Americans "did the thing that we had the most readily available capability to do," whether or not it was what was needed. The means available tended to determine what kind of action was taken. Lacking an integrated strategy and a matching perspective on implementation, the war became a collection of different approaches that might or might not fit together in a complementary fashion producing a coherent result. In the words of Townsend Hoopes, "For the enemy, the war remained fundamentally a seamless web of political-military-psychological factors to be manipulated by a highly centralized command authority that never took its eye off the political goal of ultimate control in the South." For the United States, however, the war had become, by 1967, three separate struggles: the large-scale conventional war, the confused "pacification" effort, and the remote air war against North Vietnam (Komer, 1972:73).

Albert Wohlstetter suggested that in Vietnam the United States had two choices: "Should we concentrate on the slow, persistent attempt to help construct a viable government capable of economic and political self-development, able to protect an increasing proportion of the population from subversion and terror, and so to reduce the local support for guerrillas or infiltrated Northern forces?" Or should we "focus our major efforts on trying to hunt down and annihilate guerrillas and the main force units of the DRV?" He continues: the first alternative would have required smaller military forces than the second. It would "subordinate conventional military operations." It would attempt to prevent the establishment of base areas by the communists, but it would not expend its efforts on "search and destroy." He adds: *It would have taken years and may not have been successful at all* (emphasis added). The second alternative, the one the United States took, required the application of "brute force massively" and the impact of that strategy strained the capabilities of both the governments in Saigon and Washington (Wohlstetter, 1968).

For most Americans in Vietnam, counterinsurgency had mainly to do with guerrillas that were alien and distinct elements. It was not conceivable that they were men and women from the villages themselves, whose support and requests for food, assistance, passage, and information may be voluntarily complied with by the population. Almost no American planners realized that the guerrillas could be perceived to be champions of national independence, even if they were also communists. They were usually perceived as people sent in from outside, intruders into village life bringing with them a violent, alien, and unwanted doctrine. If this was the case, then the policies and actions of these "guerrillas"—such as, for instance, assassinating a local headman—would be looked upon by the villagers as a highly undesirable event. Many times, if the official done away with was widely detested, the event was not unwelcome (Kattenburg, 1980:110–11

By emphasizing killing instead of wooing, the United States violated the basic tenants of counterinsurgency as here defined. It was not only the practice of the liberal use of indiscriminant fire-power that was the issue, but also the sheer amount of fire-power that was available.[21] This arsenal, when used on the population under the policy of free fire zones, where anything within the area was considered fair game, the liberal use of napalm in the latter stages of the war, or the policy that made anybody running from a soldier, plane, or other manifestation of the US presence a target, was hardly calculated to win friends or influence people. The US government, as represented by its main measure of success, was interested in maximizing the killing of communists, seemingly assuming there is no collateral cost to the effort to win over the South Vietnamese people.[22] At its worst the war disintegrated into wholesale massacres such as at the village of Tu Cong/My Lai where an entire village, including a hundred children under five were killed. But symbolic of the war effort was an incident one writer recorded: an American helicopter gratuitously and with no provocation, seemingly for sport, shooting and killing a herd of water buffalo being guarded by some small boys, possibly hitting several of the boys in the process (Stone, 2007; Record, 1998:87).

One further issue must be addressed here, that of the support of the war from North Vietnam and the supplies provided by China and the Soviet Union. This issue is perhaps presented most starkly by Harry G. Summers, who makes the thesis of his book virtually the opposite of what I have argued here. He argues that the failure to address the outside role of the communist powers and their interference in South Vietnam was the crucial flaw in the West's strategy. The answer from the perspective of this study is that the political solution is treated here as a sine quo non for resolution of the Vietnam problem in favor of the West. Without a political solution the cause is lost. That said, as military intervention from the North or its allies increased, the chances of resolving the problems decreased.[23] Solving the political problem would have gone far to immunize South Vietnam against interference from outside; not solving it meant that no amount of fending off northern interference would have saved the situation.

CONCLUSION

This study has focused on two issues. Whether or not the United States had a feasible security interest that justified the Vietnam War, and second, whether or not the methods by which that war was fought were appropriate to the objectives. To both questions the answer is negative.

The first problem for the United States, given its objective of preventing a communist takeover of South Vietnam, which would have extended North Vietnamese influence, was to construct a stable and legitimate political base for a government in South Vietnam that would enjoy the loyalty and support of the people and would provide support for the necessary military effort to defeat the communists. In a situation where the intervening power is dependent on a client state, wielding influence is almost always difficult. The client state wants to preserve its influence, but if it has not already succeeded in establishing a legitimate and popular government, it probably needs assistance to do so. But in addition to the likely struggle for influence between the local government and the intervening government that is likely to ensue, they are both likely to be placed in a dilemma, a sort of catch-22 situation where no matter what they do, the results will be inadequate. If the client government is left alone to improve its position on its on, it will not be successful. If on the other hand, the intervening government plays a strong role in promoting reforms or even taking over some of the functions of the client government, then it will compromise its legitimacy, its capabilities, and its standing with the populace. Since this sort of dilemma is almost impossible to solve, it suggests that a power contemplating intervention should not intervene, unless one of two conditions exist: either a legitimate and capable government is already functioning, in which case the intervention may not be necessary in any case, or there exists an overwhelming security interest that justifies high risk intervention. In the case of Vietnam, there existed a relatively quiet time in the late 1950s when, if progress were going to be made in bolstering the support and legitimacy of the Saigon government, it should have been done. Since it did not occur then, during the first few years of the 1960s the situation might still have been turned around without excessive American involvement. Again it was not, but again the United States persisted. There was a US determination, in the face of evidence that the South Vietnamese government could not be reformed, to redouble the effort.

The second reason for continuing intervention, even in the face of evidence of the intractability of the problem, would have been the presence of overwhelmingly important security interests. Whatever the value of holding the line against North Vietnamese influence in a place so difficult as Vietnam, it soon became evident that because of the development of the Sino-Soviet dispute, protecting South Vietnam from the North was not synonymous with resisting either Soviet or Chinese power.

There is no doubt that one of the big obstacles in deciding what US security interests in Vietnam were and how the United States should respond was the lack of clear analysis and communication among the policy-making elites about the problem. The discussion often did not move beyond platitudes, and as the discussion of the "domino theory" suggests, almost never included robust arguments that invoked empirical evidence to make a compelling case. The arguments revolved around empty abstractions unattached to supporting evidence. Even the abstractions were not consistent. According to Sir Robert Thompson, "I have asked many Americans what the American aim is in Viet Nam and have never yet received the same reply" (Thompson, 1968:448). It is hardly surprising that US allies and the rest of the world were at best unenthusiastic, and more often baffled at what the Americans were about in Vietnam.

Ernest May is probably right that the appropriate approach in South Vietnam would have been something closer to a police action instead of the massive military operation that ensued (Hoffmann, 1981:9). In Vietnam, there was a problem in the disproportion of ends and means in two senses. The limited security issues at stake did not justify the effort given to the war, and the means used to fight it were excessive and inappropriate for what was being attempted. Ignorance and arrogance are a deadly combination, and both were on display as the American missionary spirit combined with overwhelming military power to work disruptive and in many cases horrendous effects on Vietnamese society. The effort, however, was still inadequate.

CHAPTER 6

BOSNIA—1991–1995

The city will be divided into Muslim, Serbian, and Croatian sections, so that no ethnic groups will have to live or work together."
"Do you mean," I asked, "that Sarajevo will be like Berlin before the wall was destroyed?"
"Yes," he answered, "our vision of Sarajevo is like Berlin when the wall was still standing.

> Radovan Karadzic, the Bosnian Serb leader, on his vision for the future of Sarajevo, responding to US ambassador to Yugoslavia Warren Zimmermann during their last meeting in 1992

The US intervention in Bosnia-Herzegovina (hereafter Bosnia) stands out from the other case studies in that it is the only case where US policy makers were doubtful that there was an American security interest at stake. They avoided intervention as long as possible. But, unlike the other cases where intervention resulted in difficult and protracted war in the target country, in Bosnia once a serious military effort was made to end the conflict, it was quickly successful and with no loss of American life. But even in Bosnia, a difficult political dilemma lingers. The success of the effort in Bosnia has been primarily to stop the violence and transfer the conflict to the political arena.

While violence erupted in or involved numerous of the republics and autonomous areas that made up Yugoslavia, Bosnia was unique with its ethnic mix of 31 percent Serbs, 17 percent Croats, and 44 percent Muslims (and 5 percent "Yugoslav"). The disintegration of multicultural Bosnia was a follow-on of what happened to the larger Yugoslavia. In contrast to the clear-cut domination of Serbia, Croatia, and Slovenia by one ethnic group, in Bosnia the fragmented ethnonational make-up of the country, and the degenerating situation there, meant there was no power center able to counter the constantly increasing centrifugal forces breaking apart the republic. "In many respects the republic of Bosnia and Hercegovina became the last bastion of genuine Yugoslavism." Moreover, "in no republic was Tito's stature greater than in Bosnia, the home of the partisan movement and of his most disciplined and faithful party organization" (Donia and Fine, 1994:191–94).

The intensification of Serbian nationalism, in turn stimulating a similar development in the other provinces, proved a key development in the dissolution of Yugoslavia. An early momentous event was the publication in 1986 of a memorandum by the Serbian Academy of Sciences and Art. The memorandum portrayed the Serbs as victims of Tito and communist rule and accused Croats and Albanians of "genocidal" policies. Described by one scholar as "wading in collective self-pity and basking in the certainty that the Serbs were uniquely victimized by socialist Yugoslavia," the memorandum was "nothing less than an ideological program for revenge and for establishing Serb hegemony over Yugoslavia's non-Serbs." Amidst ongoing purges at various levels by Slobodan Milosevic, in October 1988 he organized a large demonstration—100,000 Serbs mostly from Kosovo and southern Serbia—to demand the resignation of the leadership of the province of Vojvodina, at the time an ongoing dispute. The sense of crisis led to capitulation in the province. Milosevic was able to strengthen his position and overwhelm the opposition's resistance, clearing the way for his dominance both in Serbia proper and Vojvodina as well as in Kosovo and Montenegro (Ramet, 2002:20–31; Serbian Academy, 1986).

Meanwhile, in Slovenia, nationalist sentiment in opposition to Serbian violation of human rights in Kosovo and Milosevic's increasingly obvious moves to strengthen the Serbian hold on Yugoslavia proper was developing along a parallel track in a movement for a looser federation with Yugoslavia. In September 1989 the Slovenes amended their constitution to allow secession from the Yugoslav federation. In December 1990, 88 percent of Slovenians voted in a referendum to separate from Yugoslavia (Donia and Fine, 1994:217–19). By late 1990, reasonably free elections had been held in all republics, and uniformly, parties stressing ethnicity rather than inclusive programs had won. This was an unwelcome development since it provided incentives to governments to work for parochial goals stimulating centrifugal forces rather than encouraging integration of the polities.

Meanwhile, Croatia had been slow to respond to provocations from Serbia (Silber and Little, 1995:83). But by January 1991 evidence of a growing nationalism and a developing arms race between the two republics was visible, and appeals from the federal presidency, backing the army's position to disband all "illegal paramilitary units" only encouraged the Croatians to step up preparations for an attack. In August/September 1990, Serbs in the Krajina and other Serb-dominated areas of Croatia, urged on by the Serbian media, organized a referendum that brought an overwhelming vote for autonomy. In a direct challenge to President Franjo Tudjman and the Croatian government, the "self-styled Serbian National Council proclaimed the 'Serbian Autonomous Region of Krajina.'" Analysts have deplored Tudjman's "serious misjudgment" of Croatia's Serb community. He encouraged the resurgence of a Croatian nationalism that failed to make any concessions to Serb concerns and insecurities as a minority in a predominantly Croat republic. He also refused to renounce the conduct of Croatia during its fascist period during WWII, from which many Serbs suffered greatly. The resulting war between the Serbs and Croatia lasted from June 1991 until January 1992 (Donia and Fine, 1994:216–27).

Party and government groups in Bosnia at first pursued the interests of Bosnia within the Yugoslav Federation without yielding to the "nationalistic divisiveness" that typified the leadership in some other republics. They supported the preservation of the Federation (Donia and Fine, 1994:194). But as Serbia and Croatia sparred over the final disposition of Yugoslavia, President Izetbegovic in Bosnia and his Macedonia counterpart, Kiro Gligorov, searched for a way to preserve the integrity of their more diverse republics with their mosaic of pluralistic groups. They proposed a plan whereby Serbia and Montenegro would be the core of a new federation, Macedonia and Bosnia would be semidetached, and Croatia and Slovenia would exercise as much sovereignty inside the federation as they saw fit. But this rather vague plan never took hold. Bosnia was the last republic to face a resolution of the problem of its relationship with Yugoslavia, but also the one to suffer the most from the eventual conflagration. The complex and fragmented ethnic and religious make-up accentuated the breakup, but the designs that both of its stronger neighbors had on Bosnia had doomed it from the beginning once the country disintegrated and links were established between Bosnian minorities and their corresponding fellow republics.[1] Bosnia finally conducted a referendum on autonomy—which the Serbs boycotted—and then declared independence in April 1992. The war in Bosnia, the main act of the Yugoslav tragedy, began almost at once.

Dealing with the consequences of these historical circumstances would occupy the United States and the Europeans from 1991–95. Not perceiving a pressing US interest in the growing conflict, the United States was at first willing to pass the responsibility for the Bosnian problem to the Europeans. Sensitive to charges of impinging on European turf, weary from the recent Desert Storm initiative to eject Iraq from Kuwait, and lacking ready-made solutions, the United States was more than willing to hand the problem on. "This is the hour of Europe, not the hour of the Americans," declared Jacques Poos of Luxembourg. Even more blunt was EC Commission Chairman Jacques Delors: "We do not interfere in American affairs. We hope they will have enough respect not to interfere in ours" (Muravchik, 1996:91).

US SECURITY INTERESTS

US security interests in the Balkans became much less pressing with the end of the cold war. Yugoslavia, once a critical battlefield in the dual with the Soviet Union because of Yugoslavia's stance of nonalignment, became just another country in Southeast Europe. Southeast Europe, including Greece and Turkey, was considered a key obstacle to potential Soviet advancement and the preservation of European integrity during the period of the superpower duel, but absent the Soviet threat and with the disintegration of Yugoslavia, the strategic significance of the area diminished sharply. "Barely viable states of little consequence," was one description of the small states emerging from the breakup (IISS, 1994). As Table 6.1 shows, the newly hatched nation-states were dwarfed by American power. Their lack of economic and military power was accentuated by their tenuous viability.

But other concerns existed. By the 1990s the concept of Yugoslavia was fading. Increasingly, Milosevic's support for federal power came to be linked with the continuation of socialist government, but even more important, with Serbian nationalism. More or less free elections, which by the end of the year had been held in all the republics, increasingly reflected an ethnic vote that returned parliaments that approximately reflected the ethnic make-up of the population. As identification with Yugoslavia declined, voters increasingly were forced to choose either an ethnic group or a republic that would best represent their interests or sympathies.[2] The six Yugoslav republics—Serbia, Croatia, Slovenia, Bosnia, Montenegro, and Macedonia—Warren Zimmermann said, were engaged in "'top down' competitive nationalism" as they competed for advantage in a rapidly disintegrating Yugoslav federation (Baker, 1995:478–79).

The reaction of the United States and Europe to the crisis in Yugoslavia suggests continuity with a historical stance where the Balkans were not viewed as an area in which major security interests were at stake or major threats originated. In his memoirs, former Secretary of State James Baker stated that, unlike in the Persian Gulf, "our vital interests were not at stake." On the other hand there were too many interests involved there to ignore the region entirely. The initial US stance on a disintegrating Yugoslavia was that all changes in borders or political processes should be negotiated through an agreed process. Otherwise, violence would result. Secretary of State James Baker visited Belgrade on June 21, 1991, where he

Table 6.1 US-Bosnia war statistics

Country	GNP/GDP (bn. $)	Pop (millions)	Total armed force	Defense expend. (mil. $)	Intervention forces (peak nos.)	US casualties	Other casualties
Bosnia	14 (1991)	4.383	92,000	600			Total in Bosnian war (all sides) 215,000
Croatia	18.1	4.785	105,000	1,800			Total in Croatian war (all sides) 6,651
Serbia	16	10.821	126,500	3,100			
US	7,100	263.119	1,650,500	270,600 (outlay)	20,000 (US) 40,000 (Eur)	0	

Sources: World Bank Atlas; The Military Balance (London: IISS); Strategic Survey (London: IISS).

shuttled from room to room and talked with the heads of the individual republics. Ultimately, Baker's message favored unity, at least for the short term. He told Yugoslav Prime Minister Markovic, who was trying to hold the country together and get economic reform started:

> I agree that separation will trigger violence and bloodshed. . . . Once it starts, you won't be able to get the toothpaste back in the tube. There has to be an agreement among republics; otherwise, there is no way to prevent Slovenia from deciding to take over a border post in six weeks. It might be logical to use the army to prevent this, but that would start an explosion. It only takes one match.

Baker was very critical of Milosevic, Tudjman, and Slovenian President Milan Kucan, who he believed were not receptive to his message and focused on their own short-term concerns. On the other hand, Bosnian President Izetbegovic, Macedonian President Vladimir Gligorov, and Prime Minister Markovic were all very aware of the danger and eager to take action to head it off (Baker, 1995:478–83). Baker's fears were confirmed on June 25 when the Slovenian and Croatian parliaments voted for independence, triggering war with Serbia and the Yugoslav army (JNA). Some critics have suggested that a more effective course of action would have been de facto recognition by the West of the republics in the spring of 1991, with full recognition upon fulfillment of certain conditions and guarantees of democracy and individual rights. The United States was simply behind the curve in hoping to preserve the status quo at the late date of Baker's trip to Belgrade (Ramet, 1994:202).

It is clear, to say the least, that the Bush administration was not predisposed to intervene in Bosnia. Secretary of State Baker puzzled over the development of the conflict. He found in Yugoslavia an "air of unreality" that depressed him and his colleagues, two of which, National Security Adviser Brent Scowcroft and Deputy Secretary of State Lawrence Eagleburger, had considerable expertise on Yugoslavia. Milosevic and Tudjman had a false sense of security, not believing that the worst could happen. It is "easier to deal with Shamir and Assad than it is to try to affect Milosevic and Tudjman." But this pessimistic assessment of the tractability of the problem, instead of goading the United States into a more aggressive role, seemingly contributed to their preference that the Europeans handle the issues. It was only when the Bosnian Foreign Minister Haris Silajdzic visited him in April 1992, and upon hearing Silajdzic's impassioned pleas about the Bosnians being killed, that Baker was prodded to put more pressure on the Europeans to do something (Baker, 1995:Chapter 33; Burg and Shoup, 1999:200–05).

As the conflicts in Croatia and Bosnia unfolded in 1991 and 1992, the concerns about a wider war increased. Slovenia was no problem. Milosevic and the Serb leadership had decided there was no reason to keep Slovenia within the federation (Silber and Little, 1995:113–14). There were no Serbs living in Slovenia, so after a perfunctory ten-day war (June-July 1991), it was allowed to go.

After Slovenia, Croatia was the next theater of combat, a sort of dress rehearsal for what was to come in Bosnia, although the Croatian War was much shorter and easier to bring under control. Ever since Tudjman had come to power in 1990 he had promoted an assertive nationalism. The Croatian Serbs declared their separation from Croatia on March 16, 1991, and as both sides stockpiled arms, the Yugoslav National Army (JNA) provided arms to the Serb minority. Even more enraging to inhabitants as well as the international community was the virtual destruction of the city of Vukovar through bombardment by the JNA, an air assault on Zagreb, and assaults on Dubrovnik, a beautiful medieval city on the Dalmatian coast with no military significance. In September, in an attempt to dampen the flames of war, the U.N. Security Council imposed an arms embargo on all of Yugoslavia. A United Nations Protection Force (UNPROFOR) to help keep the agreed peace began arriving two weeks later (Donia and Fine, 1994:223–27). But by the end of 1991, the key Serbian objective, to "carve out an enclave for their people and 'cleanse' it of Croats," had been achieved (Freedman, 1994:58).

As Robert Donia and John Fine point out, the JNA used Bosnia as a staging area for operations in Croatia. This allowed it to stockpile weapons and move resources into secure locations to "facilitate mobilization" in the event the conflict spread to Bosnia (Donia and Fine, 1994:227–29). At the Lisbon Conference in late February, just prior to the scheduled referendum on independence in Bosnia, the European Community was successful—in the first of many attempts to forge an agreement among the three parties for the partition of Bosnia. The United States went along and advised Bosnian President Izetbegovic to keep the agreement he had agreed to. But Izetbegovic changed his mind, and the EC reconvened the conference in Sarajevo. Izetbegovic again agreed only to renege once again, some think on American advice. In any case, the EC announced its recognition of Bosnia on April 6 and the United States followed on the next day with recognition of Slovenia, Croatia, and Bosnia (Donia and Fine, 1996:236). Whatever the exact fate of the partition project, the reality is that it had little chance of succeeding.

It became clear that the Bosnians were essentially faced with a choice of remaining as a rump to what had in effect become a Serbian Yugoslavia or declaring independence and taking their chances on retaining their independence and territorial integrity. The Bosnian Serbs, having declared their own republic in December, boycotted a referendum on independence held in February 1992. In that referendum, over 99 percent voted for independence, but only 64.4 percent of the population voted in it (Gow, 1997:84). Undeterred by the boycott, Bosnia declared independence in April, and both the United States and the EC recognized Bosnia's statehood, while the United States also recognized Croatia and Slovenia.

The development of the war in Bosnia now rapidly accelerated. Casualties, both military and civilian, increased as Serbia and the JNA joined the Bosnian Serbs in besieging Sarajevo, carrying out ethnic cleansing and expanding the Serbian-controlled area. The Bosnian Croats played both sides of the fence, sometimes siding with the Serbs, sometimes with the Bosnians, but in the end throwing their help to the Bosnians. The war in Bosnia would go on for more than three years while the Europeans and the Americans agonized about what to do to stop the violence. It was this wider war that threatened to expand to Kosovo, Macedonia, and other points if it was not stopped. Casualties from the Bosnian war accounted for by far the largest number of the total deaths during the period 1991–1995: an estimated 215,000 dead, of which 160,000 were Muslims, 30,000 Croats, and 25,000 Serbs. In addition 2.7 million refugees were created and 20,000–50,000 were estimated to have been raped by Serb soldiers. In contrast, 6, 651 were killed in the Serb-Croat war and in the Serbia-Slovenia clash casualties were only a few dozen.[3] The size and intensity of the Bosnian war, entirely within the confines of Europe, in turn raised another security issue inviting intervention: maintaining the credibility of NATO.

Although there was little sign of concern about the credibility of NATO at the top levels of the US government, inaction on the part of NATO in the face of a growing conflict near the heart of Europe would be bound to have an impact on NATO's viability. Having never intervened militarily during the cold war, a vicious military conflagration in Europe itself with little activity by NATO would be bound to raise questions about its long-term prospects as a security alliance. While the importance of NATO in US foreign policy had certainly lessened with the end of the cold war, the intent of the members was to prolong its viability. With the demise of the Soviet Union, in fact, NATO soon, in 1993, began to consider enlargement of its membership in central and eastern Europe to accommodate the new democracies that had emerged from the Soviet bloc (Kugler, 1996:xv). An inability to put a stop to the conflict in its own backyard would not reflect well on its credibility and was undoubtedly one of several reasons that the West did eventually act forcefully on the Bosnian conflict. The problem in Bosnia was that while one could argue that NATO's credibility required action, until NATO members were convinced that important interests were at stake, arguments appealing to the need to bolster the alliance's credibility were unlikely to be effective.[4]

Bosnia is a good case of a war in which there is value in distinguishing between security and humanitarian concerns in foreign policy. There was an abundance of evidence that humanitarian needs there were great. A significant number of battle deaths, ethnic cleansing, concentration camps, rape by troops, and widespread massacre of prisoners constitutes a partial list of the atrocities occurring in the former Yugoslavia. Stanley Hoffmann argues that in today's world, one cannot clearly distinguish, as some do, between "national interests" and "national values." Even during the cold war, the United States engaged in many foreign policy endeavors that could not be clearly linked to interests or issues that did not affect the lives of American citizens. Even more in the postwar period, the distinction between these two categories is tenuous. This is not to argue that all violations of American values around the world are deserving of US intervention. Rather, the particular combination of humanitarian interests in Bosnia—widespread attacks on civilians and even genocide, the widespread violation of international norms—aggressive attacks on sovereign countries, and disregard and widespread violation of U.N. resolutions, and attacks on U.N. forces, all within the immediate vicinity of the most vigorous and effective Western alliance, constituted a combination of issues that would inevitably erode both American and European prestige and ideas of world order if not defended against.[5] As Hoffmann put it, "certain levels and kinds of distress are morally unacceptable and certain political, economic, and social breakdowns too dangerous to world order to be ignored." He rightly argues that American officials, in squirming out of their responsibilities in Bosnia, often contradicted themselves and dealt carelessly with the facts. Bosnia is not a major conflict such as we might have feared during the cold war, but a "creeping escalation of disorder and beastliness that will, sooner or later, reach the shores of the complacent, the rich, and the indifferent."[6] I have shifted my own position on the place of security interests vs. humanitarian interests in the former Yugoslavia. Whereas I originally believed that intervention had to rest primarily on humanitarian concerns, I now believe Hoffmann's argument of an indivisible connection between events there and the broader canvas of American concerns around the world is clear (Bert, 1997:68). The fate of the states originating in the former Yugoslavia, however miniscule in power terms, was of substantial concern, given the humanitarian violations and the serious threat of disorder to the modern European structures. Numerous commentators with diverse perspectives on international problems have expressed the concern that failure to deal with the ethnic fragmentation, brutality, and war in Southeast Europe would have a deleterious effect on other areas of minorities living in a volatile environment, especially in Eastern Europe and the Muslim world.[7] Over the long term, a failure to deal with the disorder would have contributed to the disorientation and weakening of the United States, Russia, the European Community, NATO, and the U.N., and would have done considerable harm to the American reputation for maintaining a world order in line with its values. Clearly, the Democratic candidate for president, William Clinton, was also moving in this direction. On August 5, he called on President Bush to "do whatever it takes to stop the slaughter of civilians, adding, "we may have to use military force."

IMPLEMENTING INTERVENTION

Sabrina Ramet suggested that early recognition of the disintegrating polity of Yugoslavia and prompt efforts to recognize the emerging states with the proper safeguards might have avoided violence by preempting the continued efforts toward consolidation by Milosevic and the army. James Gow has alleged that the point at which the outbreak of the Bosnia War in the spring of 1992 began to appear likely, after seizure by the Serbs of some 30 percent of Croatia's territory, would have been a time for the West to stand firm and, if necessary, take military action to end it (Ramet, 1994; Gow, 1997:83).

When Yugoslavia began to unravel, what most outside governments, many of which eventually became involved, wanted more than anything was for the problem to just "go away quickly, quietly, inexpensively and with all refugees back where they came from" (Switzer, 2001:285). They were caught unprepared—the issue was messy and complex and might require a real foreign policy effort and related costs, both material and political, to solve.

PARTITIONED BOSNIA VS. INTEGRATED BOSNIA

The issue of a partitioned Bosnia as a solution to the conflict runs like a red thread through the dispute over Bosnia, from the debate in the Bosnian parliament prior to the referendum and the start of the war in early 1992 through to the present. The controversy is still not quieted, and if anything is more central to the country's future than ever. The Serbs have consistently favored partition and the Muslims have favored an integrated state. The continuing tension speaks volumes about what remains to be done. After a three-and-a-half-year war, endless conferences, and a fifteen-year occupation, the key issue dividing the involved parties is still nearly as salient as before.

The United States supported an integrated multiethnic state, but this view was not so popular in Europe. One Western official said that Croatian president Tudjman accurately reflected the views of many Western governments when he said Europe would not tolerate an Islamic state in its midst, and therefore division of Bosnia into Serb, Croat, and Muslim communities was inevitable (The *New York Times*, 1992:16; 1994:IV:1). The British preference for partition as a solution is deeply ingrained" (Magas and Zanic, 2001:306).[8]

A second example of a potential settlement package, beyond that proposed at Lisbon, was the Vance-Owen (V-O) agreement, promoted by the cochairs of the International Conference on the Former Yugoslavia (ICFY), a continuation of the London Conference. The London Conference was called at the end of August 1992 as the level of violence in Bosnia continued to increase. It attempted to "isolate and threaten Serbia and Milosevic personally, for aggression against Bosnia." There was agreement among the warring parties to end ethnic cleansing, to cease hostilities, have international supervision of heavy weapons, and to respect human rights. This was progress, but unfortunately there were no provisions for implementation of the measures the conference adopted (Burg and Shoup, 1999:212). Although some optimistically believed all problems would be settled by Christmas, the reality was that little actually changed on the ground as a result of the conference. The ongoing process produced, however, another plan for establishing order and ending violence in Bosnia. The V-O plan, presented in January 1993, would have created a decentralized state with ten provinces. The national government would involve all three ethnonational groups, as would the provincial governments. The special area of Sarajevo would have equal governmental representation of each group, while the ten provincial governments would have "political structures proportionately based on ethnic distribution in the 1991 census." One advantage of this scheme was that it would have reversed some of the changes to the status quo achieved by ethnic cleansing. The division of Bosnia into ten self-governing provinces provided some of the safeguards the Serbs were looking for, in that heavily Serb provinces would have disproportionate government by Serbs. At the same time, the plan had the advantage of "recapturing some of the democratic and moral ground lost . . . in the 'cantonisation' [partition] scheme" discussed in Lisbon the year before. It also nullified "any prospect of unified Serb lands" resulting from contiguous territories.

Some critics, including the United States, missed these points and insisted on seeing V-O as a continuation of the "cantonisation" project of Lisbon, an acceptance of ethnic cleansing and the attempt to establish new borders through the use of force. As we have seen earlier, Gow believes that a strong push by the United States for acceptance and implementation of V-O could have made a significant difference in quelling the violence.[9] Even if it was defeated, the tentative plans for both Europe and the

United States to put troops into Bosnia for implementation of V-O could have been implemented until some new arrangement was developed.[10] Fighting now was limited not only to Serb-Muslim or Serb-Croat clashes but increasingly intensive Croat-Muslim conflict was taking place. In any case, it seems clear that the US-European differences on the desirability of V-O were detrimental to the potential ultimate acceptance of the plan. Particularly salient was the American distaste for what they considered the concessions to ethnic cleansing as well as the reluctance to make the commitment to implement it. But it would not be the last time this US-EU difference over partition would impede progress.

After the demise of V-O, the cochairs met with Milosevic, Tudjman, Izetbegovic, and Karadzic as well as Mate Boban (Bosnian Croat) and Bulatovic (president of Montenegro) to discuss what became the foundations for three later plans: the Union of Three Republics (also known as the Owen-Stoltenberg plan), the EU Action Plan, and the Contact Group plan. These plans all gave the Serbs their own contiguous area for a republic within a Union of Bosnia-Herzegovina (Owen, 1996:190).

The Contact Group, including representatives from the United States, Russia, France, Germany, and the United Kingdom, formed in April 1994, was able through 1995 to provide the basis of a common conception for a settlement, for the first time involving all the major players including the United States. "Despite their divergent perspectives and preferences," the military and political stalemate that emerged in the beginning of 1994, the major players were now attempting to act, together and decisively as one, on an agreed political objective. The objective was to consolidate Muslim-Croat cooperation (already formalized in the creation, as a US initiative, of a Federation of Croatia and Bosnia-Herzegovina) in February 1994 in a fashion that would allow them to control 51 percent of the land, with 49 percent left to the Bosnian Serbs. The Croats were too weak to fight on two fronts, that is, in Croatia and in Bosnia, and they were anxious to be taken seriously by the West. Not only would the Croats and Bosnians now be cooperating against a common enemy instead of against each other, but it would make it easier to smuggle weapons into a common entity. Since the Bosnian army had enough manpower, but was short of weapons, this was likely to strengthen them vis-à-vis the Serbs

THE POLITICAL WILL TO END THE CONFLICT

Many Americans found the war in the former Yugoslavia maddening, as the quote from Secretary Eagleburger illustrates (note 6). The behavior of the main actors was irrational, the war made no sense, the players' behavior was unpredictable and erratic, and the war was complex beyond belief. All of which is to say that it was a different kind of conflict than the United States usually encountered, and lacking models as precedents, it left Americans—as well as the Europeans—at a loss as to the preferred solution. A particularly obvious question in such a situation is who is responsible for the war, who is the enemy? Significantly, these case studies have revealed that picking the enemy is often a difficult task that depends frequently on how one understands or frames the conflict. In the case of the former Yugoslavia, the most popular positions were one country (usually Serbia) or, alternatively, each of the countries was equally culpable. Neither U.N. Security Council resolutions nor the Dayton documents have ever named an aggressor in the conflict, but speak instead of "warring parties" (Divjak, 2001:152).

What is not in dispute is that each of the main protagonists in the war in Bosnia was involved in ethnic cleansing, each was involved in violence against civilians, each broke its share of agreements and cease-fires, each had paramilitary groups assisting the more standard military units, and each had detention camps. Many would maintain that on many indices of these actions the Serbs had the edge in the use of force and brutality, and Muslims are often viewed as least guilty, but exact numbers are hard to come by. Some believed the media focused excessively on Serbian exploits because they were more visible (Crnobrnja, 1994:181–82).[11] The reputation of the Serbian units was hurt particularly by several major incidents, of which the number of casualties and victims could not be matched by any single incidents carried out by the other militaries. In the early part of the war in Croatia the city of Vukovar was almost completely destroyed by Serbian artillery during a three-month assault by shells, missiles, and grenades, driving its inhabitants and defenders into their basements for a precarious survival or fleeing for their lives (Tus, 2001). Military offensives were directed at towns in eastern Bosnia including Gorazde, Zepa, and Srebrenica as they filled with refugees to five or six times their normal size, people driven from the countryside by ethnic cleansing. "The tactic was similar to that applied at Sarajevo: encircle and intimidate into submission by cutting off vital supplies" (Crnobrnja, 1994:180–83). In the spring of 1995, the fall of Srebrenica made international headlines as the meager defenses of the Dutch soldiers guarding the "safe area" were overrun. United Nation's and other investigations showed that more than 7,000 persons, over 3,000 civilians, were killed by the Serbs (Magas and Zanic, 2001).

If there are still doubts about Milosevic's intentions and his methods, a review of his trial in The Hague is useful and enlightening. According to testimony Milosevic played an important role in instigating and supporting rebellion by the Serbs in Croatia; he exerted control over three armies, including the JNA, the Bosnian Serb army, and the Croatian

Serb army; he wanted to establish a "greater Serbia" and had no interest in maintaining the old Yugoslav federation; he used two chains of command, one through the JNA and the territorial defense units, the other through the Serbian security services and involving paramilitary units; and Zeljko Raznjatovic's (Arkan) notorious Tigers were under the control of the Ministry of the Interior (Gow and Zverzhanovski, 2006).[12]

Tudjman, along with Milosevic, was interested in gains for Croatia in Bosnia and he was promoting his own nationalism. We have seen above that Milosevic and Tudjman had talked explicitly about dividing Bosnia between them. Noel Malcolm, writing about a recently published new book on the wars in Yugoslavia, stated that one of the things most noticeable in the book is "the degree of President Tudman's co-responsibility for the war in Bosnia—which, while it may not reach full equivalence with the responsibility of Milosevic, must now be seen as approaching it more closely than previous evidence had suggested." Elsewhere in the book, the editors point out that because of the occasional overlap between Belgrade's and Zagreb's interests, Belgrade was able to achieve more than its military success justified (Magas and Zanic 2001:xix, xxix). Especially from 1993–94, Zagreb not infrequently fought with the Muslim army, so that significant parts of the war did not even involve the Serbs. While prior to the war, Izetbegovic did not seem to believe that the problems would come to war, and even though the Bosnian government was ill prepared to fight one, he was willing to take his chances with independence. Izetbegovic has sometimes been accused by his distracters of prolonging the fighting in hopes of encouraging Western intervention, which they thought, would give them a larger share of any settlement. He was a devout Muslim, and some have alleged that his "Islamic Declaration" is a tract promoting extremism. There is no doubt that he himself, and to some degree the Bosnian government moved to a more Islamic position with less stress on building a multicultural society in the latter stages of the war. There is also a school of thought that believes the Bosnian government was short-changed by the Dayton settlement since it ended up with less land than it should have or possibly could have had if the fighting had continued. But it is clear that neither Tudjman nor Izetbegovic was up to playing the role of villain with the panache that Milosevic mustered.

The initial reaction to the crisis, common to both the Europeans and the Americans, was to keep Yugoslavia together. The United States and Germany quickly got beyond that when it became clear that Slovenia and Croatia were gone, but Britain and France tended to a more pro-Serb stance in line with their historical connections and preferences. French-Serb unity predated not only the breakup of Yugoslavia, but also its creation, extending back to the WWI military alliance between the two countries. The sympathy many French officers felt for the Serbs the Americans found puzzling and disquieting (Cogan, 2003:60). And as James Gow points out, by the start of the war in Bosnia in 1992, it had been clear that the Serbs had been preparing for the destruction of Bosnia for some time (Gow, 1997:80). Milosevic had a vision and the determination to implement it that could not be matched by the other groups in the former Yugoslavia.

There was great controversy over the role of the U.N. in Bosnia. Even by 1992, there was a growing feeling that the secretary general was opposed to U.N. involvement in Bosnia, considering it a "rich man's war" (Gow, 1997:94). The involvement of the U.N., which also had a veto on the use of force even if the NATO countries all agreed, often created chaos, especially in the early years of the war when the vetoes on military action came from New York rather than in the field. The frustration with the U.N. forces stemmed not just from the extreme caution of Boutros-Ghali, but from the complexity of the U.N. mission and the Security Council resolutions (Gow, 1997:138). UNPROFOR was also at the heart of the delivery of humanitarian supplies. These supplies, usually going to Croat or Muslim communities, were regularly subject to a 20 percent off the top payment to Bosnian Serbs. UNPROFOR, because of very limited mandate for the use of force—primarily just self-protection—were often seen as in danger of being hit by bombing runs. The contradiction between American preference for the use of force and the European concern about the fate of their (UNPROFOR) troops on the ground was significant. Many were critical of the camaraderie and seeming congruence of attitudes between UNPROFOR personnel and the Serbs. There was also a substantial difference in the mind-set of UNPROFOR, on the one hand, and the United Nations High Commissioner for Refugees (UNHCR), on the other. The latter were more willing to run risks to deliver humanitarian assistance (Bert, 1997:167–70). But "[a]s a result of UNPROFOR's relative impotence, the warring armies in Bosnia increasingly came to despise it and humiliate it" (Gow, 1997:117).[13]

An equally or more important reason for the reluctance of the United States to get involved in Bosnia was the tepidness of support at home for such an adventure. The success of the Gulf War of 1991 notwithstanding, American foreign policy elites and citizens were very wary of risky military involvement abroad. In spite of President George H. W. Bush's assertion that we had kicked the Vietnam syndrome, that experience was still very much in the minds of foreign policy elites. The general question of "Should the U.S. get involved in Bosnia?" received consistently negative answers throughout the war. To a more specific July 1992 Gallup poll on whether the United States should take the lead in seeking U.N.-supported air strikes if Serbian forces continued to impede the delivery of relief supplies, 35 percent said yes and 45 percent no. By August, support had increased and 53 percent supported either US participation in U.N.-backed air strikes or ground action against Serbian forces and remained stable well into 1993, but at the same time roughly a third continued to oppose intervention. Generally, the level of public interest in the war remained low, and when the public was asked for a reason for intervention, it was clear there was little feeling of urgency on their part.

As Elizabeth Drew put it, the divisions among the president's advisers contributed to "a division in the mind of a President who had few strong instincts on foreign-policy questions." Put differently, there was a different policy for each individual crisis (Bert, 1997:217–18). As Thomas L. Friedman perceptively noted, Clinton was trying to get the symbolism right, but unfortunately that didn't fit with the actual costs that would have to be paid for actually doing something. "Clinton senses that the voters want more moralism, but not an invasion." The public mood seems to be, "Do what is right, but not with my boy or girl." The substitution of humanitarian air drops, which the president initiated, for meaningful action toward settling the dispute reflected this attitude.

In May of 1993, following the rejection in April of V-O by the Bosnian Serbs, Secretary of State Christopher was sent to Europe to test the reaction to a program of "lift and strike," lift the arms embargo on the former Yugoslavia and use airpower to strike those promoting the conflict on the ground. Throughout the conflict, the issues inherent in lift and strike were at the heart of the differences between the Americans on the one hand, and the British and the French, on the other. Many Americans, believing the arms embargo was unfair to the Muslims and the Croats and should never have been imposed in the first place, believed it should be lifted to compensate for the Serb advantage in weapons. Britain and France believed this would lead to an influx of arms for all sides that would increase the intensity of the conflict. Once the UNPROFOR forces were on the ground, largely made up of British and French soldiers, the Europeans became very sensitive about any policy that would mean a more dangerous environment for their troops. Some said they had purposely put in the UNPROFOR forces to ensure the Americans could not use force. Then, if the Americans threatened to use force, they could just threaten to withdraw their troops and cease the humanitarian action (Magas and Zanic, 2001:306).

When Christopher went to Europe with Clinton's plan, it was this objection he met there. Lifting the embargo would be like throwing gasoline on a fire. It would bring the Serbs into Bosnia in greater numbers. It would end negotiations and lead to the withdrawal of UNPROFOR. The arms going to the Muslims would have to transit Croat-controlled territory, and the Croats would take some off the top. Anyway, the

Muslims weren't trained to use the arms. The Bosnian government testified repeatedly that it was willing to risk the removal of UNPROFOR and the humanitarian benefits if that was the cost of lifting the embargo. Ejup Ganic, a member of the Bosnian presidency said the arms were needed to force the Serbs to the table. The Serbs say privately that they will not negotiate with someone who cannot match their military capability ([Senate] Committee on Armed Services, 1994:29, 43, 58, 62).

Americans were divided on the issue. Lee Hamilton, chair of the House Foreign Affairs Committee, believed that unilateral lifting of the embargo would threaten the peace talks, signal that the United States was entering the war on the side of the Bosnia government and make it responsible for their fate, and encourage others to violate sanctions elsewhere. General Wesley K. Clark of the joint staff thought a unilateral lifting of the embargo would lead to a precarious withdrawal of UNPROFOR, a drop in humanitarian assistance, Croatia would be encouraged to reenter the war, and the United States would be under intense pressure to provide greater assistance to Bosnia. But in 1995 there were threats by the US Congress to force President Clinton to lift the arms embargo whether or not the U.N. went along.

James Gow persuasively argues that there were five points at which a peaceful conclusion to the breakup might have been obtained, where a different international response might have made a crucial difference (Gow, 1997:325–29). All of these focus on more creative diplomacy, more careful considerations of first principles, and a systematic blueprint for settling the conflict. More care, attention, and planning could have produced a more imaginative and flexible Western involvement in negotiations. The West was simply not enough involved. Three of these opportunities potentially had as one segment the use of military force. We have examined the factors that discouraged military assertiveness by the West during the conflict: on the European side, pro-Serb sentiment, timidity at the possibility of encountering military opposition without strong domestic support, and the lack of a European capability for intervention (Gow, 1997:320); on the US side, a preoccupation with the domestic consequences of intervention, an unprepared president with initially little interest or expertise in foreign affairs, and a somewhat chaotic decision-making process. Of these, timidity over taking military action without strong domestic support was undoubtedly the most important. Vietnam was still a fresh memory, along with events in Somalia, and for the British, Northern Ireland.

Policy makers in the Bush administration were worried by the consequences that would flow from a threat made by the United States if there was no intention of follow-through. If the Serbs disregarded the threat and the United States did not react, this would harm the US reputation and credibility and make it less effective in future confrontations. Eagleburger recounts an incident in the Adriatic. During the war in Croatia the Serbs were shelling the city of Dubrovnik on the Adriatic coast and the president of Croatia requested that the United States sail the Sixth Fleet, already in the area, along the coast past Dubrovnik as a signal of US concerns. Eagleburger refused to do this, since further action would be needed if the Serbs disregarded the message conveyed by the warship (ABC News, 1994; Bert, 1997:118–19). This carries caution to an extreme, since the message to be conveyed could be interpreted variously, and was subject to a denial by the United States that the movement was anything except routine and no message was intended. What was there to lose by trying it and hoping the Serbs would act on the intended signal? One might think that the Bush administration would have been concerned about the implications for American prestige of watching a situation in Yugoslavia develop *without taking any* substantial action, but apparently they did not believe that this would undermine US prestige or credibility. At other times, threats or minor actions were quite effective in changing Serb behavior, as in June 1994 at Gorazde when Western resistance convinced the Bosnian Serbs to refrain from taking the city (Silber and Little, 1995:Chapter 26).

Clearly, the attitude of the Bush administration was not well suited to effectiveness in Bosnia. They still subscribed to the cold war perspective that a war is all or nothing, that getting a little involved may suck you in to a gigantic project from which there are no early exits, or at least none that will allow you to leave with your "national honor" intact. It is worth quoting Eagleburger, an illustration of the continued effect of Vietnam as well as American impotence.

> I'm not prepared to accept argument that there must be something between the kind of involvement of Vietnam and doing nothing, that the *The New York Times* and the *The Washington Post* keep blabbing about, that there must be some form in the middle. That's, again, what got us into Vietnam—do a little bit, and it doesn't work. What do you do next?
> US Department of State, 1992a

The State Department would find that most future wars were not going to be the full-scale wars of attrition like WWII or the 1991 Gulf War. Bosnia was a war where you needed a limited and carefully calibrated military response, one that could be applied and then withdrawn as the occasion required. It took the United States about four years to figure out that there had to be something between just negotiating and all-out war, and just how this kind of war should be waged. The Bosnia response by the West was, as one commentator said, "too little, too late," but it was also better late than never (Meier, 1995:244).[14]

INEFFECTIVENESS OF BOSNIAN SERB FORCES

So far we have concentrated on what went wrong in Western attempts to halt the war in Yugoslavia. But there were also advantages that put this intervention among the more successful of the case studies in that the violence was decisively stopped, even though the process of getting there was long and arduous. One reason the process was so protracted is that it was assumed that taking on the Serb military machine would be a formidable task. The British, afraid of finding another Northern Ireland, even more cautious than the Americans were about finding another Vietnam, were "carefully plotting the radiating consequences of every move, spying the countryside for that dreaded 'military quagmire' where credibility has been known to disappear without a trace," wrote one analyst sarcastically (IISS, 1994:99). But these fears were not borne out. Far from being an intransigent foe, when the time came, the Serb military machine collapsed like a house of cards, whether in the face of Bosnian advances, Croatian routs, or American bombing. What happened to this fearsome foe that had perpetrated a myth of invincibility for so many years?[15]

The Serb war effort was handicapped by a low level of commitment, poor morale, personnel shortages, poor leadership, and dysfunctional civil-military relations, in spite of inheriting the JNA and an initial advantage in organization and equipment (Cigar, Magas, and Zanic, 2001:xxix). Once Croatia struck in the Krajina, Izetbegovic pushed ahead in Bosnia and NATO finally began bombing seriously in the summer of 1995, the whole edifice of Greater Serbia collapsed, to be followed soon by the Serbian hold on Kosovo. The whole deadly experiment was ended, but at great cost to the former Yugoslavia.

THE ROAD TO DAYTON: COMBINING MILITARY AND DIPLOMATIC MEANS

A confluence of events and forces combined to create the military situation that made the Dayton Conference possible. The Muslim-Croat federation that had been created in February 1994 reduced the fighting between the two groups and contributed to their military strength and consequent gains against the Bosnian Serbs. The growing military strength of this block made it possible for them to strengthen their position as prelude to serious negotiation to end the conflict. The final military positions of the two sides, the Bosnian Serbs, on the one hand, and the Federation of Croatia and Bosnia-Herzegovina, on the other, matched almost exactly the Contact Group map on which the Dayton settlement was based. Still, the Sarajevo government was dependent on both the Croats and the United States for military supplies and the United States could use its leverage against either of these to compel negotiations (Gow, 1997:280).

Second, as we have seen, the offensive by the Croatian forces against the Serbs in the summer of 1995 and the complete rout of the Croatian Serbs was both a military and a psychological assist. This was done with substantial preparation and assistance from the United States. The United States had communicated to the Croatian government, on instructions from Washington, that it had no objection to a Croat plan to assist the Bosnian government in getting arms, especially from Iran (US Congress, 1996). The Croats would also acquire arms from such a deal. The Croats received a substantial amount of training from the Americans as well, including instruction from retired military officers. Some even detected US and NATO influence in the strategic maneuvers of the Croatians. There was also a substantial amount of ethnic cleansing and shelling of women and children as a result of the Serbian rout by Croatia. It was the biggest forcible displacement of people in Europe since WWII (Silber and Little, 1995:350). Holbrooke upbraided Tudjman for the "brutal treatment of the Serbs" that followed most Croatian military successes, and John Shattuck, an assistant secretary of state, later criticized Croatia for creating a stream of refugees driven from their homes (Holbrooke, 1998:160,189). It virtually eliminated the Serb presence in Croatia as civilians left in droves for either Serbia or Bosnia. This offensive dissolved once and for all the myth of the invincibility of the Croatian Serb military, and demonstrated decisively that the Serbs in Croatia, and by extension those in Bosnia, were on their own and not Belgrade's concern. An attack on radar installations at Udbina and Knin by US naval aircraft just before August 4 when the Croatian operation Storm was launched may have led Belgrade to believe they were facing a coordinated NATO-Croatian attack (Zunec, 2001:76). A Canadian officer was struck by the lack of military readiness among the Krajina Serbs. He called the leadership "corrupt, incompetent, and complacent" (Silber and Little, 1995:348).

Equally important was the improvement of the context for the use of military power against the Bosnian Serbs. The United States was engaging in significant shuttle diplomacy aimed at a convergence of opinion on a settlement. The Europeans, especially the French, were planning to withdraw their UNPROFOR soldiers, and a decision was made to deploy Rapid Reaction Force (RRF) troops, following air strikes against Pale at the end of May. The coincidental timing of a Serb marketplace shelling in Sarajevo that killed over 30 people provided the occasion to begin an aerial bombardment against the Serbs. The effects of the NATO airpower and the RRF put pressure on Milosevic and left him in a much stronger position to act as the negotiating representative for Karadzic and Pale, since they obviously had nowhere else to go (Gow, 1997:276–79).[16] The arrival at Dayton reinforced the truth of Richard K. Betts' belief that in a serious dispute one cannot carry out both, a limited and an impartial intervention and achieve success. There must be either total intervention where the intervening forces determine the terms of peace, or there must be an end to impartiality, so the resources of the winning local forces can be used to force a settlement (Betts, 1994:21). The 1995 intervention finally turned decisively against the Serbs and tipped the balance so that a settlement was possible.

It speaks well of the flexibility of the West's position that in the negotiations at Dayton, Richard Holbrooke was able to consider the positions of all parties and factor them into the final agreement. Holbrooke and his colleagues conducted an intensive round of negotiations to lay the groundwork for Dayton, even while the fighting was still going on and before the ceasefire was to take hold. They traveled all over the former Yugoslavia, Europe, and to Washington and Moscow, and Anthony Lake also traveled in Europe. Once the conference started, it was a long and grueling process with stubborn participants and changing positions, colorfully portrayed in Holbrooke's book.

Holbrooke, no shrinking violet when it came to tough negotiations, was not averse to knocking heads together—figuratively, of course—to resolve differences within governments as well as between them. The split between Izetbegovic and his prime minister Haris Silajdzic was sometimes particularly troublesome. Milosevic was remarkably willing to sell out the Bosnian Serbs, notably in his willingness to give up control of Sarajevo. These rounds of negotiations mark another aspect of US behavior that contributed immensely to the success of the US intervention in the former Yugoslavia. It was done with skill, and perhaps most essentially, with support and close cooperation with the president and Washington, although the public and some critics were less than supportive. The summer's work in general showed the value of coordinating and combining diplomacy with military coercion. It was a display of skill and policy that had not been in evidence in the attention Washington gave to the prior periods of the war.

The accords promised an integral state, but divided the state into two entities, the Federation of Bosnia and Herzegovina (51 percent of the land) and the Serb Republic (49 percent), attempting to meet simultaneously Izetbegovic's preference for a multicultural state and the Serb demand for autonomy. The central government was to have responsibility for foreign affairs, customs and immigration policy, monetary policy, law enforcement, communications, transportation, and air traffic control between the two entities. There was no provision for linking up ethnic communities in Bosnia with either Croatia or Serbia. A narrow Posavina corridor ties the two parts of the Srpska Republika together. All people have the right to move about freely and the requests and rulings of the war crimes tribunal are to be respected. IFOR (NATO international implementation force of approximately 60,000 troops) was put in place to help provide security. Both entities were allowed to keep their armies, troops were withdrawn behind agreed upon cease-fire lines, and the arms embargo and the sanctions on Serbia were lifted (Bert, 1997). In some ways, the Dayton accords met fewer of Sarajevo and Washington's objectives than V-O, in that the two separate entities rewarded ethnic cleansing and gave the Bosnian Serbs contiguous territory as opposed to individual provinces. V-O also would have required greater demilitarization, thus encouraging further integration. Holbrooke later regretted allowing both sides to keep their own armies. The Dayton accords, on the other hand, were easier to implement than V-O would have been (Gow, 1997:307–15).

The key problem, which has persisted since 1995, is the resistance to disserting ethnic identification and interests in favor of the creation of a multicultural and integrated Bosnia. One reason little progress has been made is that those least invested in the success of Dayton were the most involved in implementing it. "Revanchist attitudes have been banked, but not extinguished," as another critic puts it (Chollet, 2005:24; Switzer, 2001:296).

CONCLUSION

This Bosnia case is unique in that in the perception of US policy makers national security interest in Bosnia was problematic. The Bush administration declared that there was no vital American interest there. The Clinton administration campaigned on getting involved and stopping the conflict, but their emphasis was more on humanitarian than security interests. My judgment is that there was a US security interest at stake in Bosnia, since any major threat to the values that underlie a US-inspired world order does affect security. While political elites may have appreciated more the security dimensions of the conflict for the United States as the war dragged on, it is clear that the public as a whole never really accepted it. The 70 percent opposition to sending troops for IFOR is clear testimony to that. It was also clear that both policy makers and the public were still thinking of the traditional war of attrition, with two clear-cut sides and unambiguous military targets, inviting an "all or nothing" kind of involvement that Eagleburger talked about. This war was plagued from the beginning with confusion and disagreement on who was responsible for the war and what needed to be done to end it. There was no clear political framework, and without that one could not find an effective military approach. For reasons historical and otherwise, the Europeans could not agree among themselves about the role and blame of the various participants in the war.

Disagreement in the international community was only one factor that impeded effective prosecution and ending of the war. One reason that Leslie Gelb's admonition that "diplomacy without force is farce" was not heeded was that the outside intervening countries did not have the stomach for military action (Gelb, 2009). The Europeans simply didn't have the capability, and the Americans were still suffering from the inhibiting effects of being bogged down in Vietnam, and the difficulties in Somalia. Only after long and unnecessary procrastination did events come together in a way that allowed an effective combination of political and military action that brought the war to an abrupt end. Milosevic and the Serb military were shown to be "paper tigers," to borrow a metaphor from another conflict. In this way this case differs considerably from the other case studies analyzed here. The four other "enemies," as we will see, were anything but pushovers. Mary Kaldor characterized Bosnia as a "new" and unique war. This war is the one case that is not just "low intensity," but very low-intensity war. The low degree of mobilization of the Serb fighting forces and the fickleness of both the leadership and the troops when the going got rough make it unique.

The uniqueness of the war is also reflected in the aftermath. Almost a decade and a half after the end of the fighting, little progress has been made in building an integrated Bosnia that can stand on its own, notwithstanding that the effort was funded at a high level. From 1996 to 2007, $300 per capita per year was donated by the international community, making the reconstruction of Japan and Germany look modest. This amount compares with $65 per capita pledged annually for Afghanistan since 2002 (McMahon and Western, 2009). The difficulty of finding a permanent solution reflects the fact that the final settlement did not depend on just the battlefield results but also on negotiations, where everybody got something, and nobody ended up an abject loser. It remains to be seen whether a long-term settlement can be arranged, but what is clear is that more attention early on to the breakup of Yugoslavia and the grievances of the individual republics could have resulted in understandings or actions that would have avoided much of the violence.

CHAPTER 7

AFGHANISTAN—
2001–PRESENT

I can hear you. The rest of the world hears you. And the people
who knocked these buildings down will hear all of us soon!
> President George W. Bush responding to rescue workers at
> ground zero in New York City after 9/11

I said, 'General Petraeus, winning the hearts and minds of the Afghans
is not the job of a soldier. That's the job of an Afghan.'
> Mohammad Umer Daudzai, President Hamid Karzai's
> chief of staff

The difficulty facing the United States in trying to bring stability to
Afghanistan was nicely summarized by Secretary of State Condoleezza
Rice in her 2006 statement that, five years after the United States
intervened militarily in 2001, the country was in danger of becoming a
failed state (Rotberg, 2007:3). In the modern era, two themes have run
through Afghan history: the struggle for development and reaction to
foreign security threats (Jalali, 2007:24). Development, as well as cultural
change, has been slow and difficult. Foreign security threats have been
numerous. The United States is the third major power to have engaged
Afghanistan in less than a century, after an Afghan war with the Soviet
Union and a series of wars with Great Britain.

Afghanistan hits bottom on many socio-political-economic indicators, and "[i]t is no surprise that a terrorist network found a base in
Afghanistan: just as Lenin might have predicted, it picked the weakest
link in the modern state system's rusty chain" (Rubin, 2007:62). The
U.N. Development Program described the Afghan educational system as
"the worst in the world" (Jones, 2006:209). In 2005, the average annual
per capita GDP was estimated to be about $300. The country ranked

155 out of 162 nations on the UN Human Development Index, and 176 out of 178 on a corruption index. One American official called it a "vertically integrated criminal enterprise" (Rotberg, 2007:6–7; Filkins, 2011). Afghanistan is sorely lacking in infrastructure, including transportation and especially railroads. Much of the country has been destroyed by the international and civil wars that have wracked it for the past few decades. When the post-Taliban regime and the international community took over Afghanistan, it lacked state institutions, a legal order, formal economy, and any sense of a security order (Rais, 2008:206). Jon Lee Anderson reported that, after traveling in northern Afghanistan after the 2001 attack, he entered a brightly lit Kabul, the first Afghan city he had seen that had a functioning electrical system" (Anderson, 202:108).

Since the fall of the Taliban, Afghanistan has once again become a virtual narcotics state. It produced 93 percent of the world's opiates in 2007, but production has declined somewhat in recent years (Nautilus, 2011). Economic growth after 2001 had been impressive, mostly because the country started from such a low point. Between 2001–2002 and 2004–2005, real GDP grew 60 percent, but it has been erratic in recent years. It had recovered to at least the highest point reached before the wars (McKechnie, 2007). Afghanistan badly needs revived and reformed institutions. Especially in the provinces, it needs decentralized governance to provide services to a scattered and ethnically diverse population. It has one of the world's most centralized governments, in a land of geographical and ethnic diversity (Rubin, 2007:62; Lister and Nixon, 2007).

While the imperative for development is a relatively new phenomenon, Afghanistan's problems with foreign penetration go back centuries. Since Afghanistan has never produced enough wealth to pay the cost of governing or defending itself, it has been stable only when its neighbors or imperial powers agreed to strengthen it to meet their own security interests (Rubin, 2006:15). It became a pawn in the "great game" between Britain and Russia, where "a succession of ambitious Tsars and ruthless generals crushed the Muslim people of Central Asia and occupied their lands" (Hopkirk, 1992:xv). During the first of three Anglo-Afghan wars (1839–42) and due largely to inept leadership, 4,500 British and Indian soldiers and 12,000 civilians attempted to flee from Kabul to Jalalabad to escape Afghan wrath in a full-scale uprising against the British. Between repeated attacks and the ravages of the weather as the group made its way through mountain passes in winter, only one person made it to Jalalabad alive.[1]

In spite of a history of conflict and subjugation, Afghanistan is still lacking a "national sense of belonging or loyalty" that extends much beyond family, clan, or village. Even during the struggle to expel the Soviet Union, seemingly the very embodiment of a national cause, the response was also

Table 7.1 US-Afghanistan war statistics

Country	GNP/GDP (bn $)	Pop (million)	Total armed force	Defense expend. (mil. $)	Intervention forces (peak nos.)	US casualties	Host country casualties
Afghanistan (2001)	2.[a]	24[b]	Taliban forces				(government soldiers and police)—10,000 (civilians)—11,000, fighting; 20,000, indirect
US (2001)	10065.	285	1,367,700	310,500	104,000—US; 46,200—NATO[c]	1109 (8/4/10)	

Sources: World Bank Atlas; The Military Balance (London: IISS); Strategic Survey (London: IISS); New York Times, December 1, 2008; DoD http://www.defenselink.mil/news/casualty.pdf, accessed 8/4/10; Washington Post, February 18; July 1, 2009; Foreign Policy, July/August 2009; BBC News online, news.bbc.co.uk/2/hi/south/asia/8389351.stm, accessed 8/4/10.

[a] 1999
[b] 2000
[c] projected—8/2010.

"decidedly local, organized on tribal, clan, family, ethnic, or sectarian lines and focused not on national but on local objectives" (McChesney, 1999:5). According to one analyst, the ethnic and social forces of Afghanistan are more conscious today of their separate identities than at any time in the country's history (Rais, 2008). "The entire Afghan population has been displaced, not once but many times . . . Kabul has turned . . . into the Dresden of the late twentieth century. The crossroads of Asia on the ancient Silk Route is now nothing but piles of rubble . . . complex relationships of power and authority built up over centuries have broken down completely" (Rashid, 2000:207–08).

US SECURITY INTERESTS AND INTERVENTION

These case studies focus on the immediate question of American security: if and how it was threatened in each of the cases, what American goals were in intervening, and whether the resulting intervention was effective. Such a limitation excludes—in order to keep the study within manageable limits—detailed examination of past policies and their effect on the present circumstances. In the case of Afghanistan, however, the impact of immediate past policies was so important that they merit a brief discussion.

The Soviets alleged that outside powers were meddling in Afghanistan, while President Jimmy Carter's administration charged that the Soviets were interested in access to warm water ports and the oil of the Persian Gulf. The proximate reason for the 1979 invasion was more likely the unpopularity of the Soviet-supported Afghan government and the consequent threat of instability. Regardless, by organizing highly motivated groups of mujaheddin and transiting weapons and supplies through Pakistan, the Afghan opposition, with Pakistani and US support, was soon making life difficult for the Soviets (Ewans, 2002). The acquisition by the mujaheddin of the US Stinger shoulder-held ground to air missile was particularly helpful to the cause. The mujaheddin were highly motivated, but operated, often quite autonomously, under seven different leaders. After the 1988 agreement for Soviet withdrawal and the implementation of the withdrawal in 1989, the mujaheddin continued the struggle against the pro-Soviet government then in power. The United States and Pakistan ignored the Geneva stipulation that they stop arming the insurgents, leading to collapse of the government and state failure (Rubin, 2007:64). The conflict between the groups of fighters then continued as a civil war over who would become the dominant authority in the country. The American response was to cut off support and ignore the conflict. The Soviet Union having dissolved, the United States believed it no longer had any interests to defend (much less a humanitarian obligation). The result was a costly and debilitating struggle between the mujaheddin groups through the mid-1990s (Bearden, 2001; Rashid, 2000).[2] No less a figure than US Defense Secretary Robert Gates has admitted his role in supporting the build-up of the mujaheddin—"I was pumping arms across the border to some of the same guys" the US is fighting today—and lamented the mistake of "turning our backs on Afghanistan after 1989." For that, he says, "we paid a price" (Will, 2008).

The result was to make the reassembly of the Afghan state and the building of a strong and stable supporting society considerably more difficult. The effect of the Soviet occupation and the conflicts among the fragmented opposition was very detrimental to strengthening a common identity and the ethos of cooperation necessary to the functioning of a modern state. The United States had set in motion the spirit of jihad and the belief among our surrogate soldiers that, "having brought down one superpower, they could just as easily take another." Ironically, Jalaluddin Haqani, the CIA's favorite mujaheddin commander, who often hosted bin Laden and received bags of cash from the agency, would, after 9/11, emerge as the number three target of the US forces in Afghanistan (Crile, 1988:521–22). A wiser policy would have been at the least to remain engaged after the Soviet withdrawal to attempt to fashion some kind of settlement that might have ameliorated the forces of Islamic fundamentalism and hastened the beginning of a healing process in Afghan society. The case for this kind of policy, however, was difficult to make to a US populace and Congress weary of the cold war and relieved that it was finally over.

WHAT KIND OF WAR?

History aside, what should have been US objectives after the attack of 9/11? Reading Bob Woodward's account of the Bush decision to go to war in Afghanistan, one is struck by how many assumptions from the conventional wars of the past were accepted by the decision makers and how few questions were asked about these assumptions and their suitability as a basis for the pending decisions. The attack on the United States was the first since Pearl Harbor at the start of WWII, and a more costly day in casualties. The terror attacks "clarified America's post–Cold War foreign policy in one blow," and seemed to change everything, sharply discounting history and precedent (Hirsh, 2001:161).

At the same time, the nature and execution of the attacks, in addition to being highly unorthodox and unprecedented, in some ways seemed almost mundane. Instead of a cold war threat of nuclear multiwarhead ballistic missiles that could devastate the globe and kill tens of millions of people, this threat involved the hijacking of passenger planes to be crashed into skyscrapers by 19 terrorists, most of whom were citizens of our important ally, Saudi Arabia. But the actions were executed without the acknowledged complicity of any nation-state. The unexpected and startling, almost incomprehensible nature of the attack was indicated by the fact that in spite of warnings conveyed to policy makers of probable terrorist attacks, so few policy makers had the insight or imagination to take serious actions to thwart them or even conceive of the incarnation in which they might appear. Traditional indicators of power or threat were of little use in interpreting this threat. In such a situation, according to Michael Hirsh, President Bush erred in stating that the fight against terrorists is a war for survival or existence. The "enemies of freedom" he referred to in his speech to Congress are not powerful industrialized countries like Germany or Japan. They were "mere ragtag holdouts, tiny 'cells' of misfits who failed even to seize power in their own small home countries. However dangerous it might be, this global war is more like a mop-up mission, courtesy of US Special Forces, the CIA, and the FBI."[3] Small-time tyrants such as Milosevic and Adid were too insignificant to "rouse Americans to action," but at the same time "too annoying or brutal to be ignored by a civilized superpower." It is the responsibility of presidents to deal with these kinds of crises. The president is the "global go-to guy" who is called upon in such crises. He is "President Pothole," called upon to maintain the global system (Hirsh, 2001:162–63).[4] The one caveat to this perspective is use by terrorists of nuclear or biological weapons. A widespread fear is that terrorists will assemble a relatively simple and easily detonated device to be set off in a major city, with widespread damage. Analysts differ on the probability of such an attack. The other danger is that the targets of al Qaeda's actions will be panicked into doing foolish things that play into the terrorists' hands. Bin Laden has said that it is "easy for us to provoke and bait. . . . All that we have to do is to send two mujahidin . . . to raise a piece of cloth on which is written al-Qaeda in order to make the generals race there to cause America to suffer human, economic, and political losses" (Mueller, 2006:3).

Throughout the deliberations, President Bush and the National Security Council (NSC) were obsessed with quick decisions that would allow the speedy implementation of a military strike. The concern was that delays in hitting some specific targets that the public approved would risk political support and fear of political repercussions from a disgruntled public. Americans felt that the country had suffered at the hands of al Qaeda and retribution was in order. The leadership was also afraid the country would lose focus. "You don't have months," Secretary of Defense Donald Rumsfeld said. He wanted a plan for attacking Afghanistan quickly, in days or weeks. The president wanted to keep attention riveted on the long-term struggle. "The American people want a big bang," he said. "I have to convince them that this is a war that will be fought with many steps." Bush wanted military action that would hurt the terrorists, not just make Americans feel better, he told British Prime Minister Tony Blair (Woodward, 2002: Chapter 4). Still, you can sense the urgency: "My instincts were beginning to tell me that there was kind of an anxiety beginning to build. And I wanted to make sure that our coalition [of other countries] knew we were tough." And the people at ground zero in New York City, they were "looking at you in the eye, these tired faces, 'You go get 'em.' And we're going to get 'em, there's no question about that" (Woodward, 2002:145). And then there was the press corps. "They want the war over yesterday. They don't get it" (Woodward, 2002:295).[5]

The gaps between the traditional assumptions being made during the meetings and decisions and the nature of the new reality stemming from the new and startling kind of attack they had experienced soon surfaced. One problem was the tendency to think in terms of targets as countries. Bush was aware that the country faced a new kind of "faceless enemy," an enemy that "runs and hides." He and the NSC were grappling with the fact that the attack had come from a stateless actor, which had a seemingly formless and inchoate organization. Vice President Cheney said that in some ways states were easier targets than the "shadowy terrorists." In his book on Cheney, Barton Gelman frequently makes the point that Cheney believed that major events originated with states, not with transnational movements (Gelman, 2008). Al Qaeda was the enemy, Bush said, but there was a tendency to revert to thinking in terms of states, just as in previous conflicts. CIA Director Tenet called it a "60-country" problem. To that, the president responded, "Let's pick them off one country at a time."[6] The problem, according to Rumsfeld, was not just al Qaeda and bin Laden, but other countries that supported terrorism. Frequently, this kind of thinking led to Iraq. On September twelfth Rumsfeld had raised the issue of attacking Iraq with the president, and Wolfowitz conducted a Pentagon press briefing in which he suggested a "campaign" that would target a series of countries, not a single action. The president himself said that he believed that Iraq was involved, but that he was not going to strike them then. He didn't have the evidence at that point. "What the hell, what are these guys thinking about?" Secretary of State Colin Powell asked of the chairman of the joint chiefs of staff, Hugh Shelton, "Can't you get these guys back in the box?" Finally, the president sent the message that he had heard enough debate on Iraq. He wanted to strike Iraq, too, but for the moment the priority was Afghanistan (Woodward, 2002:33, 41, 60–61, 85, 99). Interestingly, this state-centered focus is reinforced by aspects of neoconservative thinking that attach great importance to state actions, particularly in regard to the promotion of terrorism (Rapport, 2008:290).

Another point of friction in preattack thinking was between traditional military thinking and the realities of Afghanistan. A refrain throughout the Woodward book is the absence of meaningful military targets in Afghanistan. A weak, poor, and underdeveloped country already destroyed by war—before the war even begins—and with little infrastructure, there were few civilian or military targets for the proposed US bombing campaign. Finding anything to hit would be hard. "What can we do to Afghanistan that Afghanistan hasn't already done to itself?" one close adviser to the president is reported to have asked (Keegan, 2001). Rumsfeld in particular was concerned. He advocated starting another front so that success in the war would not hinge solely on what happened in Afghanistan. The targets were meager. What could they actually accomplish? (Woodward, 2002: 33, 137) He was evidently sensing, even if he didn't articulate it well, that in this conflict the overall political context would be more important than specific military actions. Or more precisely, the military conflict would have to correspond to and support the political framework of the war if it were to be successful.

The whole tenor of the debate in the administration prior to the intervention in Afghanistan raises questions about whether the president and his advisers fully understood the context in which intervention in Afghanistan should be viewed. Despite Bush's assertions that "[t]his is a new world" (Woodward, 2002:62), there is a surprising lack of curiosity in the discussions as to the dynamics of that world. At no point in Woodward's account is there any discussion of basic questions about the people who carried out the attack on New York, or basic questions about al Qaeda. One would expect that questions about the motivation of the terrorists would have arisen. Are they driven only by religious motivation or, as one might surmise, by both religious and political objectives? This is not a frivolous question, since many local terrorist groups, for example, Hamas and Hezbollah, are strongly driven by nationalistic political agendas. An argument that nationalism and resentment of US influence—American troops stationed on the Arabian Peninsula or strong support by the United States for Muslim governments viewed by many Muslims as illegitimate—is more significant than Islamic fundamentalism in motivating al Qaeda is made in Pape (2005). The United States has moved its troops out of Saudi Arabia since 9/11, although it is unclear if appeasing the terrorist movement was a factor in that decision. Certainly some explanation by government decision makers for terrorist actions that went beyond the president's hackneyed statement that they hate our freedom, would have been welcome. One commentator makes his dissenting opinion crystal clear: "Bin Laden has been precise in telling America the reasons he is waging a war on us. None of the reasons have anything to do with our freedom, liberty, and democracy, but have everything to do with US policies and actions in the Muslim world." In his view, it is the Gulf royals—not Osama bin Laden—who hate us for what we are, not what we do (Anonymous, 2004:x). If political motivations are present, then changes in US foreign policy, if they do not compromise important US interests, should be considered. Answering questions about terrorists' motivation, strategies, and likely responses to specific US policies could provide important information about the preferable US policy.[7] Implicit in such an evaluation are considerations such as what troop placements might be most offensive to terrorists or hostile national governments; how significant is the US attitude on settlement of the Palestinian issue in provoking resentment and terrorist action; are there specific aspects of US policy toward Muslim countries that may provoke or offend that could be eliminated cost free; how do differing Sunni and Shia attitudes toward terrorism and the likelihood of engaging in it affect the West; and other similar questions. There is little evidence that these kinds of questions were given any in-depth consideration in the Bush White House, or to the extent that they were, the general assumption that was usually made was that all of the impetus for reform or change belongs to the other side. US policies were justified; those of the terrorists were not. No further discussion is necessary.[8] As the *New York Post* put it, no doubt reflecting a popular position in American society, "Why do they hate us? That's what the so-called deep thinkers are asking about America's Islamic enemies . . . Who cares? Osama [bin Laden] ordered the deaths of some 6,000 innocent people, mostly Americans, on American soil. What difference does it make why? . . . And the only question that matters is how can they be eradicated most quickly" (Lieven, 2004:73). This approach, however, contravenes Sun Tzu's much cited principle that in order to win wars, it is necessary to know your enemy. No rational and effective policy can be developed to counter an enemy until one understands the adversary. Further, surely the fate of the Soviet Union in Afghanistan little more than a decade earlier was relevant to the proposed US invasion, but there is no mention of that experience or its relevance in the accounts of the NSC debates (Anonymous, 2004:103, 31).

Remarkably, no plans for attacking Afghanistan seemed to exist. Rumsfeld became increasingly impatient as he waited weeks for a plan of attack and repeatedly made inquiries to General Franks as to when it would materialize (Woodward, 2002). Given previous attacks by bin Laden on American embassies, the ship USS Cole and the fact that bin Laden had moved to Afghanistan in 1996, this is surprising. When the intelligence community has regularly been giving warnings that bin Laden has plans for further attacks, including on the United States, it would seem likely that the military would have been prepared to go after al Qaeda quickly if and when the situation presented itself. As Robert K. Betts has written, "Only in America could the nation's armed forces think of direct defense of national territory as a distraction" (Anonymous, 2004:25).

There were several options open to the administration for dealing with al Qaeda and the Taliban. One critic maintains that the proper approach to a strike in Afghanistan would have been an immediate and brutal strike fatal to both al Qaeda and the Taliban. When that option was not pursued, because of inadequate preparation and the belief that a coalition should be put together first, the United States missed a "one-time chance to blow al Qaeda and the Taliban to the stone age" (Anonymous, 2004:224). Such a "decapitation" exercise would have hit our enemies hard. Exactly what the details of such a strike would have been and its impact on Afghanistan, not to mention on Americans, we are never told. John Keegan makes a second suggestion. Drawing on great powers' previous experiences in Afghanistan, he suggests that "efforts to occupy and rule usually ended in disaster. But straightforward punitive expeditions, for limited objectives or to bring about a change in Afghan government policy, were successful on more than one occasion." Reliance on this type of limited intervention rested on the assumption that Afghan society is "unstable, fractious and ultimately ungovernable." These limited campaigns of penetration with the purpose simply of inflicting punishment, can succeed so long as the punitive forces "remain mobile, keep control of the high ground and are skilful at tactical disengagement" (Keegan, 2001). Others also warn of the peril of trying to occupy Afghanistan (Bearden, 2009). Especially in retrospect, such a "punitive expedition" would have had advantages. The primary need to strike directly at al Qaeda and devastate it could have been accomplished, although the potential of al Qaeda retaining a refuge from which to launch future activities would have been present if there was no long-term US presence. Whether the American public would have been satisfied with such a "temporary" solution is an open question. If the Taliban had continued in power, and if they had continued to host al Qaeda, then repeat attacks might have been required. On the one hand, such an approach might have sidestepped the delicate and seemingly intractable question of how to deal with the Taliban that ran like a thread through Woodward's account of the preinvasion discussions. However seductive such an approach appears in retrospect, there would have been no guarantees that the Americans would have avoided further involvement in Afghanistan. What if the strike had bruised Taliban authority just enough to unleash another round of civil war? Such an unsettling development, inviting anarchy and disintegration to terrorist activity would have tempted further attempts at fixing the situation. What if the first strike had not fully disabled al Qaeda, as indeed happened with the invasion? The United States would have likely been sucked in for at least a second try. Still, a skillfully planned strike using special operations personnel to strike al Qaeda and then disappear would have diminished many of the risks of a prolonged stay.

The US attack and its delay and inept management of the war allowed many leaders, including bin Laden to escape and disperse personnel, military stores, and funds, both within the country and across the border into Pakistan. Frederick W. Kagan, reversing the thrust of the argument for a quick strike, has argued that having adequate American ground forces in place in Afghanistan would have allowed the United States to direct the initial attack in a way to prevent the escape of Osama bin Laden and al Qaeda, but also would have made it possible to limit the military gains of the Northern Alliance, thus increasing US influence in the formation of a government more acceptable to the Pashtuns. A more representative government would have been more likely to shape a stable and durable peace acceptable to all Afghans (Kagan, 2003).

Yet another approach would have been to ally with and negotiate with the Taliban for the delivery of bin Laden and al Qaeda personnel. Given the shortage of time and the difficulty of dealing with the Taliban, a more plausible variation on this was to deal with a faction of the Taliban receptive to this approach. Yet a third possibility was to use the Northern Alliance to overcome the regime by military means, but it was militarily weak and could not take over the south nor eliminate al Qaeda. In addition, for the Northern Alliance to form a government would alienate the Pashtuns. Through the Pakistanis, following option two, the United States appealed to the Taliban to give up bin Laden. Two visits by the Pakistani Inter-Services Intelligence (ISI) Directorate to Kandahar on September 17 and a second on September 28 were unproductive. The United States continued to appeal to the Taliban, in the words of President Bush on October 12 to "cough up [bin Laden and al Qaeda] today, then we'll reconsider what we are doing to your country. You still have a second chance." In the view of Gilles Dorronsoro, two factors worked against a negotiated solution and led to the use of the Northern Alliance to overcome the Taliban. One was the ambiguous position of the Pakistanis, who found it difficult to go against the Taliban, and second, the fact that the United States preferred for domestic political reasons to give the Taliban an ultimatum and was reluctant to conduct negotiations, as the State Department preferred (Dorronsoro, 2005; Tyler and Bumiller, 2001).

The Bush administration believed it was justified in identifying and attacking Afghanistan with the goal of eliminating bin Laden and al Qaeda. They saw abolishing the base from which bin Laden had launched the attacks as crucial and therefore legitimizing an attack on Afghanistan. Osama bin Laden and the core leadership of al Qaeda had been located in Afghanistan since 1996 where he continued the tradition of the Afghanistan jihad, a cause celebre in the Muslim world in the 1980s. From dozens of training camps there it supported insurgencies in Chechnya, Kashmir, and Tajikistan. US officials believed that 10–20,000 foreign volunteers were trained in Afghanistan after bin Laden located there in 1996. An FBI report stated that "hundreds" of terrorists were trained in Afghanistan as opposed to "thousands" of guerrillas. As a State Department counterterrorism coordinator noted, "Afghanistan was the swamp these mosquitoes kept coming out of" (Byman and Pollack, 2007:108–10). The perpetrators of 9/11 were a lethal threat to the United States, and future attacks on the United States and its allies were likely to be conceived and launched from there. Whatever the myriad strategies and tactics that could and should be used to fight terrorists, if they could be identified, it was important to eliminate them and their organization and any supporting infrastructure and political arrangements that could be used again. Initially, the administration was willing to forego war if the Taliban were willing to give up Osama bin Laden and to change their ways. In the run-up to the war, policy was still ambivalent. CIA Director Tenet suggested holding off on the Taliban; attacking the Taliban could destabilize President Musharraf's government in Pakistan. Powell said propaganda and diplomatic pressure on the Taliban should be the focus. The goal at the outset should not be to change the regime, but to get the regime to do the right thing. "We'll sneak up on the Taliban issue." Vice President Cheney agreed, "We don't want to hit the Taliban up front for we don't want to discourage them from changing the leadership and breaking with al Qaeda." Later, he talked about a short-term hope of winning over moderate Taliban, but in the long run, he said, "we need the Taliban to be gone." The NSC initially was uncertain how much the Taliban would need to be disturbed. The main objective was to eliminate al Qaeda, and attack the foreigners (Arabs) rather than Afghans. But as deliberations went on, there seemed to be a growing realization that eventually the Taliban would have to go. Tenet in particular was ambivalent on the issue, at times talking about splitting the Taliban and al Qaeda, at other times saying they were inseparable. Rumsfeld, always concerned about finding military targets, wasn't sure what to hit if he were limited to al Qaeda (Woodward, 2002: 89, 123–24, 128, 154, 192). And the close relationship between al Qaeda and the Taliban, Taliban statements supporting al Qaeda and historical support, certainly raised questions of whether it was realistic to expect that al Qaeda could be dealt effectively while leaving the Taliban in power.[9]

Having made the decision for major and direct US involvement in the war, however, why the United States failed to commit American troops to the operation in Tora Bora designed to capture the al Qaeda top leadership and prevent them from escaping to Pakistan raises a major question about US objectives and strategy. There were serious questions about the motivation and capability of Afghan troops to detain or destroy the al Qaeda leadership. The United States had forces available that could have been successfully deployed to operate in the very difficult terrain, and Gary Berntsen, the commandant of the operation to attack bin Laden and al Qaeda, repeatedly requested them. It was clear that bin Laden and up to a thousand al Qaeda personnel were at Tora Bora in November 2001 and US political and military officials knew it. But after initial success in surprising al Qaeda with air strikes called in at great risk to the spotters, the job of apprehending the fighters was turned over to indigenous forces. Some of the commanders have admitted that their troops were paid to help al Qaeda troops escape. And some of the Afghan fighters closing in on Osama bin Laden insisted on going home at dusk to break the Ramadan fast instead of finishing their military task (Nasr, 2010). The handling of this phase of the operations has been called the "biggest flaw of the campaign" (Krause, 2008; Bergen, 2009).

THE PAKISTAN PROBLEM

Another major US error in setting objectives to repair the security breach that 9/11 represented was failing to recognize the degree to which the Taliban was important to Pakistan and to its stability. Moreover, Pakistan, regardless of the promises of Musharraf, was unlikely to give up its sponsorship of the Taliban, since its premier foreign policy objective is defense against India. It views its alliance with the Taliban and related groups as a major key to retaining influence in Afghanistan which provides an ally and in-depth defense against its main target, India. When Secretary of State Powell after 9/11 gave the Pakistanis an ultimatum that they must side with the United States, he had told the president that whatever action he took in Afghanistan it could not be done without Pakistan. He and Richard L. Armitage, the deputy secretary of state, put together a list of seven demands for Pakistan and told the Pakistanis that they were not negotiable. All must be accepted. Surprisingly, the Pakistanis agreed to abide by the demands.

Even though the United States invaded Afghanistan to eliminate al Qaeda and its bases, seven years later it is clear that this objective has not been accomplished. A recent report stated that

> . . . it is increasingly clear that the Bush administration will leave office with Al Qaeda having successfully relocated its base from Afghanistan to

Pakistan's tribal areas, where it has rebuilt much of its ability to attack
from the region and broadcast its messages to militants across the world.
                                                    Mazzetti and Rohde, 2008

There are many factors that have contributed to this situation, to be
explored below, but the point here is that, given Pakistan's relationship
to the Taliban in 2001, the objectives of the United States were too
narrowly defined. The problem of the hosting of al Qaeda was so intertwined in the complex relationship between Afghanistan and Pakistan
that the involvement of Pakistan in supporting the Taliban should have
been treated as inseparable from the Taliban's survival. It appears that
among the US leadership there was a considerable amount of illusion
about Pakistan-Taliban relations from the beginning. On November 21,
2001, for instance, to reporters' requests about Pakistan's continuing
diplomatic ties with the Taliban and possible assistance to the Taliban,
State Department spokesman Richard Boucher said: "Pakistan has clearly
broken with the Taliban. Pakistan has clearly made its views known on
the Taliban, and Pakistan has supported the effort against the Taliban.
So I don't think there is much question anymore about any quality relationship there" (Boucher, 2001). Since this element of the problem was
not adequately acknowledged at the beginning, the result was neglect of
the Pakistan side of the problem; a "farming out" to the Pakistanis of
the feeding and care of the Taliban sanctuary problem, to the point that
Washington has only recently recognized the reality of the relationship.

Pakistan has a long history of meddling in Afghanistan's politics. As we
have seen, it has long seen Afghanistan as a "strategic reserve" should its
troops need to redeploy because of an Indo-Pakistani conventional conflict.
The Taliban's links to Pakistan's Pashtun borderlands were forged through
two decades of war and life as refugees in Pakistan. "The Taliban were born
in Pakistani refugee camps, educated in Pakistani madrassas and learnt
their fighting skills from Mujaheddin parties based in Pakistan. Their families carried Pakistani identity cards" (Rashid, 2000:185). Direct support of
the Taliban by Pakistan started under Prime Minister Benazir Bhutto, who
in her own words was "slowly, slowly sucked into" support of the Taliban.
Starting with covert aid (fuel, machinery military spare parts, and training),
the Pakistanis were eventually supplying trade concessions and cash grants.
"Once I gave the go-ahead that they should get money," Bhutto recalled,
"I don't know how much money they were ultimately given . . . I know it
was a lot. It was just carte blanche" (Coll, 2004: 293).

By 1999, every Pakistani general whether liberal or religious, believed
in the jihadists. For Musharraf, who came to power in 1999, as for many
generals, jihad was not something he believed in personally, but was rather

a "professional imperative." The jihadists had proved themselves over many years "as the one force able to frighten, flummox, and bog down the Hindu-dominated Indian army," Pakistan's number one obsession. The Kashmir issue increasingly became the "prime mover" behind Pakistan's Afghan policy and its support of the Taliban (Coll, 2004: 478–79; Rashid, 2000:186).

Pakistan and the Taliban were collaborators in a common cause, and that collaboration continued after 9/11.[10] Pakistan needed the Taliban to carry out the main thrust of its foreign policy, tying down India, and to be assured this "strategic depth" it forged a relationship with the Taliban. Powell's instincts had been correct when he expressed "surprise" that Musharraf agreed to full cooperation with the United States (Woodward, 2002:59). Bush needed to pay more heed to the motto of his political mentor—Ronald Reagan—on international negotiations: "trust but verify."[11] The Pakistan connection merited close and continuing scrutiny after 9/11, both to alter Pakistani policy toward the Taliban and to promote democratization within Pakistan.

IMPLEMENTING THE WAR

The US attack on Afghanistan began with the insertion of special operations forces and CIA paramilitary teams to work with the Afghan opposition—the Northern Alliance—to depose the Taliban. Preparatory work had included working with Afghanistan's neighbors, especially Uzbekistan and Tajikistan to get air and ground access to Afghanistan. Bombing was used to destroy military targets and facilitate the advance of the US and Afghan personnel on the ground. The special forces troops worked with warlords and other contacts deploying military force or sabotage capabilities, with the Americans supplying weapons and supplies. The CIA had fewer contacts in the south among the Pashtun than in the north where they had worked steadily with the Northern Alliance, but one of the southern contacts was Hamid Karzai, who later became president. On October 7, 2001, the offensive began, the small group of special forces and CIA people working in conjunction with the Afghan troops and coordinating activities with the available air power when needed. For the first month, progress was slow and the press was beginning to write about a "quagmire," but on November 9 Mazar-e Sharif was taken, and soon Kabul. There were reports of attacks in Kandahar in the south, and by December 7, that city had fallen leaving the Northern Alliance, its Pashtun allies, and the United States in control of the country (Woodward, 2002). The speed of the victory in Afghanistan showed a new innovativeness in US strategy. It seemed to validate Rumsfeld's emphasis on a streamlined military that traveled lightly. He was reportedly delighted with pictures of special forces troops on horseback and with laser designators calling in precision air strikes with their hand-held radios (Rodman, 2009:243). US elation with the speed of the offensive was marred primarily by the failure to find and detain Osama bin Laden who apparently escaped from the Tora Bora region. Another worrisome factor was that the Northern Alliance had entered Kabul, thereby influencing the shape of the postconflict settlement at the expense of the Pashtuns in the south. This had been a source of concern throughout the White House decision making, especially for George Tenet.

There had been remarkably little planning for how postconflict Afghanistan would be handled, although such planning could have contributed substantially to postconflict stability. One limiting factor in the postconflict planning was that there was no real coherent concept of what the goal should be. Bush, and others, especially Rumsfeld, were clearly emotionally opposed to an ongoing US involvement, as the president's frequent pejorative references to nation-building indicate. On the other hand, there was a feeling that there was little alternative to US involvement, since some kind of postconflict governance had to be contrived. At an NSC meeting on October 4, when Wolfowitz and Rice talked about getting money from other countries for rebuilding, the president asked, "Who will run the country?" Belatedly, Rice realized that they should have addressed that. The vagueness of the postconflict thinking was reflected in the concern (especially by Rumsfeld) about whether to take and enter cities. On the one hand, they wanted to ensure order and continuation of everyday life. On the other, they preferred to do this through proxies, if possible, so they did not have direct responsibility (Woodward, 2002:193–95, 306, 310). The rapid fall of the Taliban and the quick collapse of their regime under attack from the Northern Alliance created a favorable environment for a war-weary people and for the United States and the Afghans to move quickly to consolidate their gains, but they were not able to take advantage of it (Giustozzi, 2008:233).

NO COMMITMENT, NO PLAN, NO MONEY

Expatriate and Northern Alliance leaders met in Bonn, Germany, in late November 2001. They signed the Bonn Agreement, which established an interim successor regime, established a plan and timetable for achieving peace and security and reestablished key institutions in the country. Both the pressure to give priority to Iraq and differing outlooks in the leadership ensured that Afghanistan would get minimal help in rebuilding and the provision of security. The controversy between those at State who preferred more US involvement in Afghanistan and those at Defense and the White

House who preferred to do the minimal would be decided in favor of Iraq. Secretary Powell, joined by National Security Adviser Rice argued that it was essential that the United States not "lose" Afghanistan. In February 2002 he proposed that American troops join the small international peace-keeping force than keeping order in Kabul and assisting Karzai in extending his influence to the country outside the capital. In April 2002, President Bush gave a speech at the Virginia Military Institute where he cited the experience with rebuilding Europe and hinted that the same approach would be taken in Afghanistan (Bush, 2002b). The speech got more notice in Afghanistan than in the United States, and buoyed hope in that country. Yet, only hours after the president's speech, Secretary Rumsfeld gave his own answer, which reflected his concern about becoming bogged down in Afghanistan. "The last thing you are going to hear from this podium is someone thinking they know how Afghanistan ought to organize itself," he stated, "They're going to have to figure it out. They're going to have to grab ahold of that thing and do something.. And we're there to help" (Rohde and Sanger, 2007). As early as February 20, 2002, Senator Bob Graham reports, he was told by CENTCOM commander Tommy Franks that "military and intelligence personnel are being redeployed to prepare for an action in Iraq. The Predators are being relocated." Senator Graham remarks that this was the first time he had heard not only that a decision to go to war in Iraq had already been made, but also that it was being implemented at the expense of the war in Afghanistan (Graham, 2004:125–26). Senator Graham was chair of the Senate Intelligence Committee. One scholar asserts that "from January 2002 through the war of 2003 the question of what the Bush administration should do about Saddam Hussein's regime became the dominant issue in US foreign policy and, indeed, in all of American politi-cal life" (Mann, 2004:332). General Hugh Shelton, chairman of the joint chiefs of staff during 9/11, said that the war in Iraq was the main factor in the United States losing out in Afghanistan. The United States does one thing well. It doesn't do several things at a time well (Shelton, 2010).

But despite the president's remarks in Virginia, no detailed reconstruc-tion plan was forthcoming, reflecting, former officials now say, tension and division in the administration over how large a role the United States should play in "stabilizing a country after toppling a hostile government." Regarding Powell's proposal, Richard N. Haass, the former director of Policy Planning at State, remarked that "[t]he president, the vice presi-dent, the secretary of defense, the national security staff, all of them were skeptical of an ambitious project in Afghanistan. I didn't see any support." Western officials put together a loose plan for Afghans to secure the country themselves, dividing up their assistance among them. The United States would train a 70,000-member army. Japan would disarm some 100,000 militia members, Britain would run an antinarcotics program, Germany would train a 62,000 member police force, and Italy would reform the justice system. "It was state building on the cheap, it was a duct tape approach," recalled Said T. Jawad, Mr. Karzai's then chief of staff and later Afghanistan's ambassador to Washington (Rohde and Sanger, 2007). The defect in the plan for years was that nobody was in charge, nobody was really coordinating to eliminate redundancy and ensure complementarity. That problem was to follow the allies' effort for years to come. The result was different approaches with mixed results, and little attempt to ensure cooperation and an integrated result.

In interviews conducted around the globe among former participants in the Afghan effort, *New York Times* reporters David Rohde and David E. Sanger found wide support for the proposition that the postconflict effort had insufficient resources and a lack of commitment from Washington. James Dobbins believed that the perception that Afghanistan hated foreigners and the Iraqis would welcome us was wrong, a belief that contributed to the effort to have a "light footprint" in Afghanistan. The reality was the exact opposite. Robert P. Finn, the US ambassador in 2002–03 said, "I said from the get-go that we didn't have enough money and we didn't have enough soldiers. I'm saying the same thing six years later." Ronald E. Neumann, a later ambassador made the point that the idea that we could just hunt terrorists and didn't have to do nation-building was "a large mistake." Dobbins notes that Afghanistan was the only time in an American intervention in which the United States spent more money and had more troops five years after the intervention than it did in the first year or two (Robichaud, 2007:4).

The US amounts were far below the amount of money committed to Iraq. One estimate is that donors had provided to Afghanistan barely 5 percent of that provided to Iraq. The per capita amount committed to the Afghan reconstruction was far below that of many other attempts to reconstruct failed states such as Bosnia, East Timor, Kosovo, and Iraq (Rubin, 2006; Dobbins et al., 2003). Long delays in appointments and funding had been common, and aid was often ineffective. It took a year before the State Department appointed a full-time coordinator for the reconstruction in Afghanistan (Rashid, 2008), and far fewer troops were committed than many believed necessary. James Dobbins, Bush's special envoy to Afghanistan, argued that another 25,000 troops were needed to keep order in cities beyond Kabul. He was rebuffed (Jones, 2008a:25). Following the 9/11 attack, NATO offered to send troops to fight with the Americans in Afghanistan. The United States first declined the offers, fearing that expanding participation in the coalition beyond Great Britain and modest personnel and equipment contributions by a few other NATO members would introduce "unwelcome political complications."[12] That changed as the situation deteriorated in 2005 and Washington admitted it needed helping stabilizing the south (NYT Editorial, 2007; Chayes, 2006). Washington and Defense Secretary Gates began demanding that the allies do more, while some of the allies were seeking to avoid fighting, often in response to opposition to casualties back home, or putting limits on what they would do or where they would operate. The British, the Canadians, and the Dutch were carrying the brunt of the non-US fighting mission (Anderson, 2007). Allied dissatisfaction with the initial US management of the war did not contribute to their enthusiasm for participation in the later stages. After years of US mistakes and misjudgments, deferral to the war in Iraq, and the resulting chaos in Afghanistan, the United States badly needs the rest of NATO, but now their publics are much less enthusiastic.

General Dan McNeill, head of US forces in Afghanistan, had the problem of how to extend the US presence without having to provide too many troops or too many resources and annoying Rumsfeld (Rashid, 2008). Hamid Karzai, in an interview in March 2009 was asked about the extra 17,000 troops that are scheduled to go to Afghanistan. He remarked that in 2002 he had pleaded for more troops that could go out to keep peace in outlying towns in the further reaches of the country. But he said his pleas were to no avail; he never got the troops he wanted. The troops being sent in 2009 are in response to the sharp upsurge in the insurgency. These troops, he said, are seven years too late (Karzai, 2009).

WARLORDS AND EFFECTIVE GOVERNMENT

The Bush administration was confronted with promotion of one of two policy alternatives for governing as the initial invasion wound down. By the summer of 2002 the warlords were becoming stronger, and the Karzai regime was too weak to compete. US policy was in effect to leave Karzai stranded and ineffectual in the capital, protected by foreign forces, while simultaneously relying on the warlords to keep order in the countryside and the US special forces to hunt down al Qaeda. As Ahmed Rashid put it:

> It was a minimalist, military intelligence-driven strategy that ignored nation building, creating state institutions, or rebuilding the country's shattered infrastructure. By following such a strategy, the United States left everything in place from the Taliban era except for the fact of regime change.

An alternative strategy would have been to use "power, money, and recently won influence and goodwill" to supplement Karzai's power, thus giving Karzai more control and involving the central government in the beginning of an effort to rebuild the country's institutions from the center out (Rashid, 2008:133).[13] Instead, Kabul became in essence one player among many as regional warlords, often using traditional patrimonial rule rather than developing modern bureaucratic institutions, dominated the countryside. As Ali A. Jalali, the former Iraqi Minister of the Interior states, "The United States has long hesitated to support the removal of defiant warlords . . . [failed] to hold [militia leaders] accountable . . . [and] continues to undermine the establishment of the rule of law" (Rubin, 2006:20). While this propensity to indirect rule was congruent with Bush's preference to avoid "nation-building," it was hardly consistent with building a responsible government that could respond to citizens' needs and provide the security they needed to get on with everyday life. The result was a state where citizens gradually lost faith in the government's ability to perform services and provide resources, and where outside of Kabul, security was haphazard, justice was arbitrary, and, especially in the east and south, the Taliban and its allies gradually regained the initiative. Public opinion polls showed that the increasing power of warlords was very unsettling for many Afghans (Jones, 2008a:26).

Sarah Chayes reports on her successful effort to help traditional Ghiljais tribal leaders in the Kandahar area go to Kabul to present their petitions and ideas and establish useful relationships with the president, the American embassy, and, eventually cabinet members, and the media, are enlightening. The whole "experiment" was bitter- sweet; sweet in the sense that the trip was successful and provided benefits on both sides; bitter in the sense that the delegation could not even enter Kabul without Chayes' intercession. "Northern Alliance fighters [guarding the Kabul gates] looked askance at their dust-daubed cars unencumbered by license plates, at their Pashtun turbans and beards, and listened with revulsion to their soft, southern consonants." Eventually an envoy was sent from the president's office—Chayes knew the Karzai family—and the impasse was broken. But what it illustrated to the Ghiljais was that this "central government of theirs, this central government that was supposed to be protecting them, was not even accessible without the intercession of a foreign woman." Kabul did not belong to them, it belonged to a "clutch of warlords from the Northern Alliance" (Chayes, 2006:223–25). These were exactly the kind of people (southern Pashtuns) whose support the president direly needed and the incident illustrates superbly both the ease with which the effectiveness and popularity of the government could be improved by interacting with local communities, and, simultaneously, the difficulty of making it happen.

Security was also compromised, and given the government's inability to either control the countryside outside of Kabul or to provide the services in the provinces, the Taliban by default are able to profit from the vacuum. RAND data show a 400 percent increase in the overall number of insurgent-initiated attacks from 2002 to 2006, most noticeably in the south and east. The number of deaths from these attacks increased 800 percent during the same period. The US military reported that the increase in violence was particularly acute in 2005 and 2006. During this period, the number of suicide attacks increased by more than 400 percent (from 27 to 139), remotely detonated bombings more than doubled (from 783 to 1,677), and armed attacks nearly tripled (from 1,558 to 4,542). Much of the learning for this innovation came from the Iraq conflict. Data also show that the use of suicide bombing increased severalfold the chances of killing someone and of instilling fear.[14] Interfactional or "green on green" fighting continued among regional commanders. The direct connection between government weakness and incompetence and the growing Taliban strength can be seen from a report from the Iraqi national directorate for security

> Individuals who flirt with the government truly get frightened as the Afghan security forces are currently incapable of providing police and protection for each village . . . When villagers and rural communities seek protection from police either it arrives late or arrives in a wrong way.

This government inability to provide security to the villagers means that once the insurgents establish a hold in a village, those who are hostile to the insurgents are often too fearful of retribution to speak out, provide information, or take action (Jones, 2008b:49–50, 65). And as time went on and the threats and danger increased, people began to contrast the present era with erratic, corrupt, and ineffective warlord rule with the time during the Taliban. Yes, oppression under the Taliban was much worse than now, but still, under the Taliban "there was a system: there was law and order . . . One knew the rules, for they were explicit. And if one only followed them, harsh and intransigent as they were, one could be relatively sure to be left in peace." In contrast to the Taliban era, "[n]ow there was no law." Oppression was arbitrary and it struck without reason (Chayes, 2006:193).

The identification of the US-supported government with the warlord society was not a good sign for US foreign policy. Why did the United States insist on resisting efforts to carry out reform at the expense of the warlords? There are several answers to this. To begin with, the CIA and special forces had worked closely with many warlords during the war in the fall of 2001, and they were reluctant to disturb the established arrangements. In a comment that speaks volumes about the implicit deal that the US and Karzai governments have with the status quo, an American official told the *New York Times* that the United States doesn't go after the drug kingpins because they are "the guys who helped us liberate this place in 2001," and the people the United States still relies on to hunt al Qaeda, the Taliban, and Osama bin Laden (Jones, 2006:266). Instead, the United States harassed the poppy-growing peasants.

Second, reintegrating former combatants into peaceful society remains a challenge. The second phase of a program to do that targeting nearly 2,000 illegal armed groups began in 2006, and was known as the disbandment of illegal armed groups program. The upsurge in Taliban-led violence in 2006 slowed the program, and also drove the government to rearm militias and assign them to serve as auxiliary police forces in some districts (Rotberg, 2007:33). One report in autumn 2007 reported that the revival of insurgent activity is leading to ex-militia leaders hoarding arms. It reported that "former warlords still hold considerable sway" (Semple, 2007). The whole thrust of the US strategy has been too little on reform and guaranteeing an active state that could provide services and a sense of legitimacy that would well serve the average citizen, and too much obsessed with hunting al Qaeda and finding a military solution to the Taliban.[15] The priority should have been on negotiating with "influential tribes" and rebuilding the infrastructure and the institutions of government (Rais, 2008). Such a focus on negotiation, reconciliation, and rebuilding of the economy is not something that came easy to the Bush administration, and most especially not to the Defense Department. Nor did the Karzai government take advantage of opportunities. The extent of corruption in the government in 2011 is phenomenal (Filkins, 2011).

In the initial period after operation Enduring Freedom, neither the Afghans nor the Americans really took the insurgency seriously. The United States was focused on Iraq and the Afghan campaign was left directionless. The Afghans in turn assumed that the Americans, with their overwhelming power would rid them of their enemies in the remote countryside and in Pakistan. Karzai and his cohorts concentrated on building a structure of power without much consideration of the effect of these efforts on the ongoing insurgency or the popularity of the government. While polls initially showed Karzai with high popularity, some of those traveling in the country had different impressions about the government's popularity. By 2006 when the insurgency "struck back with a vengeance," it was already "well past the incubation state" (Giustozzi, 2008:161). Any doubt that the situation has improved under the Obama administration cannot survive perusal of some of the latest reports on loss of confidence in the government, the persistence of warlordism, and reports on Ambassador Karl W. Eikenberry's view of Karzai (Witte,

2009; Filkins, 2010; and Schmitt, 2010). Karzai's legitimacy was further blemished by sponsoring a dishonest presidential election.

PAKISTAN (AGAIN)

Following the overthrow of the Taliban in 2001, there were three reasons Pakistan needed ties with the Taliban: (1) to balance against India, especially because of New Delhi's close ties with the Afghan government, (2) to hedge against US and NATO withdrawal from Afghanistan; in such an event, the Taliban would serve as Pakistan's proxy in Afghanistan; and (3) to preempt a move among Pakistan's Pashtun population toward closer relations with the Afghans, should Afghanistan become more secure and prosperous (Jones, 2008b:54). The Pakistanis have long been concerned that the relationship with their neighbor remains within the right range of cordiality. General Zia-ul-Haq, Pakistan's dictator from the 1970s again and again told General Akhtar Abdur Rahman, director-general of ISI, "The water in Afghanistan must boil at the right temperature" (Coll, 2004:63). General Musharraf himself told the Pakistanis in 2000 that their country had to cooperate with the Bush administration in order to keep Afghanistan and the Taliban from being harmed. He has therefore been all too happy to adhere to American guidance to concentrate on fighting al Qaeda and ignore the Taliban (Rubin, 2007:58–59). Pro-Taliban and pro-al-Qaeda former leaders gave widely reported speeches at Pakistani government and military institutions "calling for jihad against the United States and the Afghan government" (Jones 2008a:32). Musharraf and others often complemented their praise for the Taliban with acidic criticism of Afghan President Karzai (Rashid, 2008:369). The West needs to remember that the "overwhelming majority" of Pakistanis at every level of society are sympathetic to the Afghan Taliban, hate the US strategy, and believe that "9/11 was a CIA and/or Mosad plot intended to justify a US invasion and conquest of parts of the Muslim world" (Lieven, 2011:17).

Throughout the 1990s, the Pakistan military and the ISI provided arms, ammunition, and financial aid to the Taliban. Their ties were extensive and well documented. Still, the United States was tone-deaf to problems between Pakistan and Afghanistan. There was little attention to the controversy over the border between the two countries, the Duran Line. Afghanistan had never recognized the tentative border, which was proposed by the British back in the nineteenth century. As Barnett Rubin comments, Pakistan is unlikely to respect a border that Afghanistan does not even recognize. The United States largely relied on cooperation from Pakistan for action against al Qaeda and Taliban sanctuaries in that country. Afghanistan, to the other hand, wants the United States to reduce unpopular actions in the country, intruding upon citizens by searching their homes and using excessive firepower that kills civilians to eliminate suspected insurgents, and instead to put pressure on Pakistan to end the sanctuary it gives insurgents and eliminate the cross-border flow of men and material (Jones, 2008a,b; Rubin, 2006). A possible solution to the difficult problem is international negotiations in which Pakistan, but also India, Russia, and Iran would each be given assurances regarding their concerns with and demands on Afghanistan that would allow a permanent agreement to bring stability to Afghanistan and restore it to a version of its historic role of buffer state in the region (Giustozzi, 2008:233). Some have gone further and suggested a formal guarantee by the international community of the permanent neutrality of Afghanistan, perhaps on the model of Switzerland (Jones and Pickering, 2008:38). Unfortunately, the United States, and initially the United Nations, showed little interest in involving Iran in the Afghan problem, even though Iran expressed its willingness to get involved, both diplomatically and in construction and troop training (Dobbins, 2008:46, 121, 143, 153.

Evidence of Pakistan's continuing role in sponsoring the Taliban is abundant and easily available. The provincial governor of Khost province on the Pakistan border, Arsala Jamal, told Defense Secretary Gates in December 2007 that the tribal areas just across the border in Pakistan have been a haven for Taliban and al Qaeda forces to regroup and organize. Some members of the ISI provided weapons and ammunition to the Taliban, as well as paying the medical bills of wounded fighters and providing financial assistance to Taliban training camps. They also helped train Taliban and other insurgents destined for Afghanistan and Kashmir in various areas in Pakistan. Based on interviews with senior U.N., NATO, Afghan and Pakistani government officials, Seth Jones contends that "[t]he Pakistan government repeatedly stated that it was not providing assistance to the Taliban, but the evidence to the contrary appears overwhelming."

A 2006 US, NATO, and Afghan report definitively documented the real situation, concluding that the "insurgency cannot survive without its sanctuary in Pakistan" (Rubin, 2007; Rashid, 2008:368). Put more directly, one US intelligence officer said: "Pakistan is supposed to be our ally in the war on terrorism. Sometimes it's helpful in capturing or killing insurgents, and sometimes it helps groups trying to kill us. How's that for an ally?" (Hoffman and Jones, 2008:50).

Complicating this issue is the coincidence that "only the Pashtuns have ever demonstrated an interest in the type of jihad being waged by the Taliban." The Pashtuns live by a distinct culture that tends to make them even better suited for insurgency than other Afghans. The Pashtun social code, Pashtunwali, has core tenets such as self-respect, independence, justice, hospitality, forgiveness, and tolerance. It is the keystone of the Pashtun identity and social structure and "shapes all forms of behavior from the cradle to the grave." It makes the Pashtuns natural warriors and encourages their independence from Kabul. The tight-knit nature of Pashtun social organization helps explain the ties between Pashtuns on both sides of the Pakistan-Afghanistan border, and in fact renders the border virtually irrelevant from their perspective. The nagging fear for both Islamabad and Kabul is the emergence of a Pashtun state loyal to neither capital (Johnson and Mason, 2008:59, 64). The new civilian government elected in 2008 has shown itself little more capable or willing than Musharraf to control the extremist jihadist elements in Pakistan society.

The relevant question is why it took the Bush administration so many years to focus on what was really going on, since the United States' "willingness to ignore Pakistan's conduct was integral to the continued and increasing violence" (Cordesman, 2009). Condoleezza Rice had briefly raised the issue in June 2006 when she was in Islamabad, but Musharraf denied any Taliban presence in Pakistan. Bush declined to raise the issue of the Taliban sanctuary in Quetta at a tense tripartite dinner for Musharraf and Karzai at the White House on September 28, even though Karzai brought it up, and Musharraf himself had admitted before coming to Washington that there were Taliban in "both Afghanistan and in Pakistan." Bush had passed up a similar opportunity in Islamabad in March. While acknowledging and addressing the problem, there is no evidence that the Obama administration has made any progress in solving the problem (Bumiller, 2010). On the contrary, increasingly the "problem" of hosting al Qaeda is acknowledged to exist as much or more in Pakistan as in Afghanistan as the recent capture of Osama bin Laden in Pakistan so vividly illustrates.

EXCESSIVE FORCE, RELATIONSHIPS WITH LOCALS, AND CULTURAL SENSITIVITY

President Karzai has complained frequently and bitterly about excessive and inappropriate use of force by Americans. In April 2008 he declared that although civilian casualties had dropped substantially since the past year, they needed to cease completely (Gall, 2008). The shortage of ground troops led to "reliance on air strikes and artillery barrages," complicating the job of winning over civilians. Sometimes casualties are caused by local chiefs providing information motivated by personal grudges and a desire for revenge rather than affiliation with insurgents. The more recent efforts of General McChrystal and the Obama administration have focused on limiting civilian deaths with mixed results. Relations with the local population were a frequent problem, ranging from lack of respect for local customs to arbitrary arrests and killings. Unauthorized access to homes was a major problem, to the point that US forces were required to rely on Afghan security forces for home searches. "Recreational" looting of agricultural fields also contributed to resentment toward foreign troops. Reportedly, there was little understanding among the local population of US security requirements, such as the ban on drivers overtaking US convoys. This helps to explain how simple road accidents could spark riots, as happened in Kabul in May 2006 (Giustozzi, 2008:163–64, 191). In other cases hunting teams have insulted villagers by searching their women, or desecrating cemeteries by exhuming their dead and sometimes refusing to allow assistance for the victims of air strikes (Jalali, 2003:184). According to a meticulous report, around 3,000 Taliban prisoners were massacred by the Northern Alliance forces, and by some accounts the atrocity was witnessed by American soldiers. Despite the seriousness of these reports and the known locations of communal graves, the U. N. declined to carry out an inquiry in order not to embarrass the Afghan and US governments (Dorronsoro, 2005:326–27).

RECONSTRUCTION AND DEVELOPMENT

It doesn't take much reading in the literature on the Western attempts at reconstruction and development in Afghanistan to see that there are some major problems in translating foreigners' good intentions into tangible results appreciated by the Afghans. The problem of attempting to do reconstruction in the face of inadequate security is a problem that is omnipresent in Afghanistan (Rashid, 2008; Jones, 2008b).

Even though much of the money is dedicated to state ministries, when it arrives it is handed over to NGOs like Oxfam or Care, for the construction of schools and hospitals. The result is the "slow and steady erosion of the host state's responsibility" (Cohen et al., 2008). Moreover, evidence of the attraction of antiforeign appeals is apparent. Hamid Karzai has criticized the wasteful overlap, cronyism, and unaccountability among foreign NGOs in Afghanistan. According to CBS veteran news reporter Lara Logan, corruption is rampant in the international aid effort, as bad as in the Afghan government, (Logan, 2009). The counter argument is that the government is too often wasteful and inefficient and dollars go further if they are dispersed through the private sector.

Two seasoned observers of the assistance process in the country note that

> the extent to which policy was set by people who knew nothing about Afghanistan was frightening. It could have been anywhere. That political,

social, and economic history is important in determining what is possible in a country was not part of the thinking: it was simply cut and paste. Many of those responsible for the writing hardly left their offices in Kabul, and never ventured outside the city. Some of them hardly stayed long enough for the entry stamp to dry in their passports.

Johnson and Leslie, 2004:181

Ann Jones recounts receiving consistent refusals for international funding for a proposal to train high school teachers. A colleague later told her that the problem was that her proposal was not expensive enough. She notes that many schools in Afghanistan are built on a standard $174,000 blueprint, ensuring a school that is "too expensive for communities to maintain, too big to find enough teachers, and too 'centralized' for girls from outlying villages to walk to." Senator Joe Biden had an alternative idea of building 1,000 neighborhood schools in Afghanistan at a cost of $20,000 each and staffing them with teachers who had lost their jobs to the Taliban (Jones, 2006:236–69). Jones found inappropriate schools purchased at excessive cost, but no textbooks to go with them; inappropriate textbooks; school projects that are started, but terminated a year early because of funding termination, causing the Afghans to lose face (not to mention an education), and one woman to ask her: "What's wrong with America? Why do they keep starting things they can't finish?" In other words, projects in Afghanistan often suffer from contracts given to big corporations with enormous fees when going through local government and getting local workers to plan and participate in the work would benefit both the Americans and the Afghans and help ensure the practicality and continuity of the project (ICG, 2007).

Instead, the omnipresent Western military and aid workers bring two habits strictly frowned upon by Muslims, permissive sex and dress and drinking of alcoholic beverages. Jones cites a widely rumored figure of 6,000 sex workers in Kabul in 2005, with 80 brothels. In the view of many Afghans, foreign aid is something that foreigners enjoy, living in big houses and driving SUVs, many of them spending the evenings drinking and in brothels. Meanwhile, half the city still lies in ruins, many Afghans are jobless and live in tents; women in tattered burqas still beg and may turn to prostitution; hospitals and schools are overcrowded and inadequate.

CONCLUSION

The Bush administration gave priority to military tasks, but still failed to apprehend bin Laden, perhaps the biggest flaw in the entire Afghan effort. Having chosen to fight the Taliban and the insurgents, instead of expeditiously giving resources and encouragement to Kabul to restore public services in the countryside, promote the government's legitimacy and jettison the warlords as fast as possible, the administration temporized, trickling in resources and aid, and hanging on to warlords to provide security, and increasingly as time went on, killing civilians in military actions that eroded the government's legitimacy. Recent revelations add additional understanding of the basic flaws of past and present strategy in stressing military rather than political issues. The United States in the early years of the conflict was not interested in exploiting opportunities to reintegrate the insurgents into the Karzai government, following the establishment of that government. It is alleged that much of the senior Taliban leadership agreed in principle to find a way to abandon the fight, but a lack of political will in Kabul and American opposition meant that it came to nothing. Similar probes in the following years were equally fruitless (Gopal, 2010). According to Kati Marton, the wife of the late Ambassador Richard Holbrooke, Obama's special envoy to the region, he believed before he died that the whole conflict was still too militarized and more emphasis should be put on political and diplomatic approaches (Kristof, 2011). The United States first shunned NATO's help, and then used it in an uncoordinated and inefficient manner. The command of all NATO and US troops in Afghanistan was finally consolidated under one person, General David McKiernan, but as of March 2009, this kind of coordination has not been done for aid and development programs (Fick and Nagl, 2009). More than a few of these many difficulties can be blamed on the unseemly rush to leave the apparently solved Afghan problem and get on to the project in Iraq.

Another egregious weak spot in the United States Afghan policy was its reluctance to admit the troubling contribution of Pakistan in supplying and encouraging the Taliban. As we have seen, it was evident from the start that Pakistan's willingness to give up its investment in the Taliban was dubious. The Bush administration should have worried less about the "axis of evil" and more about some of its "friends" like Pakistan.[16] Early attention to the problem *might* have allowed the United States to encourage a more democratic government in Pakistan in exchange for intensified attention to the Afghan problem. The corollary of this problem has been the reluctance to acknowledge, as the conflict wore on, that increasingly the main nub of the al Qaeda problem was not Afghanistan but Pakistan (Lieven, 2011). The crucial time to recognize this reality should have been the early months of the Obama administration, before the decisions to expand the effort in Afghanistan. Now, there is still major focus on the Afghan result, when more and more what happens there is dependent on what transpires in Pakistan, and of less importance than Pakistan. The effort, however, has not been adjusted to recognize this.

The three major problems that have thwarted US progress in Afghanistan are: the switching of priorities to Iraq only months after the October 2001 attack; the Pakistani sanctuary for the insurgents; and the low legitimacy level of a Kabul government that is corrupt, does not produce security or services, and tolerates warlord rule. The priority given to Iraq is over and in the past. The Obama administration has also sharply increased troop levels and resources. The problems of Pakistan and government performance, however, seem almost intractable. The United States is dependent on the behavior of secondary actors—Pakistan and the Kabul government (see quagmire problem in Chapter 9)—for results. The Taliban are now reported to be more radical than early in the conflict, much more global and not easily separated from al Qaeda. The two groups are said to be joined at the hip (Williams, 2009). To the Karzai government's sorry record of governance, there now can be added massive electoral fraud to further debilitate its legitimacy.

Learning from the situation in Iraq, the Obama administration has made a sincere and apparently successful effort to implement a real counterinsurgency strategy in Afghanistan. General McChrystal's report before he was relieved speaks the real language of counterinsurgency, and his replacement General Petraeus seemed particularly concerned about a major irritant to the Afghans, the occasional killing of civilians. But the question remains: after a decade of war and given the best of strategies and intentions, can the situation be saved given the lack of a responsive government in Kabul and continued Pakistani collaboration with the insurgents? There is a gnawing worry that the Obama administration has still not faced the reality in Afghanistan, nor the questionable expediency of continuing the present policy.

CHAPTER 8

IRAQ—2003–2010

> We're an empire now, and when we act, we create our own reality. And while you're studying that reality—judiciously, as you will—we'll act again, creating other new realities, which you can study too, and that's how things will sort out. We're history's actors . . . and you, all of you, will be left to just study what we do.
>
> A senior adviser for President Bush, to Ron Suskind

In none of the cases in this study is the decision to go to war more perplexing than in the case of the attack on Iraq in 2003. Initiated when the United States was already involved in one unconventional war in Afghanistan and having no readily discernible connection to the events of 9/11, a full-scale assault aimed at the toppling of Saddam Hussein was undertaken without even one formal decision or cost-benefit review of the likely results (Fallows, 2006:119; Davis, 2006:21). George Packer quotes Richard Haass, formerly director of Policy Planning in the State Department, as saying he will go to his grave without knowing why the United States went to war in Iraq (Packer, 2005:46). While the process of decision making in the George W. Bush administration was unique and even bizarre, the American obsession with Iraq and Saddam Hussein, which goes back to the Reagan administration, is in itself puzzling given Iraq's relatively minor power position and unimaginative leadership. The Baath regime, which came to power in 1969, has always been authoritarian and hardly an obvious ethical match for the United States. The primary concern for the Americans in the Gulf area had been preserving some kind of counter to Iran after the overthrow of the Shah in 1979. There has been a "triangular rivalry among Iran, Iraq and the Gulf Arab states led by Saudi Arabia." An attempt to balance between Iran and Iraq was replaced after the Gulf War by dual containment (Buzan and Waever, 2003:191–201). The United States initially sought to balance Iran by supporting Iraq, as it did during the Iran-Iraq War in the early 1980s, when the United States sold Saddam $200 million worth of weaponry as well as gave billions in loans and credits for agriculture and energy projects, and supplied US intelligence data to Iraq. Diplomatic relations, which had been severed in 1967, were restored in 1984. The Reagan administration got interested in supporting Saddam when the tide in the war turned against Iraq, and it saw an opportunity to draw Iraq away from the Soviet Union. It was just as the Iraqis started using poison gas against the Iranians that Ronald Reagan appointed Donald Rumsfeld to be his special emissary and sent him to Iraq. Rumsfeld neglected to discuss the use of gas on the battlefield with Saddam, but did raise the issue with Deputy Prime Minister Tariq Aziz. The United States had a valid concern in worrying about Iranian dominance of the area, but American support of Iraq in the war was sullied both by the gas issue and the carnage of the war in which a million people were killed. Additionally, Saddam Hussein gassed at least 5,000 of his own people in villages in the Kurdish areas, again with no US protest (Galbraith, 2006).[1] The validity of previous concerns about Iran is supported by recent fears about the extent of Iranian influence in postwar Iraq. The concern is particularly acute that once the Americans are gone, the Iraqis will not be able to cope. According to one border policeman, "when the Americans leave, it will be miserable for all of Iraq. Not just the border. Iraq is like a big cake that everyone wants to eat, and the Iraqi army is not strong enough" (Londono, 2010).

Just prior to the 1991 Gulf War, controversy revolved around then American Ambassador April Glaspie who seemingly condoned Saddam's pending attack on Kuwait in 1990. "I have a direct instruction from the President to seek better relations with Iraq," Glaspie told Saddam, after hearing broad hints about what he had in mind. For the decade following the Gulf War, however, the emphasis continued to be on the containment of Saddam. For none of the presidents involved, George H. W. Bush, Bill Clinton, or George W. Bush, was containment a fully satisfactory process. There was considerable doubt about the ability of the weapons inspectors to gather reliable information on the extent and success of Saddam's programs for building WMD. Further, there was a consensus that the coalition developed to contain Saddam could not be maintained. This was believed especially in the Arab world, but also to some extent in Europe. The report on the impact of the economic embargo in killing and shortening the life of Iraqi children was particularly effective in diminishing enthusiasm for the embargo, and corruption also played a role in decreasing its effectiveness. Iraq was able to play on the "sanctions fatigue" afflicting the participants in the multilateral effort, in turn decreasing the efficacy of the efforts to control Saddam and increasing the cost of what was accomplished. Iraq was able to impede the work of the weapons inspectors, to frustrate the efforts to maintain the no-fly zones, and to repeatedly force the U.N. forces to deploy "expensive naval build-ups in the preparation for military hostilities for the multiple occasions when Saddam violated a string of U.N. Security Council resolutions" (Davis, 2006:3–4).

Whatever the frustrations of containment, however, few policy makers shared the determination and singleness of purpose for regime change as the group known as neo-conservatives and the national security people in the George W. Bush administration. Their view of the international system has been described as one where states "face a situation of crisis, in which action is crucial to combat existential threats" (Rapport, 2008). This group initiated an action for policy change during the Clinton administration and helped prepare the 2003 attack that began the war. The success of their venture during the Bush administration owed a great deal to the permissive atmosphere created for radical foreign policy departures by the 9/11 incidents. Eighteen activists on Iraq policy, including Paul Wolfowitz, Donald Rumsfeld, William Kristol, Robert Kagan, Richard Perle, Zalmay Khalilzad, and others sent a letter to President Clinton on January 26, 1998, urging a US policy of removing Saddam Hussein from power and offering their full support for such an endeavor. It stipulated that acting to "end the threat of weapons of mass destruction against the U.S. or its allies" would be in the "most fundamental national security interests of the country," whereas accepting "a course of weakness and drift" would put our interests at risk (Clinton Iraq Policy Letter, 1998).

The neoconservatives, the primary drivers advocating a more aggressive policy toward Iraq, got their start during the Reagan years, when, disillusioned with the transformation of the Democratic Party during and after the Vietnam War, Democrats Irving Kristol and acolytes of Democratic hawk Henry "Scoop" Jackson such as Richard Perle and others transferred their loyalty to the Republican Party. They had strong support from people such as Donald Rumsfeld and Dick Cheney, more closely identified with traditional Republican conservatives. The foreign policy neoconservative activists such as Perle, Paul Wolfowitz, and Douglas Feith had a long history of working together for common causes, charges of abusing their access to classified information, and close ties with Israeli officials. Their behavior often reflected the Trotskyite background of the first generation of neoconservatives, including a tendency toward paranoia toward the most recently identified threat or enemy and a tendency to slant information in a direction favorable to their cause.[2]

This group clashed on Iraq with another group of foreign policy experts identified with Bush senior's administration and usually categorized as realists, especially Brent Scowcroft, James Baker, and Lawrence Eagleburger. All warned against invading Iraq in August 2002. Scowcroft, who later stated

"I'm a skeptic about the ability to transform Iraq into a democracy in any realistic period of time," had also penned an op-ed piece critical of invading Iraq, when he could not gain access to the White House. He argued that Saddam had no direct designs on the United States but rather countered US interests in the Middle East. Containment was working to thwart the threat from his activities, and any direct assault on him would distract from the American priority of fighting terrorism, with which Saddam is not significantly involved. Any attack would be costly and provoke outrage in the region, and likely result in a costly long-term occupation. The United States would be better served by working for an Israeli-Palestinian settlement, the real obsession of the region (Scowcroft, 2002).

In any case, as Mann points out, the debate among Republicans in the summer of 2002 was "America's only serious public debate about the war in Iraq," with Republicans Chuck Hagel and Colin Powell also expressing reservations about the Iraq plans. The Democrats were divided and hesitant to challenge the president on Iraq (Mann, 2004:337–43). Anatol Lieven has persuasively argued that many supporters of the Democratic Party such as Michael Tomasky, Michael O'Hanlon, and Michael McFaul in essence backed the neoconservatives in their call for maintaining a dominant US military position in the world, promoting democracy, and opposition to the status quo (Lieven, 2004:75–80).

US SECURITY INTERESTS AND IRAQ

The concern of policy makers through several administrations with Saddam's Iraq is understandable. Saddam was a constant nuisance who would not go away. The Baath Party in Iraq had a dreadful human rights record from the beginning, and Saddam proved himself ruthless in the extreme (al-Khalil, 1989). Iraq perhaps surpassed any other third world country in approximating the ruthlessness and efficiency of Stalin's autocratic rule. After starting two major wars, with Iran (1980) and Kuwait (1990), he was ejected from Kuwait by a U.N. coalition and ignominiously forced to retreat to Baghdad, with his WMD programs a shambles. Notwithstanding these setbacks, however, he continued to thumb his nose at the world community and was a constant challenge to US interests in the Middle East. On the other hand, Iraq was a small relatively weak power with a military that was less than effective when matched against a competent force (Table 8.1). A clear difference in the priorities of the Clinton and George W. Bush administrations toward this "minor strategic annoyance" was revealed when they met during the transition. Clinton had surmised correctly that the top priorities of the new administration were national missile defense and Iraq. Clinton then suggested a different

Table 8.1 US-Iraq war statistics

Country	GNP/GDP (bn $)	Pop (million)	Total armed force	Defense expend. (mil. $)	Intervention forces (peak nos.)	US casualties	Host country casualties
Iraq	26,1 (2002)	22.95	389,000 (active)	18,664			(Insurgents) U.S. military: 18,832—9/2007 (Civilian and police) U.S. military: 77,000—2004–2008; Iraq Human Rights Ministry: 85,694; Iraq Body Count: 108, 398; Johns Hopkins: 600,000—10/06
US	10,946	291	1,427,000	329,616 (2002)	180,000	4,404 (8/2010)	

Sources: World Bank Atlas; The Military Balance (London: IISS); *Strategic Survey* (London: IISS); *USA Today* online, http://www.usatoday.com/news/world/iraq/2006-10-10-iraq-dead_x.htm; DoD, http://www.defenselink.mil/news/casualty.pdf, accessed 8/4/10; Iraq Body Count, iraqbodycount.org, accessed 12/05/08; *Washington Post*, December 31, 2007; *USA Today* online, September 27, 2007 at http://www.usatoday.com/news/world/iraq/2007-09-26-insurgents_N.htm, accessed 3/10/11; *The Associated Press*, December 29, 2010 at http://www.armytimes.com/news/2010/12/ap-iraq-war-deaths-drop-in-2010-122910/, accessed 3/11/11.

set, to include al Qaeda, Middle East diplomacy, North Korea, the South Asian nuclear competition, and, only then, Iraq. Reportedly, Bush did not respond (Layne, 2006:185; Gordon and Trainor, 2006:13).

One knowledgeable source in the administration in 2003 attributes the decision to go to war with Iraq to President Bush and three advisers (Cheney, Rumsfeld, and Wolfowitz). He lists five reasons why the 2003 war with Iraq was initiated:

- To clean up the mess left by the first Bush administration when, in 1991, it let Saddam Hussein consolidate power and slaughter opponents after the first US-Iraq war;
- To improve Israel's strategic position by eliminating a large hostile military;
- To create an Arab democracy that could serve as a model to other friendly Arab states now threatened with internal dissent, notably Egypt and Saudi Arabia;
- To permit the withdrawal of US forces from Saudi Arabia (after 12 years), where they were stationed to counter the Iraqi military and were a source of anti-Americanism threatening to the regime;
- To create another friendly source of oil for the US market and reduce dependency upon oil from Saudi Arabia, whose government might someday be overthrown (Clarke, 2004:265).

All of these are credible components of a rationale for war, although none are really a convincing explanation of why by 2003 war had suddenly become imperative, nor do they explain the exaggerated claims made by many about the enormity of the threat made by Elliot Cohen, Dick Cheney, and others, or the urgency of dealing with Saddam (Kaufmann, 2004:6; Western, 2005:193; Gelman, 2008). In an interview in *Vanity Fair* after the war, Paul Wolfowitz, who Bob Woodward called the intellectual godfather and "fiercest advocate" for toppling Saddam (Woodward, 2004: 21), suggested that the WMD rationale for the war was settled on as the primary justification because it was one on which everyone could agree.[3] Intelligence supporting the existence of WMD was faulty, and as many have suggested, there was never a case made for the war that provided a sharp favorable contrast with the containment regime. Another major rationale provided by the Bush administration for the invasion was the *implicit* assumption that somehow al-Qaeda and Iraq were linked and cooperating to promote terrorism throughout the world. No reliable evidence has been produced of any substantive cooperation of that sort. Administration pronouncements, however, consistently framed terrorism and Iraq together, thereby implying that Iraq was somehow directly involved in 9/11. This myth was finally disowned, but only belatedly. Meanwhile, this particular rationale had provided one of the most convincing justifications for war as far as public opinion was concerned.

> Only in September 2003, only after occupying Iraq, only after Vice President Cheney had stretched credulity on *Meet the Press*, did the President clearly state that there was "no evidence that Iraq was involved in the September 11 attacks."
>
> Clarke, 2004:268

The effectiveness of the arguments from the administration's perspective, however, was high. Polls showed that even a year after the invasion 47 percent of the public believed that clear evidence that Iraq was supporting al Qaeda had been found in Iraq (Kaufmann, 2004:33). It was the assumption of Saddam's aggressive tendencies combined with his supposed links to terrorists and the possession of chemical, biological, and potentially nuclear weapons that formed the heart of the case for war.

Following the 9/11 attack, R. James Woolsey, one of the signers of the Iraq letter to the president and director of the CIA in the early Clinton administration, told James Fallows: "We don't know where this attack came from, but the response has to involve Iraq" (Fallows, 2006:xi). Everyone in Washington was receiving similar signals, according to Fallows. As we have seen, the decision making on Afghanistan involved considerable discussion of attacking Iraq with the implicit assumption that that job would have to be done, but with the president mandating that Afghanistan should get priority. These specifics follow from the administration's peculiar way of viewing the Middle East. That perspective posits, first, that the status quo was unacceptable. Autocratic and backward regimes that have been supported by the United States in the past no longer threatened just the welfare of their citizens, but with the development of terrorism the rest of the world as well. Many regional thinkers were also hostile to the status quo. Another assumption was that Saddam Hussein, the WMD, and the autocratic regime pose an unacceptable threat to world peace and must go. Regime change in Iraq and the democratization of the Middle East are the keys to making the region safe for the world. The Bush administration also believed that the Israel-Palestinian dispute could best be solved after these fundamental changes took place. Many other observers believed the opposite, that changes in that relationship had to precede other kinds of progress in the Middle East (Gordon, 2003).

No doubt part of the problem was that it was difficult for the leadership to adjust to the fact that an act such as bringing down the twin towers could be done by a small group of extremists without direct involvement of a state sponsor. As Paul Wolfowitz complained to Richard Clarke, "You give bin Laden too much credit. He could not do all these things like the 1993 attack on New York, not without a state sponsor. Just because FBI and CIA have failed to find the linkages [with Iraq] does not mean they don't exist" (Clarke, 2004:232). The potential ingenuity of Saddam Hussein seemed easier for some high officials to grasp. As Vice President Cheney explained to a skeptical House Majority Leader Dick Armey, "Saddam could put drone aircraft on a freighter, steam them across the Atlantic and use the route-planning software to dispatch lethal microbes anywhere from Miami to Boston" (quoted by Barton Gellman in Heilbrunn, 2008).

In his 1995 book recounting the Gulf War, former Secretary of State James Baker laid out the reasons against going to Baghdad and implementing "regime change" in Iraq after Saddam was thrown out of Kuwait in 1991. At that time, there was considerable controversy over the advisability of such a course. "I believe this idea is as nonsensical now as it was then," said Baker, "and not merely for the narrow legalistic reason that the U.N. resolutions did not authorize coalition forces to undertake anything beyond the liberation of Kuwait." The president's decision not to go to Baghdad was an "absolutely correct" judgment on which there was little debate. At the least, to march on Baghdad would have made a nationalistic hero out of Saddam, and he would have been difficult to find. It would have turned the war to liberate Kuwait into a "war of conquest." Iraqi soldiers could have been expected to resist enemy occupation of their country "with a ferocity not previously demonstrated on the battlefield in Kuwait." If Saddam were captured and the regime overthrown, American forces would still have the task of a military occupation of "indefinite duration to pacify the country and sustain a new government in power." Finally, there was a strong fear among neighboring Arab countries that such actions would lead to the fragmentation of Iraq and the enhancement of Iran's power and the export of their brand of fundamentalism (Baker, 1995:436–37). This is a fairly accurate summary of the difficulties actually encountered after the invasion of Iraq in 2003.[4] Baker recounted that whereas the decision not to march to Baghdad was originally controversial and stimulated questions when he was on the lecture circuit, but when complications developed after the start of the 2003 war, he no longer heard those kinds of questions.

But whereas Baker and others emphasized the difficulties of overthrowing Iraq, the Bush administration and the neoconservatives emphasized the ease with which it could be done. Vice President Cheney quotes Professor Fouad Ajami predicting that following liberation, the streets of Basra and Baghdad "are sure to erupt in joy in the same way the throngs in Kabul greeted the Americans" (Western, 2005:199–200). Another former Reagan official with close ties to the advocates of war, Ken Adelman, famously characterized the coming war with Iraq as a "cakewalk." He noted the drastically reduced size of Saddam's degraded military and lampooned those who thought the new high-tech military would not be effective against Iraq (Adelman, 2002).

IDEOLOGICAL RIGIDITY

If looking for the motivation for Iraqi policy in the security realm appears to be a will-o'-the-wisp, can the motivation for the policy be better explained by the messianic strain in American history, an assumption of cultural and institutional superiority that should be transplanted to foreign soil, a victory of morality and civilized culture over immorality and barbarism? Two approaches have been taken to Bush's focus on a religious and moralistic approach to ideals and their combination with American nationalism as a guide to US policy. One perspective sees these ideas as reflected in Bush's personality serving as a more or less literal guide to choosing goals and making decisions in foreign policy. Beliefs about American virtue and exceptionalism serve as a guide to foreign policy formulation. A second approach, taken by Jacob Weisberg, sees the ideological content of Bush's pronouncements as convenient but not deeply held beliefs that provide justification for his need to achieve more pressing objectives, in this case to prevail against the shortcomings of his father's policies and vindicate his family. In this construction, the ideas may or may not serve as an accurate indicator of the actual direction of foreign policy. His ideological and religious views were superficial and not deeply felt; superficial masks for other motivations. While there can be no empirical test of such hypotheses, there seems little doubt that justification of the attack on moral grounds—overthrowing Saddam, bringing democracy and good government to the Iraqi people—played a role in garnering public support. That is not to say that the public did not believe in a legitimate security objective, but rather that they also believed such an objective coincided with a morally viable and attractive policy goal of removing Saddam. The moral overlay therefore was an assist in increasing support for a policy the public already believed could be justified in terms of security.

There is a strong strain of moralism in the neoconservative movement, indeed, as we have seen in Chapter 1, in American foreign policy in general. This element is especially strong in the thinking of President George W. Bush, and according to some, it extends beyond ideology, religion, and his perspective on the world to include a personality predisposed to making "gut" decisions, rigidly adhered to, without the dispiriting burden of doubt. In the case of Iraq, these factors combine to confirm his belief that in carrying out the "liberation" of Iraq the United States was fulfilling its "providential mission to restore freedom to the oppressed" (Langston, 2007; Suskind, 2004).

George W. Bush believes in values that are universal, God-given rights to which people all over the world are entitled. He makes no allowance for differences in right and wrong based on culture-specific preferences and historical development.[5] "So it is the policy of the United States to seek and support the growth of democratic movements and institutions in every nation and culture, with the *ultimate goal of ending tyranny in our world*" (emphasis added) (Bush, 2002a; 2005). "Wilsonian in boots" is Pierre Hassner's phrase for the forceful imposition of democracy (Ikenberry, 2004).

According to Bruce Bartlett, who worked for both President Reagan and the first Bush, George W. Bush believed he was on a "mission from God" (Suskind, 2004). Bush became especially close with Michael Gerson, like the president a "born again" member of his staff originally hired as a domestic speechwriter, who later filled in as a policy advisor as well. Bush delivered a speech to a joint session of Congress on September 20, after 9/11. After the speech, Bush thanked Gerson, who replied "Mr. President, this is why God wants you here." "No," Bush responded, "this is why He wants *us* here" (Kaplan, 2008:132). Woodward reports he pressed Bush a "dozen times" on what his father's advice—the initiator of the 1991 Gulf War—might have been on the later invasion of Iraq. Bush maintained he couldn't recall, but finally stated that "[h]e is the wrong father to appeal to in terms of strength. There is a higher father" (Woodward, 2008:432).

If one takes things on faith, then one knows what needs to be known; there is no need for getting detailed answers to tough questions. As Suskind notes, "Absolute faith like that overwhelms a need for analysis. The whole thing about faith is to believe things for which there is no empirical evidence. . . . Faith heals the heart and the spirit, but it doesn't do much for the analytical skills" (Suskind, 2004). In his masterful portrait of Bush's family history and persona, Jacob Weisberg stresses the degree to which Bush's religious beliefs have been subordinated to political objectives originating in his family history and attempts to best his father. It is more useful to understand Bush's view of the world as dressed up in religion rather than driven by religion. Weisberg spends a chapter on Bush's religion, concluding his interests in it are more in its instrumental use than specific theological content or beliefs to which he was strongly attached. Similarly, Bush's ardent promotion of democracy and human rights is congruent with American values, but his eight-year administration hardly showed excessive concern with parsing and enhancing those values domestically. In his view, Bush's faith and his liberal democratic values are part of a "constructed persona" rather than a framework through which he looks at the world. The problem is that in the end Bush's ideals disintegrate into vacuousness. As Weisberg says,

Bush's problem wasn't his broadest goal [spreading democracy and human rights through the Middle East] but his relentless ebb into abstraction, incompetent execution, and glaring inconsistency. In a matter of four years, the president's view had reversed itself completely. In 1999, Bush rejected the very notion of nation-building. Now he was embracing *region*-building [emphasis in original].

However sincere Bush is about his beliefs, or how important the substance of them are to his thinking, they provide a convenient way of dealing with contradictions that others might find troubling. As Weisberg notes, Bush has a "habit of pious oversimplification," a useful tool if faced with resolving the contradictions between ideals and the realities of US foreign policy. Bush seemed to face no such dilemma since he maintains that US interests are identical with US ideals, as he often put it. The reason Bush could surmount such dilemmas, the reason he was so "flexible" in choosing various rationale for the intervention depending on the time and setting was, according to Weisberg, that he was not intellectually invested in any of them, he was primarily interested in "finishing his father's business." He had spent the first 40 years of his life desperately trying to emulate his father, now he was desperately trying to differentiate himself from him, to outdo his father and to vindicate his family (Weisberg, 2008:210).

Leaving aside the question of motivation for beginning the war, what does seem clear is that, in Bush's skilful hands, the carefully constructed and promoted rhetoric of national liberation was an asset at selling the war, to a public that was extremely receptive. Bush's small town Texas roots and ideas were very much in tune with the rural southwest conservative constituency he was closest to. These ideas in turn have a long history of resonating with the mainstream of the American public.

THREAT INFLATION AND PUBLIC ACCEPTANCE

Once the war was accepted as a priority, a very aggressive selling job commenced. The context for the administration's promotion of the war had two elements: exaggerated hope and optimism on the part of the advocates and easy acceptance and abundant credulity on the part of the public. If the case for war in terms of security was shaky, the administration compensated for it through "threat inflation" (Kaufmann, 2004).[6] Here we will examine four factors that allowed the administration to make its case for war and that complicated accurate discussion and dialogue on the war: overstatement of Saddam's aggressiveness and recklessness; exaggeration of Iraq-al Qaeda cooperation; exaggeration of Saddam's WMD capabilities and the refusal of the administration to take seriously the results of the

United Nations weapons inspectors' (UNMOWIC) investigation; and the complicity of the press and the public in providing support for the war. In a leadership that eventually united on the war, after Secretary of State Colin Powell bought into it, the president from the start was obsessed with Iraq, while Cheney and the other major players all constituted a powerfully influential prowar force that was unified in stating its case (Packer, 2005; Western, 2005). All that remained was to sell the public and as many allies as possible on the war.

The introduction of most Americans to Saddam Hussein as a villain dates from the Gulf War in 1991. After Iraq invaded Kuwait, George H. W. Bush consistently compared Saddam to Hitler, implying he was a ruthless tyrant bent on world domination. During the 1998 debates over Bill Clinton's bombing of Iraq and the passage of the Iraq Liberation Act, the public by a "solid majority" supported US military action to remove Saddam Hussein.[7] In February 2001, there was still a majority supporting the use of ground troops to remove Saddam by a margin of 52 percent to 42 percent. As Jon Western writes, for nearly a decade Americans had been exposed to Iraqi behavior, first the invasion of Kuwait, then the alleged plot to assassinate President George H. W. Bush, then the violations of U.N. resolutions and the expulsion of the weapons inspectors. So Saddam Hussein was familiar to Americans. When the United States was attacked by terrorists, "most Americans were willing to assume Iraq's complicity, absent any compelling evidence to the contrary" (Western, 2005:192).

The Bush administration played on this general perception and further intensified it as the build-up to the war progressed. One of the chief assists in this process was a book by a liberal not normally identified as either a neocon or a member of the Bush administration. Kenneth Pollack's book (2002) was very influential in converting doves to hawks. One of his arguments was that Saddam Hussein was "one of the most reckless, aggressive, violence-prone, risk tolerant, and damage-tolerant leaders of modern history." Chaim Kaufmann refutes this reasoning, arguing against Pollack on the basis of the seven cases of Saddam's historical behavior he cites. Others have also argued Saddam historically was quite susceptible to deterrence, including Pollack himself in an earlier publication (Kaufmann, 2004; Mearsheimer and Walt, 2003; Byman et al., 1999).[8] Moreover, there were plans to streamline the embargo and there were alternative solutions to invasion and regime change.

A second prong of the administration argument was that a link existed between Iraq and al Qaeda, which resulted in detrimental cooperation between Saddam and terrorists intent on inflicting harm on the United States. One of the key links in this supposed arrangement was a meeting alleged to have taken place in Prague between Mohammad Atta, the pilot of the first plane to hit the twin towers in New York, and an Iraqi intelligence official in April 2001. Both the CIA and FBI confirmed that the single source that reported this alleged event was not credible, and that Atta in any case had been elsewhere at the time of the alleged meeting (Kaufmann, 2004:17). A second claim was made that Abu Musab al-Zarqawi, the head of a Jordanian and Palestinian terrorist group, had had substantial cooperation with Saddam. Both of these claims were discredited, and indeed many knowledgeable people doubted that a secular and suspicious Saddam would ever cooperate with terrorists in a way that would allow him to be linked to and blamed for any incidents that might result in attacks on Iraq. There was selective use of intelligence, in analyst Paul Pillar's view, that created the impression of an alliance between bin Laden and Saddam. There was a "rhetorical coupling" in which Bush administration officials repeatedly mentioned Iraq and 9/11 in the same breath (Isikoff and Corn, 2006:411). Tenet, however, makes clear what the early position of his agency was on the connection. A few days after 9/11, a CIA analyst attended a White House meeting where he was told that Bush wanted to remove Saddam. According to Tenet the analyst responded:

> If you want to go after that son of a bitch to settle old scores, be my guest. But don't tell us he is connected to 9/11 or to terrorism because there is no evidence to support that. You will have to have a better reason.
>
> Powers, 2007

Third, there was general agreement, both in the United States and among allies, that Saddam still had WMD and programs to develop more, although there had not been inspectors in Iraq since 1998. The administration set about providing as convincing evidence as possible that Saddam not only had biological and chemical weapons, but that he was close to developing a nuclear capability as well.[9] As it turned out, however, there were a few dissidents on some key points, and the strength of the administration's case lay in effectively eliminating or glossing over these points and the dissidents' case. The declassified sections of a CIA NIE from October 2, 2002, suggested that Iraq had continued its WMD programs in "defiance of U.N. resolutions and restrictions" and that if left unmolested it would "probably have a nuclear weapon during this decade." Because of Baghdad's denial and deception, the CIA judged that analysts were seeing only a portion of Iraq's WMD efforts. The NIE judged that the Iraqis "started reconstituting" the nuclear weapons program about December 1998, the time when UNSCOM inspectors departed. The NIE also judged that the offensive chemical and biological warfare program was active and more advanced than before the Gulf War, that Iraq was also developing missile systems that exceed the U.N. mandated range of 150 kilometers, and that unmanned aerial vehicles (UAVs) could threaten Iraq's neighbors, US forces in the Persian Gulf, and possibly the United States.

The verdict in the US intelligence community was not unanimous, however. The Bureau of Internal Research in the State Department dissented, indicating that they lacked "persuasive evidence that Baghdad has launched a coherent effort to reconstitute its nuclear weapons program." State also attacked a key part of the NIE's evidence, since they were not convinced that the claim that aluminum tubes Baghdad was allegedly acquiring to be used to develop nuclear programs was accurate. Instead, they were likely going to be used for constructing artillery rockets. The Department of Energy concurred with State that the aluminum tubes were probably not part of a nuclear program. The NIE also refused to confirm that Iraq had succeeded in acquiring yellowcake for uranium, although this was part of the administration's case. State specifically noted that these claims were "highly dubious," a judgment later confirmed. These reservations substantially weakened the administration's case. Regarding potential Iraqi attacks on the United States or its allies, the CIA conceded that Iraq would probably take clandestine action against the United States and allied interests in the Middle East "in the event the United States takes action against Iraq"; it believed it would not conduct terrorist attacks with conventional or CBW against the United States unless it feared the demise of the regime was "imminent or unavoidable" (CIA, 2002; Cirincione et al., 2004:23–24)).

In 2002 and early 2003 US officials, including Cheney, Rice, and the president all made speeches stipulating that Iraq certainly had WMD and was in the process of developing nuclear weapons. They argued that it was better to stop Saddam sooner rather than later, when he had already developed nuclear weapons. Many questions were raised by lower-level analysts and officials who had access to evidence but did not have the influence necessary to challenge the official version directly. One analyst reported interviewing a dozen intelligence officials who agreed—and none disagreed—with an analyst who said that "[a]nalysts at the working level in the intelligence community are feeling very strong pressure from the Pentagon to cook the intelligence books" (Kaufmann, 2004:40).

Others were raising questions, however. Hans Blix, then working for the IAEA, had reported in October 1997 that no discrepancies existed between Iraq's past nuclear program and Iraq's "latest declaration." Blix, in his report to the Security Council on the same day, basically confirmed this perspective. On the basis of his knowledge of the situation, he could not say if Iraq had disarmed. The inspections suggested a mixed picture. "Cooperation had accelerated, but I noted that it had not come immediately, and while it was resulting in the destruction of missiles that we had judged proscribed, it had not straightened out any question marks." Even with a cooperative attitude, more months would be needed to verify disarmament, and after that a monitoring system would need to remain in place to detect any revival of programs. In its rush to carry out regime change, the US government's plan to attack Iraq was scarcely delayed by the findings of Blix's U.N. Monitoring, Verification and Inspection Commission for Iraq (UNMOVIC). As Blix says, sarcastically,

> That the professional inspectors, who had by then visited many hundred sites of the most varied kind, including sites based on intelligence tips, and analyzed many thousands of documents, had not come to confirm US/UK assertions was apparently not an overwhelming concern of the administrations.
>
> Blix, 2004:216

Blix said later that if given two more months, he could have made a definitive statement about the existence or absence of WMD in Iraq (Blix, 2008). Thus the risk to go to war without pausing to investigate the gap between the inspectors' findings and the dogma long perpetrated by the US government was one of the key landmarks in the long list of mistakes in Washington's Iraq policy.[10] It shows a most incautious and arrogant disregard of empirical evidence and common standards of prudent decision making.[11] As David Kay, the Bush administration's handpicked weapons inspector (and war supporter), said after an exhaustive post-Saddam search for WMD in Iraq, "[t]here were no stockpiles of weapons of mass destruction at the time of the war" (Boehlert, 2006:227).

The seriousness with which accurate intelligence was taken by the administration can be judged from the remarks of the deputy chief of the CIA Iraq Task Force. Responding to an apprehensive email he had received from a Defense Department employee working at the CIA, he noted that Powell's speech to the U.N. had relied heavily on evidence provided by "curveball," an informant that the Germans had warned was unreliable. "Let's keep in mind," wrote the deputy chief, "the fact that this war's going to happen regardless of what Curveball said or didn't say, and that the Powers That Be probably aren't terribly interested in whether Curveball knows what he's talking about" (Ricks, 2006:91). "Curveball" confirmed in early 2011 that he lied, motivated by his desire to see Saddam attacked and overthrown by the United States.

THE PUBLIC CONTEXT

We have discussed the world of officials. What was the stance of the public toward the war? As discussed earlier, Americans were traumatized by the terrorist attacks in New York and Washington, and thus more receptive to believing in linkages and connections that a more stable public opinion might have rejected. The administration played this advantage to the maximum. Bolstering the administration's focus on Iraq following 9/11 was a corresponding shift in public awareness of Iraq and an increase in the support for the president following the incursion into Afghanistan. The president's approval numbers soared and then "hovered around 90 percent." This substantial support, however, quickly became bifurcated once the invasion occurred and the war began to bog down as resistance to US forces grew. The war quickly became one of which Republicans approved and Democrats disapproved as polarization grew rapidly. The partisan difference in approval ratings exceeded 70 percent in 74 of 94 Gallup polls taken between January 2004 and June 2006, a difference level never previously reached going back to Eisenhower. In a *Los Angeles Times* poll asking whether, in light of the failure to find either WMD or an active program to produce them, Bush's decision to go to war had been correct, "90 percent of Republicans but only 10 percent of Democrats answered 'yes'" (Jacobson, 2007).

DISTORTING US INTERESTS AND MISJUDGING REALITY

We started this discussion of whether the United States should have invaded Iraq by noting that Iraq is a small and weak country that hardly presented a major threat to Americans. As Stephen Walt points out, even a state with modest capabilities may justify a reaction by others if it is perceived as "especially aggressive" (1987:25). While Iraq had started two regional wars, one in 1980 and one in 1990, the consensus among most international relations scholars as well as many US officials, was that Saddam had been effectively contained, or "kept in his box." Moreover, the evidence of both connections between al Qaeda and Iraq as well as the evidence for the existence of advanced development of WMD was unreliable. A puzzling aspect of the attack on Iraq, as Richard A. Clarke suggests, is that Bush's selection as an "object lesson for potential state sponsors of terrorism," was not a state that had engaged in anti-US terrorism, but one that had not (Clarke, 2004:244). It is difficult not to conclude that one reason for attacking Iraq was that it did not yet have an advanced nuclear program and therefore was a relatively easy target. Both Iran and Korea, on the other hand, presented more complications. The main lesson other rogue nations would draw from the Iraq example was that in order to avoid an attack by the United States, it is necessary to develop a nuclear deterrent (Record, 2004:61).

The balancing structure between Iran and Iraq discussed earlier was drastically changed by the US invasion and the downward trajectory of the war in Iraq. Iranian power increased substantially as stability in Iraq decreased and it alarmed US allies in the region. King Abdullah of Saudi Arabia said that the United States had handed Iraq to Iran on a golden platter. "You have allowed the Persians . . . to take over Iraq" (Woodward, 2008:347). Not only did the American scheme for democratization work in Iran's favor, since the majority Shiites were brought to power by the electoral process, but the chaotic fighting among ethnic and religious groups and against the American occupation weakened the Iraqi government, and both factors provided many opportunities for an increase in Iranian influence. Iran has been able to take advantage of the chaos in Iraq to increase its influence with both domestic groups inside Iraq and other regional groups such as Hamas and Hezbollah. Sources disagree on the extent of Iranian support, but there is general agreement that it goes beyond moral support to substantial amounts of armaments. This has led to protests by the United States as well as efforts to put more pressure on the Iranians (Shadid, 2007; Sheridan, 2008b; Ignatius, 2008). As Richard Clarke has stated, the attack on Iraq was an "*idée fixe.*" Iraq was portrayed as the biggest danger threatening US security. It was a rigid belief and received wisdom that "no fact or event could derail" (Ajami, 2006:140). The Bush administration was the instigator of the war, but it had many accomplices. Air Force General Richard Myers, chairman of the joint chiefs of staff, was widely viewed within the military as "the best kind of uniformed yes-man—smart, hardworking, but wary of independent thought." The vice chairman, Marine General Peter Pace was viewed by many as "even more pliable." But most telling was the demeanor of the Congress. It was clear that many in the Congress lacked information and had many questions, but the administration was not about to provide satisfactory answers. Instead of holding out and making demands, they were willing to go along. Five weeks before the war began (Ricks, 2006:86–90), Senator Byrd took the floor to state

> This chamber is, for the most part, silent—ominously, dreadfully silent. There is no debate, no discussion, no attempt to lay out for the nation the pros and cons of this particular war. There is nothing. We stand passively mute in the United States Senate, paralyzed by our own uncertainty, seemingly stunned by the sheer turmoil of events.

Many Democrats were leery of and apprehensive about the war, but they had been beaten up so many times in past years over a "soft" foreign policy that they were reluctant to take the political risk of opposing another war. Not coincidentally, the vote was timed to precede the mid-term elections.

IMPLEMENTING THE WAR

Anyone nonplussed by the rationale for the US intervention in Iraq is bound to be further perplexed by the way the war was implemented.[12] Planning for the postwar occupation, commonly called phase IV, suffered from numerous complications and problems. Stephen Hadley, Rice's assistant and later her replacement, who had worked on a plan beginning in late November, 2002, had a broader perspective than the military, who were mostly interested in achieving stability. In his view, the president's goal was to achieve democracy, and there was a big difference between a minimum goal of stability and achieving the more difficult goal of democracy. An important complication to planning, as to so many other aspects of implementing the war, was the chasm that separated the views emanating from Colin Powell and the State Department, and those from Defense under Rumsfeld. As Woodward notes, more than the usual differences existed between State and Defense. Each had a "fundamentally different definition of what was possible, and what was necessary."

Douglas Feith came to talk to Hadley about locating a cell in the Pentagon that would handle both postwar planning and implementation of the plans. The cell would be interagency, and would be in a good position to work with General Franks and CENTCOM in the postinvasion environment. Defense would have people who could work continuously on these problems after the end of military operations, and this was the most effective way to handle phase IV. Powell thought this made sense and posed no objection to it. This was the first time that the State Department would not take charge of a postconflict situation (Diamond, 2005:29). This decision had tremendous implications because of the gap between the thinking of State and Defense, and due to DoD's disinclination to cooperate with State. National Security Presidential Directive (NSPD) #24 set up the Office of Reconstruction and Humanitarian Assistance (ORHA). ORHA was to both plan and implement those plans for the full panoply of issues that would be confronted in post-Saddam Iraq. Rumsfeld chose General Jay M. Garner to head ORHA. Powell sent over the "Future of Iraq" study, a plan for handling postwar Iraq that the State Department had had underway almost a year and had input from experts on a wide range of topics. He also sent the names of 75 State Department Arab experts, including Thomas Warwick, who had headed the study, and Meghan O'Sullivan, a sanctions specialist who Powell thought highly of (Woodward, 2004:280–84).

Rumsfeld was not really interested in sharing information and responsibilities with other agencies and Powell was startled to find that O'Sullivan and Warwick's services were rejected. They had written and said things that were not supportive of the war, according to Rumsfeld. This was an ironic verdict indeed given the incredible work O'Sullivan eventually put into the war. Only after Powell raised a ruckus with Rumsfeld were O'Sullivan and five others that he demanded be included accepted on the insistence of the White House (Woodward, 2004:284). Garner was given few resources and had a concept of his duties mostly oriented toward humanitarian and refugee work. Garner did not learn about the State Department "Future of Iraq" study until a month after he was appointed, when he attended a February 21–22 meeting to discuss planning, two months before the war would begin. Planning for the postwar transition in Germany and Japan had begun in 1942, two and one-half years before the end of the war (Ferguson, 2008:Chapter 2).

The invasion itself was well planned and, compared to phase IV, was a masterpiece of competence and precision. In a few days, the coalition was doing to Iraq what the Iranians could not do in eight years (Terdoslavich, 2006:11). In contention from the beginning of the planning, however, was the issue of the number of troops that would be needed. There was an assumption among many of the war planners that the troops would be received with cheering and flowers, much like American troops in Europe during WWII, thus obviating the need for large numbers. General Shinseki testified before Congress and suggested several hundred thousand troops would be needed, a figure that he had earlier put at approximately 350,000. There was a widespread belief in the military that the civilians in DoD did not know how to determine the required number of troops. Rumsfeld and Wolfowitz believed that no more troops would be required for postconflict operations than for the invasion itself. Others, including an NSC briefing that, comparing the number of troops that had been used in Bosnia and Kosovo, suggested that larger numbers of troops would be required in the postconflict phase, 364,000 or more. The White House, however, viewed this assumption as based on the way things were done in the Clinton administration and believed the model of Afghanistan better fit what the Bush administration would need in Iraq. In the end, Defense and the White House discredited Shinseki's testimony and went with lower numbers (Gordon and Trainor, 2006). Almost everyone intimately acquainted with Iraq on the ground seems to believe more troops were needed, including army officers (Diamond, 2005:98). George Packard points out, unless you had an ideological stake in it, the controversy over whether there were enough troops "didn't survive your first contact with Iraqi reality" (Packard, 2005:245).

There was substantial planning done for the postwar period. In addition to the State Department study, the Army War College at Carlisle, Pennsylvania, had done a detailed, accurate, and prescient study that circulated widely in the government. It investigated historical experience in general with postwar occupations, what had worked and what had not. It also focused on the specifics of the Iraq case, what the problems were likely to be and how they should be dealt with. This included topics such as how to prevent looting, how to put in place a police force, how to get utilities up and running, and how to protect hospitals and doctors. Given this effort at preparation represented by this study and others, how can one explain the extent to which postconflict Iraq became so chaotic and ill-governed?[13] James Fallows was intrigued by this question and conducted interviews to find out. He concluded that the problem was lack of connection between the people doing the planning and those actually carrying out the occupation. They were two completely different groups of people and there was little communication between them (Ferguson, 2008).

LOOTING

This oversight showed itself in the chaos, the breakdown of law and order and the looting that occurred almost immediately following the cessation of major military operations. James Fallows has posited as the greatest mystery of postwar Iraq: why the military didn't do anything to control the looting (Ferguson, 2008:127)? Some argue that this period was the most crucial period for setting expectations among Iraqis and influencing the rest of the occupation period. There are several reasons why this period immediately following the military conquest was so crucial. First, it sent a signal to the Iraqis about American intentions and competence. Refusing to keep order in this crucial period suggested two alternative explanations to the Iraqis, and neither was to the advantage of the United States. One explanation was that the Americans were incompetent. They ran a quick and effective military operation to conquer the country, but then were unable to keep order after they had deposed the government. The need to maintain order is such an elementary need that failure to do so disastrously deflates expectations. Not only did the response to looting set a tone for the rest of the occupation, that is, if the occupation forces are not able in stopping looting by unarmed people, presumably they can also be rolled later on when the stakes become higher and the ferocity of battle intensifies. On the other hand, if order is firmly and fairly maintained, it would help to set an expectation that order would be strictly maintained and violence effectively punished in later stages of the occupation. An alternative explanation for American behavior that many Iraqis latched on to was that the Americans did not care about Iraq and they intentionally allowed the looting, which furthered American interests and illustrated a complete indifference to Iraqi interests. As US Army Major Rod Coffey put it (Wright and Reese, 2008:92)

> The looting creates the perception [for an Iraqi] that 'my country is being destroyed' . . . The looting feeds all those myths that the Americans are here and they just want to take all our oil and they want us to be weak.

The implications of this perspective becoming widespread among Iraqis are too obvious to need elaboration. Second, the loss of materials and the cost of buying new materials and rebuilding the buildings and arrangements that were destroyed were tremendous, and greatly delayed the work of stabilizing and rebuilding Iraq. One CPA estimate of the cost of the initial looting was $12 billion. The literal material cost of the looting of furniture, records, buildings, and vehicles must be added to the immense psychological and symbolic implications in creating an atmosphere that created many unnecessary obstacles to rebuilding Iraq and greatly prolonged the process.

The extent of the looting was phenomenal. Many of Charles Ferguson's interviewees commented on the "extraordinary destructiveness of the looting, and its almost pathological, obsessive thoroughness." It started in the first border towns that US troops went through, such as Safwan, where looters converged on a big fuel storage tank and sucked the content out. It continued unchecked as the troops moved toward Baghdad, giving at least two weeks' notice that the problem would be monumental in the capital. There, thousands of buildings were looted and gutted, then burned. "I found a city that was on fire, not from the war, but from the looting," said Paul Bremer, who arrived in mid-May. Huge reels of electrical cable, refrigerators, rooftop air conditioners were carted off. Printing presses were looted and parts of power plants were removed with industrial cranes. Hospitals, hotels, department stores, universities and schools, police academies, and Saddam's palaces were ransacked, as was the national museum in Baghdad where valuable treasures were lost (Ferguson, 2008:106; Filkins, 2008a; Ricks, 2006:158; Bensahel et al., 2008:88). At one point, there was so much copper being exported from the looting in Iraq that it depressed the market for scrap in Jordan. Looting of weapons and ammunition persisted for months. Marc Garlasco, a national intelligence analyst, recounted how he came upon large weapons caches of rockets, mortars, and bombs being looted by Iraqis with AK-47s. They could not interest British or American troops in stopping the looting since they didn't have the necessary troops to handle the situation. Weapons were everywhere after the main fighting stopped. Large caches were in a zoo in Baghdad, and along the riverfront in Basra. In Baghdad, there were big antiaircraft rocket launchers under highway overpasses. Local groups could not get the US military to remove them; children played on them and the ten-foot-long rockets occasionally exploded (Ferguson, 2008:122, 373–74). Even racehorses originally owned by Saddam's sadistic son Uday were being rounded up and led away by ordinary citizens (Filkins, 2008a:97). As the looting continued, it began to mutate into organized crime. One contributing factor undoubtedly was that Saddam had released nearly 100,000 prisoners from his prisons before the American invasion. According to journalist Nir Rosen, the reception rate of murder cases at the Baghdad morgue rose from one a month to twenty-five a day within a month of the takeover of Iraq. Women stopped going out because of the danger of rape and kidnapping. Under Saddam, whether Sunni or Shia one could walk around Baghdad at three or four in the morning and not feel threatened. In a matter of weeks after the invasion, Iraqi women were being sold into sex rings in Amsterdam (Ferguson, 2008).

The importance of this period in setting the tone for the effectiveness of the American stay in Iraq and the need to handle it well is so obvious that the mind boggles at the failure of the Americans to grasp the elemental point that it was crucial to prevent the development of chaos. How can it be explained? A partial explanation follows from the fact that there were exceptions to the widespread looting. The protection of Iraq's oil infrastructure was one major success in the aftermath of the fighting. This was no accident, but the result of planning, committing resources, and the dispatch of troops to key oil fields. Needless to say, this point was not lost on the Iraqis—it only confirmed suspicions many had that the United States was only interested in oil. Similar success was evident in protecting major dams and hydroelectric facilities, especially the Hadithah dam on the Euphrates that was seized in a surprise raid on April 1. Troops were also dispatched to Mosul and Kirkuk when violence broke out there. By May, northern Iraq, in comparison with Baghdad, was relatively stable (Bensahel et al., 2008:86).

Why was "the American military machine implacable in battle, flummoxed in Peace" (West, 2008:5)? One answer is that there were simply too few troops to restore stability and stop the looting. Just as General Shinseki was criticized when he maintained in congressional hearings that more troops were needed, generally there was an optimistic view of the kind of reception that an invading force would get, and the assumption was that with that kind of reception more troops would not be needed. Wolfowitz explicitly maintained that no additional troops would be needed for the postconflict phase (Ricks, 2006:97–98). Little thought was given to the possibility of looting. Jay Garner's focus was on humanitarian emergencies and he said in an interview that he expected looting of symbols of the old regime, such as Saddam's palaces, but he was not prepared for the looting of virtually every public building in Baghdad (Rieff, 2003). The administration ignored the State Department's "Future of Iraq" report as well as a study done on this period by General Zinni, who had been told by Iraqis how hollow Saddam's regime was, particularly after the 1998 bombing. He was therefore particularly apprehensive about what might be needed (Ferguson, 2008:47). As James Dobbins, who has studied many of America's post-WWII interventions, found, "the highest levels of casualties have occurred in the operations with the lowest levels of troops." He concludes that postconflict nation-building, when undertaken with enough troops, has led to "little violent resistance" (Dobbins, 2003). It is clear that the optimistic predisposition of the administration on what policy on troop requirements would be, took precedence over any advice from outside.

Some troops who were sympathetic to stopping the looting were forced to deny the requests of Iraqis who wanted help to restore order. Some, such as ambassador and senior Foreign Service Officer Barbara Bodine, maintained that military officers were told explicitly by the Pentagon not to interfere with the looting. This view is strengthened by the fact that when Iraqis at the Baghdad museum suggested the Americans just put their vehicles in a ring around the building to discourage looters, the troops said that they had orders not to move from the spot (Ferguson, 2008:118). What seems inescapable is that the administration's ideological policy preferences were skewed away from any meaningful intervention. Rumsfeld, who appeared more than anyone else to be running the show, downplayed the significance of the looting, stating that it was nonsense to say [the United States] didn't have a plan, that "freedom is untidy," and "free people are free to make mistakes and commit crimes and do bad things. They're also free to live their lives and do wonderful things, and that's what's going to happen here." In response to Rumsfeld's remark that "[s]tuff happens. That's what free people do," Ken Adelman, up until then a close friend of Rumsfeld, later told him to his face that "[t]hat's not what free people do. That's what barbarians do" (Woodward, 2008:149). Many, including Edward Wong of the *New York Times* and Ambassador Barbara Bodine commented how frequently Iraqis even in later years would bring up the subject of the looting, to them an "epochal" event. It was the day of Rumsfeld's statement about it just being messy, Bodine believes, that the United States lost the Iraqis. That's when it became obvious to them that the "liberation really didn't have anything to do with the average Iraqi" (Ferguson, 2008: 136–37).

OFF TO A BAD START: DE-BAATHIFICATION AND DISSOLVING
THE MILITARY

Even as its army occupied Baghdad, Thomas E. Ricks writes, the United
States was not sure what it wanted to do there. "Clouds of cognitive dis-
sonance" were enveloping Rumsfeld and senior pentagon officials. They
were not finding what they expected—WMD—and they were finding
what they didn't expect—violent and widespread opposition to the US
presence. The military generally assumed that the Iraq army would be
retained, which was also Garner's intention as he tried to get his footing
in Iraq. He started assembling army units (Ricks, 2006:154–68). Garner's
approach was to retain as much as possible of the prewar institutions and
adapt them to the postwar regime. Now he was being replaced by L. Paul
Bremer, a career foreign service officer who was an expert on counterterrorism. Bremer's closest exposure to the Middle East or the Persian Gulf
was an assignment in Afghanistan in the 1960s, he spoke no Arabic and
had little management or administrative experience. As Garner said in a
later interview, Bremer was a very take-charge guy, but there is limited
information on why the administration chose to replace Garner with
Bremer (Ferguson, 2008:143). One ill-prepared team was being replaced
by another. Bremer, philosophically, was at odds with two of Garner's
approaches to dealing with postwar Iraq: that (1) the country should be
turned over to Iraqi control as soon as possible, and (2) as much as possible, existing institutions and personnel should be retained to facilitate
that transition. Bremer turned the American stay into an occupation,
he disbanded the army and he carried out a radical de-Baathification.
Bremer was seen as a man in control who wanted to be involved in every
decision. The contrast to the "inarticulate, laissez-faire Garner could not
have been more striking" (Diamond, 2005:37–39).

Garner, after learning of his dismissal—he was asked to stay on for
the transition—was again surprised when handed the de-Baathification
announcement. The idea, of course, was to eliminate those with ties to
the Saddam Hussein regime from positions of influence. Garner immediately protested to Bremer, believing it cut too deep into professional government officials and experts. Garner thought it would drive 30,000 to
50,000 people underground. Many others agreed it would be disastrous.
This turned out to be accurate. US military units themselves struggled
to cope with the effects of the order. The First Armored Division, after
failing to reestablish basic sewer and electrical services in Baghdad in
May 2003, used its own resources to find the ex-Baathist bureaucrats
and technicians who had been discharged and bring them back to work.
The Fourth Infantry Division, north of Baghdad in the Sunni heartland,

struggled to retain the services of thousands of teachers and police who had been low-level Baathists (Wright and Reese, 2008:96). The problem, as one Iraqi explained it, was that the Baath Party "had become part of the fabric of Iraqi Society, a complex, interrelated pyramid . . . to dismantle the Party, the Army, and the other structure of the state was only to replace them with chaos." De-Baathification not only relieved people of their jobs, but it destroyed their position in society along with their livelihood and their sense of being moored to some semblance of stability. As one young Iraqi clerk, a Baath Party member put it,

> We were on top of the system. We had dreams. Now we are the losers. We lost our positions, our status, the [economic] security of our families, stability. Curse the Americans. Curse them.
>
> Wright and Reese, 2008:96

One resident, after a US raid, said that he was not a supporter of the former government, but he could not accept the way the Americans treated them. When he saw things such as he had just witnessed, he said, he understood why people want to drive the Americans out of the country. If this happens more and more, he would join the resistance. And the Sunnis were a lot better organized than the Americans realized (Hashim, 2006:152).

But Bremer refused to relent. Sergio Vieira de Mello, the U.N. representative in Baghdad did an excellent job of meeting Iraqis and keeping in touch with Iraqi opinion. He was very concerned that Bremer's approach would create havoc in the country. Bremer was neither concerned nor particularly interested in de Mello's views. He thought he could get away with it (Diamond, 2005:54). He went Garner one better and surprised him with a second order disbanding the military and the Ministry of the Interior. Garner was able to convince him to exempt the ministry by arguing that the police were essential and they would be out of work if the ministry was included. The two orders put at least 500,000 men out of work in a very poor society, many of which had extensive weapons training and access to military weapons, and it deprived the government of their services (Ricks, 2006; Ferguson, 2008).

There was much confusion on who was on board and supported the orders, particularly the disbanding of the army. Hadley maintained that he learned about the orders only when they were announced. They had not gone through the interagency process and there was no presidential imprimature. Rice also had not been consulted. According to one source, neither Rumsfeld nor General Myers had been consulted, but neither of them seemed upset by the omission (Wright and Reese, 2008:85;

Woodward, 2006:197–98). One account finds that Rumsfeld did sign off on Bremer's order to disband, even though it was contrary to what had earlier been decided in the NSC with the president in attendance (Ferguson, 2008).

Bremer justified the order on the grounds that, first, the army had scattered as the Americans rolled into Iraq and reconstituting it was completely impractical for this reason. Second, the army was top-heavy with pro-Saddam appointees and many of the draftees would have refused to serve with them, and the Iraqi people would not have accepted it. Bremer claims the move was very popular with the Kurds who otherwise would not have remained loyal to Iraq (Bremer, 2006:54–56). The order for disbanding the military was described by "dozens of diplomats, policy experts, intelligence analysts, journalists, senior military officers and ordinary Iraqis . . . as an unmitigated disaster that greatly magnified, or even instigated, both the Sunni insurgency and the Shiite militias" (Ferguson, 2008). The significance of this disagreement over who did what and when lies not so much in the actual facts, but because it is yet one more example of the chaos and division in the government, the lack of coordination and information, and the failure of people, including the president, to know what was going on and the significance of specific actions. Many Iraqis had responded to the American pleas during the invasion to stop fighting, but now after they had cooperated, they were being betrayed because they were left with no means of support or ties to the new Iraq. Following the looting, the disbanding of the military represented a second landmark in the development of ever increasing difficulties in dealing with a postconflict Iraq.

GOVERNING IRAQ

One of the conundrums of postwar Iraq, debated by Americans and pondered by Iraqis, was whether the United States was a liberator or an occupier. An account of a meeting between Ambassador Hume Horan, a senior Coalition Provisional Authority (CPA) official and 279 tribal leaders in late May 2003, a little over a month after the fall of Baghdad illuminates the issue. Sheikh Munthr Abood of Amara asked Horan whether the United States believed itself to be a liberator or an occupier. Horan answered that he thought a little of both, its position was somewhere in between the two categories. The sheikh then said that if the Americans came as liberators, they were welcome as guests. If they were occupiers, then he and his descendants would "die resisting" the Americans. This assertion led to enthusiastic applause, after which one-quarter of the audience rose and walked out (Ricks, 2006:166).

One facet of the answer is immediately apparent. The prevailing view in the administration, at least among the strong advocates of the war, and especially those officials connected with the Defense Department was that the United States was a liberator. Powell thought Wolfowitz believed all of Iraq would rush to welcome the Americans in the role of liberators (Woodward, 2004:22). The Iraqis were eagerly awaiting a US liberation from the shackles of Saddam Hussein's regime. This assumption fit easily with Jay Garner's assumptions that the United States would quickly start to turn things over to the Iraqis, and the duration of the American presence would be short. "We intend to immediately start turning some things over, and every day, we'll turn over more things. I believe that's our plan," Garner said (Ricks, 2006:104). All of this, of course, changed drastically once Bremer came in, working on opposite assumptions. After disbanding of the military and de-Baathification, there would follow a laborious process of building new Iraqi institutions, including a long and complex attempt at building democracy, in which the United States would play a big role.[14] An exile returned from England to work as a professional and technical expert to rebuild Iraq who became interior minister in 2004, Sumaidaie, believed that any provisional government by Iraqis would have been better than an occupation authority. "It was a fatal mistake. We [the governing council and those working beside Bremer] were branded as collaborators. The insurgents won the mantle of patriots by fighting the occupier" (Robinson, 2008:7).

Another source of contention among the key decision makers was the question of whether the priority in postconflict Iraq would be stability or democracy. As of February, a few weeks before the invasion, what kind of government Iraq would have was clearly still up in the air. At an NSC meeting, Feith mentioned a government by Ahmed Chalabi. Bush interrupted him to say that the Americans were not choosing anyone to run the government; that was for the Iraqi people to decide. A few days later Wolfowitz, apparently unaware of the discussion in the previous meeting, brought the subject up again. The president responded forcefully that he had nothing against Chalabi, but the United States was promoting democracy. It was not going to put its "thumb on the scale" (Kaplan, 2008:155; see also Bremer, 2006:53). It should have been obvious to all that democratization would likely result in a Shiite majority and a Shiite government, thus radically realigning the power structure in Iraq and threatening instability. That this issue was so little remarked upon prior to March 19 only confirms how little priority was given understanding postconflict Iraq and the need to ensure the most favorable conditions for effective government. At the time of invasion, views on the issue seemed to run all the way from (1) set-up a democracy (Bush and Rice), to (2) achieve stability and then get out (Garner and some military), to (3) achieve stability by installing Chalabi's government of exiles (Rumsfeld, Wolfowitz and Feith).[15] As Bing West notes, the Sunnis had for centuries oppressed the Shiite majority, and the Sunnis viewed the Shiites as less cultured and civilized than themselves. Now the United States was engaged in an operation to upset the established order of society and create a new order with the Sunnis as a minority, a daunting undertaking. "Now the Shiites were poised to repay in kind while America stood guard" (West, 2008:66).

THE DESCENT INTO CHAOS

The Bush administration now compounded its errors by refusing to recognize the facts on the ground and fighting "the war we wanted to fight, not the war that was." After first characterizing it as the desperate efforts of a few 'dead-enders,' it was only belatedly recognized as a full insurgency (Bruce Hoffman quoted in Ricks, 2006:184). Following an invasion that had been successful in toppling Saddam Hussein's regime, the postconflict period would turn out to be a much less fortuitous period.

Consisting of disgruntled or unemployed Sunnis, members of al Qaeda, and eventually radical Shia militias, the insurgency would gather steam through 2003 and 2004, culminating in a major conflict reaching a peak in 2006/2007. During this time the US and Iraqi soldiers attempting to restore order were almost continually losing ground. A major turning point followed the bombing of a Shiite mosque in Samarra in February 2006, which many believed escalated the conflict to the status of a civil war between Sunnis and Shias. An alternative explanation comes from one senior military official who believed that within 30 days of Maliki's new government being seated as a result of the 2005 elections, the Sunnis had realized that it was not a government of reconciliation but rather one with sectarian objectives advanced by the Shiite prime minister. According to this official, that was when the "wheels came off" (Robinson, 2008:17). Ambassador Ryan Crocker reflected on the difficulty of brokering compromise in Iraq. The Western notion of compromise was simply not credible to Iraqis who had spent their entire adult life as "conspirators, guerillas, and insurgents, trying to topple a dictator while staying alive." Both Sunnis and Shias suffered horribly at the hands of Saddam. They all lived secretly and stayed alive by trusting no one. What might seem to us a no-brain kind of compromise does not look that way to them. There is this pervasive fear that the Baath will be back. There is a Baathi behind every lamppost (Robinson, 2008:150).

The United States, caught unprepared and reflecting the assumptions under which the army usually fought, responded to the insurgency not with the political approach to the problem that was needed, but rather with a military approach that killed many Iraqis, but did little to deal with the problems the insurgency reflected, a combination of aroused Iraqi nationalism coupled with humiliation, ethnic strife, totally inadequate services, and the insecurities of a disrupted society. An inadequate number of troops compounded the problem—or in the view of some—was at the heart of the initial inability to keep order and restore a sense of security for the population.

Central to the problems the Americans faced in trying to govern Iraq was the sheer ignorance about Iraq of most Americans in the country, a description that fit most people from the lowliest soldier to the highest official. Of seven thousand or so in the green zone, the highly fortified protected area in central Baghdad that sealed off everybody inside from the outside Iraqi world, most spoke no Arabic and knew little about Iraq or Arabic culture. Of the 600–800 in the republican palace headquarters, there were 17 Arabic speakers (Hashim, 2006:295). One Iraqi intellectual complained to Larry Diamond, an academic specialist on democracy advising Bremer, that "[t]he CPA behaves as if it knows everything. It has never reached out to the Iraqis. It is easier to go to Washington than to cross the bridge over the Tigris into the CPA" (Diamond, 2005:298).

Bremer was widely thought to be a poor choice for the job of proconsul. He was reportedly a better talker than listener. As we have seen, his administrative decisions were not only not coordinated but also not communicated before promulgation. Bremer was captive to the same imperial hubris that had put the United States in Iraq with a "democratizing mission but no real sense of how to accomplish it" (Diamond, 2005:300). Henry Kissinger, his former employer, called him a control freak (Chandrasekaran, 2006:63). Bremer himself frequently got out to speak to and meet Iraqis, at great physical risk. But he relied heavily on a few trusted employees who spoke no Arabic and had little knowledge of the Middle East; and he was reputed to "stovepipe everything." He probably did not fully trust experienced career diplomats, who were in residence and at his disposal (Diamond, 2005:298).

Lt. General Ricardo Sanchez, Bremer's military counterpart, was described by Lt. Colonel Christopher Holshek as "in over his head," and by a State Department official as "all trees, no forest." He reportedly treated neither his own men nor Iraqis with respect and he and Bremer were like oil and water, hardly a good omen for the management of counterinsurgency efforts, one of the requirements of which is united and coordinated leadership. A basic inadequacy in the US occupation was that it could not protect the population it was trying to pacify. It relied on attrition strategies of killing the enemy and diminishing the threat to gain an advantage over the adversary. This mindset was reflected at the highest levels of the administration when the president would not infrequently ask for some kind of measure, such as the number of enemy killed, that the US strategy was being effective. In the words of John Nagle, the United States was dependent on firepower and superior technology to destroy the enemy. The message that flowed from that approach was that the United States, with all its firepower, couldn't protect its allies. The idea of "separating insurgents from popular support never took hold." The conventional way to get intelligence, followed in Iraq by the United States, was to make huge sweeps and then question the Iraqis that were detained, with many going to prison, often to stay indefinitely. This strategy served more to alienate informers than to win them over. The United States consequently ended up with little useful intelligence; the fact that the insurgents were able to place as many roadside bombs as they did was an indication that the locals were not reporting on them. This also served as a political statement. In August 2003, the third major car bomb in a month killed the Ayatollah Mohammed Bakir Hakim, the leader of the Supreme Council for the Islamic Revolution in Iraq (SCIRI) and a supporter of the United States. The assassination of such a high-level figure only intensified the message of impotence regarding the American presence. As Major General Peter Chiarelli put it, "Coalition forces are forced to interact with the Iraqi populace from a defensive posture, effectively driving a psychological wedge between the people and their protector" (Ricks, 2006:221–22).

Although CENTCOM commander Abizaid, who had replaced Franks after the invasion, was more forthright than Washington in admitting the presence of an insurgency, he and Lt. General George Casey (Sanchez's replacement) were devoid of an effective counterinsurgency strategy. Casey's office did take advantage of a strategy shop they had assembled with a substantial number of PhDs with knowledge of counterinsurgency approaches. One such was Kalev Sepp, a retired special forces officer. The group evaluated Casey's approach. Sepp listed 12 best practices of winners and concluded that the US effort in Iraq had adhered to only one: emphasis on intelligence.

Sepp then listed nine unsuccessful characteristics of the US efforts that, as Thomas Ricks says, read like a "summary of the U.S. occupation in 2003–4."

- primacy of military direction of counterinsurgency;
- priority to kill-capture enemy, not on engaging population;

- battalion-size operations as the norm;
- military units concentrated on large bases for protection;
- special forces focused on raiding;
- adviser effort a low priority in personnel assignment;
- building, training indigenous army in image of US Army;
- peacetime government processes; and
- open borders, airspace, coastlines.

Although many thought that at first Casey didn't quite get it, many under him and his British advisers did and he moved toward incorporating more counterinsurgency elements into his strategy. He was effective in getting more coordination between civilian and military efforts. But the problem of putting the conflict as a whole in a political context remained. Some observers noted that the various sections of the battlefield, depending on location, "felt like a different war" (Ricks, 2006:221–22; 393–94). In other words, there was no overall consistent strategy reflecting a uniform policy.

From 2003 through 2007 the situation in Iraq gradually deteriorated, with a marked acceleration of the violence beginning in 2006. Iraqi civilian deaths, for instance, were estimated by a study by the Brookings Institution at 1,650 in May 2004, but that figure had risen to 2,700 in May 2006 and to 2,600 in May 2007. US troop deaths went from 80 to 126 in the same period, and daily attacks by insurgents, militias, and terrorists from 70 to 200 (Campbell and O'Hanlon, 2008). From a relatively benign atmosphere before and immediately after the invasion in Baghdad where foreigners could walk around safely and live in unprotected houses, the environment changed to one where security was so bad that American troops and reconstruction workers were reduced to living in the green zone and venturing out only under heavy guard. Trips to other parts of Iraq also required armed escorts as did transport of supplies on the highways.

Iraqis, meantime, lived in increasingly precarious situations and as the ethnic conflict increased, ethnic cleansing emptied whole neighborhoods of whichever group was in the minority. Ironically, Iraqi Christians, a group the Bush administration was obviously interested in, suffered greatly, much worse than under Saddam Hussein. By 2006 increasing harassment and social pressure related to dress and behavior due to pressure from conservative Shiites and militias were common. Conditions of daily life and living were such that people endured extreme stress and frustration, including shortages of power during long periods of extreme temperature. There was a constant fear of disclosing ethnic or employment or contacts with foreigners. Embassy staff were afraid to speak

English and heard fantastical and conspiratorial views of Americans, even from their own families. Some neighborhoods were unrecognizable "ghost towns" and personal safety depended on good relations with "neighborhood" governments, which barricade streets and ward off outsiders (Ferguson, 2008:349–51).

Large numbers had fled the country and those who remained lived precariously. Estimates are that almost 5 million Iraqis fled the war, 2.5 million fled the country to neighboring countries and elsewhere, while approximately 2.4 million Iraqis, nearly 9 percent of the population, were forced to move and became "internal refugees" (Bacon and Younes, 2008). Of these, roughly 80 percent were women and children, and they suffered from disease, poverty, and malnutrition. Estimating the number of Iraqis killed is a much less precise task. For the most part the Bush administration pleaded ignorance on the total number of Iraqi deaths. Figures ranged from offhand comments by the president at the end of 2005 that 30,000 or fewer Iraqis had died, to an estimate of 600,000 by a British medical journal in October 2006 (DeYoung, 2007). Many believe that figures of 100–200,000 may be most realistic. US deaths at the end of 2008 numbered over 4,000. Fallujah and Ramadi became infamous as particularly tough centers of insurgency where mistakes were made and, in Fallujah, occupation had to be postponed after four American security guards were killed, and two of their disfigured bodies hung from a bridge in front of jubilant and celebrating crowds (Packard, 2005; Woodward, 2006).

But in general through 2004 and even into 2005 the administration continued to minimize the significance of the insurgency. One National Intelligence Council estimate in the spring of 2004 found a deepening insurgency and signs of incipient civil war. There was an assumption that even the end of the insurgency would not prevent a civil war, between Sunnis and Shias. A second assessment done in August 2004 was leaked to the *New York Times* in September, just before the fall presidential election. The president called the second estimate "guesswork" and his press spokesman called it "hand-wringing and nay-saying." The president, however, had not read the second one, not even the one-page executive summary.[16]

We have discussed problems with the military strategy; it is time for a brief word on the political sphere. One persistent problem during phase IV was that the United States wanted to build democracy, but it also wanted to control events. In no period was that contradiction more in evidence than during Bremer's time in Iraq. Bremer set up a complicated calendar for ushering in a formal democratic process in Iraqi politics (see note 14). This was a schedule almost certain to produce electoral fatigue, and while it fit Western conceptions of democratic institution building, it begged the question of whether it was the procedure best suited to Iraqi conditions. There was no dearth of people who stressed the need to end formal occupation and transfer authority to Iraqis as soon as possible. Kofi Anan, attentive to his staff's findings, stated that "as long as there is occupation, the resistance will grow." This was a point of contention between Bremer and Washington. Bremer complained that Powell, Rumsfeld, and Rice all wanted to step up the schedule for turning authority over to the Iraqis. Bremer resisted, because rushing to temporary government that would give the Iraqis more authority would not fix the security problem but would only make it worse (Bremer, 2006:188). Diamond reports that he gradually realized that Bremer and his staff simply did not grasp the extent of Iraqi disaffection, suspicion, and frustration. Even more significantly, he concluded that the CPA "lacked the mechanisms—or the will—to adjust its actions and policies in response to feedback."

The signs of the disillusionment of Iraqis were there for all to see. Diamond reports that at the time of the invasion, Iraqis were approximately evenly divided on whether the United States was an invader or a liberator. Six months later in October, polls showed that two-thirds saw the United States as an occupier, only 15 percent as a liberator. But when a U.N. staffer told Diamond that the insurgents had contacted them and were eager to open a dialogue with the Americans through the U.N., Bremer—doubtless with Washington's support—was not interested. The Americans also failed to appreciate the importance and value of the Grand Ayatollah Ali al-Sistani, a moderate and steadfast defender of the Americans. One secular Shiite intellectual told Diamond that Sistani was a heaven-sent gift to the Americans. Diamond maintains that Bremer was also too slow to reach out to the Sunnis, and to allow the Iraqis to participate (Diamond, 2005). Rory Stewart, deputy governor of two southern provinces, believed most of the population disliked the US-led coalition "simply because they were the US-led coalition" (Stewart, 2006:402). Diamond quotes a CPA colleague as saying that "[t]hey are not angry about *our* freedom [as President Bush would have it]. They are angry about *their* humiliation" (Diamond, 2005:300). Stewart needed to form a provincial council, but he could not hold an election because the CPA elections were scheduled for later. In general, localities needed more authority sooner (Stewart, 2006:95, 113).

BACK FROM THE ABYSS

By mid-2006 numerous analysts were convinced something had to change in US' Iraq policy. There had to be a new strategy. The violence was terrible and getting worse. There was intense dissatisfaction with

Maliki. He was a sectarian, many felt, and showed no propensity to cooperate with Sunnis or accommodate Sunni requirements. Finally, after six months of procrastination and discussion, on January 5, 2007, the president announced the appointment of Lt. General David Petraeus to replace Casey. He also announced a new strategy that would allow American troops to hit Shia targets that the prime minister had previously vetoed. There would be new political goals and more economic aid, corresponding to Petraeus's strategy of embedding US troops in the population and increasing support for the coalition. The new strategy would be supported by a surge of 30,000 US troops.

Two early promoters of the surge were Frederick W. Kagan and retired General Jack Keane. Kagan's analytical concepts meshed with and were based on the approach that Petraeus and H. R. McMaster had used in northern Iraq at Tal Afar. That approach, in turn, derived in part from McMaster's PhD thesis on the American experience in the Vietnam War. Finally, the lessons of Vietnam were being drawn upon to correct current strategy. Petraeus, in preparation for taking command of the forces in Iraq, put together a group of talented people who shared his philosophy that the emphasis in the war should be on providing security and services for the people in order to win them over, rather than concentrating on firepower and conflict. Kagan explained that not having enough troops in Iraq was the result of not having the right approach. A population-centric counterinsurgency requires enough troops to provide security so that a bond can be formed with the population (Kagan, 2008). To put it simply, Petraeus and his team envisioned an alternative to the way troops operated in the early part of the Iraqi occupation: soldiers appeared in a neighborhood, sometimes kicked down doors to search houses, rummaged through the residents' belongings while other soldiers pointed guns at the occupants and, in Iraqi eyes, ogled the women, then after possibly detaining an occupant or two and sending them to an Abu Ghraib-type facility from which nobody knew when, if ever, they might emerge, the troops retreated to base. If, as happened at least occasionally, the wrong house had been searched, an apology would be issued if the mistake was recognized.

The advantage of the surge was that it put more troops in Baghdad, which made it more feasible for troops to remain in areas that had been cleared, thus guaranteeing the security of the population. Previously, if the troops retreated after searching and clearing, then there was no way security for the inhabitants of the neighborhoods could be maintained. This in turn cut off the badly needed flow of intelligence that could be started if the population believed that they would be protected from the insurgents. If they aren't protected, then it is suicide to convey intelligence to the Americans. If the troops remain in the neighborhood it also allows the neighborhood to proceed with rebuilding, something they cannot do if they are at the mercy of the insurgents. The new strategy, therefore, became known as "clear, hold and build." As Linda Robinson notes, the presence of the troops in the neighborhood made it possible to attain "[t]he most precious commodity [which] was the intelligence that came from the population and the volunteers as they began to trust the Americans who lived among them, instead of the soldiers kicking down their doors and leaving" (Robinson, 2008:325). From the perspective of a platoon commander, Paul Rieckhoff documents the disaster ensuing when such protection was not given for those giving information in the courts. A family with two children was assassinated for providing information on a weapons cache two days previously. The Americans had destroyed the Iraqi infrastructure providing security for such people, but had not produced a replacement infrastructure, until the new strategy began to take hold in 2007 (Rieckhoff, 2006:127).

Making the transition from a conventional attrition strategy to population-oriented counterinsurgency was not easy, especially in the bad neighborhoods. Bleak neighborhoods where the streets were deserted and people lived in fear had to be taken back by troops and cleared of the insurgents, often a bloody business, and only then could the American or Iraqi occupation force take up residence and maintain the hard-won order. Once it became clear to the population that the soldiers' presence was permanent, and equaled security, a whole new bargain could be struck, to the benefit of both sides.[17] Developments in Anbar, where alliances were developed with Sunni insurgents who had had enough of the brutal al Qaeda violence and saw the advantages allying with the coalition forces against them, to some degree provided a model for Baghdad. This "awakening," from the American perspective, was based on a strategy of "recruiting the reconcilables and grinding down the irreconcilables," or "flipping all those who could be flipped." This was a high-risk strategy. It meant taking fighters whom you had been fighting six months ago (or less) and making them your allies in the fight against al Qaeda. The Iraqi government often resisted accepting Sunni recruits for police academy admission, and Petraeus often had to go hat in hand to persuade the government to act. Many believed that rather than bringing peace, Petraeus was "organizing the next stage of the Sunni-Shia civil war." In the process of getting to know the population and lobbying the Iraqi government, Petraeus "waded into politics like no general before him had" and he directed his troops to do the same (Robinson, 2008:252–53, 324).

The extremely modest record of the United States in applying counterinsurgency techniques in war was given a big boost with General

Petraeus' success in stabilizing Iraq. The US army is quite a different one than it was at the time of the invasion. The emphasis now is on building institutions and promoting integration, not primarily on killing enemy personnel (Sheridan, 2008a). Petraeus rejected the assumption that had supported the initial US strategy when he told the president, "Mr. President, we are not going to kill our way out of Iraq." One account has assigned greater emphasis to an improved US ability to target and kill key individuals in extremist groups, but there is little dissent that, through 2008, Petraeus's approach has produced substantial dividends in an exhausted Iraq (Woodward, 2008:370, 380). The United States has also been able to focus on negotiations with Iraq's neighbors to cut cross-border flows of insurgents. In addition to the Iranian problem, as we found in Afghanistan, a major source of radical insurgents has been the American ally Saudi Arabia. In mid-2007, the United States estimated that 50 to 80 foreign fighters, many of them Saudi, were passing through Syria to Iraq each month. Of the suicide bombers active in Iraq 80 percent were foreigners, and of these, half were Saudis. Altogether, they had killed or wounded 5,500 Iraqis. None of Iraq's Sunni neighbors had embassies in Iraq, partly because of security, but also as a silent protest against the Maliki government (Robinson, 2008:288–89).

In 2007–08, tremendous progress was made in Iraq. Many of the same problems still exist, but Maliki has shown a more cooperative side as well as taking military measures against mainly Shiite extremists in Basra, Sadr City, and Mosul. The Iraqi government now controlled almost the whole of the country for the first time since the invasion. The quality of the Iraq military appears to have improved considerably. Progress was made on political objectives, including a status of forces and planned withdrawal agreement with the United States. Moreover, indicators of violence and turmoil have showed a rapid reduction between November 2006 and November 2008 while electricity production and economic conditions improved (Campbell and O'Hanlon, 2008; Campbell, O'Hanlon, and Unikewicz, 2008). Virtually everyone agrees that much progress has been made in reducing violence. The disagreement is over whether or not it will last.

RECONSTRUCTION, ETHNOCENTRISM, AND SECURITY

Reconstruction in Iraq duplicated many of the problems already documented in Afghanistan, but especially the ethnocentric approach, an inability to fashion solutions to fit the local needs and culture, and the exaggerated expense. An added element in Iraq was the explicit politicization of the process under the Bush administration, especially the determination to replicate the American free enterprise system in Iraq and the heavy recruitment of political partisans for positions in Iraq. This is richly documented in Chandrasekaran (2006). It bears repeating here that reconstruction, like counterinsurgency, is in desperate need of attention and transformation as a contribution to the US foreign policy process.

CONCLUSION

This survey of the intervention in Iraq has found few convincing security objectives that were served by the military action. One accomplishment was the removal of Saddam Hussein from office, definitely an accomplishment for both the Iraqi and the American people. A formal democracy has been installed, but unfortunately security, the bedrock of any successful democracy, is still uncertain. The change was purchased at a very high price. Larry Diamond refers to the "stark landscape of a broken, wasted country" (Diamond, 2005:119). No policy and no amount of good luck can erase the tremendous costs borne by the Iraqi people, nor the costs to the United States and damage to US foreign policy. In mid-2010, seven years after the war was started, the stability and longevity of the regime in place is still in question. Bombs killing 50–100 people go off periodically. A close but successful election was carried out in March, 2010 but seven months were required to form a government, one that seems to be backsliding on a commitment to inclusion of the Sunnis in the governance of the country, even as US troops continue their drawdown. A recent report details the pervasive fear gripping the society, an important cause of the delay in forming a government (Hiltermann, 2010). Sixty-three percent of Americans consider the Iraq War to be a "mistake." This is the "highest recorded opposition to an active war in American history," two points higher than the top opposition to the Vietnam War in May 1971(Zegat, 2008:43–44).

There is, however, one major gain for American foreign policy. The phenomenal turn around in the war brought about by the surge and the adoption of a counterinsurgency strategy in 2007 and beyond is unprecedented. Never before has the US leadership shown this kind of seriousness about implementing counterinsurgency, and the civilians and military personnel who brought it about should get credit for one extremely bright spot in an otherwise dark and discouraging saga. The big question now is whether genuine learning has taken place in the military and the government, and whether those who favor the new orientation will be able to prevail in institutionalizing this approach to war in the national defense bureaucracy. One hopes that habitual inertia can be overcome and genuine changes implemented. Success may depend on the outcome of Afghanistan, where there is an attempt to apply the lessons of Iraq, but so far with less positive results. The Iraqi saga itself, needless to say, is also still unfinished and the outcome uncertain. Whatever the long-term outcome in Afghanistan, or Iraq, the accomplishments of counterinsurgency in Iraq in the later stages of the conflict stand on their own, and should be enough to recommend changes in priorities at DoD.

PART III

CONCLUSION

CHAPTER 9

THE PERILS OF INTERVENTION

> It always surprises and grieves us to learn that other countries are sometimes incapable of appreciating the true beauty of the world system Americans are trying to build.
>
> Walter Russell Mead

Well-wishers for American foreign policy and the welfare of the United States and the world have only modest reason to be cheered by the record of the five interventions in low-intensity war chronicled here. American foreign policy has had many successes from 1898 on, but most have not involved interventions into situations requiring the fighting of unconventional war since 1945. One study of military interventions found that they typically embodied six characteristics. They were dynamic (constantly changing and unpredictable); there was a high degree of uncertainty; they were both complex and destructive; typically, there was both a lack of comparative thinking and limited learning on the part of policy makers. There is evidence among the five cases studied here justifying a similar conclusion (Levite et al., 1992:303–37). Contemplating this situation, one implication may occur to many: given the US record, perhaps it is better not to get involved in such wars in the future. Based on the findings in the cases examined here, attempting to "avoid counterinsurgencies except in extremis" seems like sound advice to US policy makers (Van Evera, 2008:19).

Bosnia seems to be the one notable success case. After a long delay, the United States finally got involved, in close cooperation with its European allies, and was successful in stopping the violence, with a peace now a decade-and-a-half old. While the political settlement of the conflict is still to be fully accomplished, the violence was stopped with minimal cost to the United States or its allies. It may not be coincidental that the success came after a long period of waiting and observing, a delay that was very costly to the Bosnians. It is also ironic that this was the one case where many people believed no US security interest was involved, and many others argued only half-heartedly that there was one.

In Afghanistan, most foreign policy specialists as well as citizens believed there was a security interest involved following the 9/11 attacks. The only question was what form the intervention should take. I have argued that there was a dearth of imagination among the decision makers in assessing what had happened and what course of action to take. Certainly the decision makers did grapple with the issue of how to relate to the Taliban given that al Qaeda was the main enemy. Whether or not the intervention showed the correct focus and approach, what is certain is that mistakes were made later on, including the decision to open another front in Iraq. The one key problem, the ineffective partnership and government of Hamid Karzai, I have argued, is a frequent problem in this kind of war. Often there is little the intervening country can do to choose its partner, or, alternatively, if it has a choice, it cannot know which candidate would be best. This circumstance is the best argument for accepting the advice proffered above, to avoid intervention in unconventional war, except in extremis. The outcome of the Afghan conflict at this point is still unknown and very contentious.

In three of the cases studied, the Philippines, Vietnam, and Iraq, I have argued that realist criteria for determining the security interests for intervening did not provide a justification for intervention, although key decision makers at the time of intervention obviously judged differently. Ironically, a few years after the Philippine War ended, Theodore Roosevelt, while still believing it was the US duty to "hold" the islands, had grown much less enthusiastic about carrying out that duty. There was confusion over what the US objectives should be and whether there was a security interest as stake, just as in later wars. The clueless McKinley is in some ways similar to later presidents, such as Johnson, in his mixed feelings about his war. The key issue in the beginning from a security perspective for the Philippines was: did the Americans need to take over sovereignty of the Philippines to protect US security interests? There is no reason to believe they did.

The Vietnam War is still contentious in the United States,[1] and there was considerable outcry about the imprisonment, executions, and other repression that followed the takeover by Hanoi. But there seems to have been little in the way of security repercussions from the American loss there. Vietnam ended up defending itself against China in a war—just the possibility Morgenthau suggested—and today it is a "bourgeoisie" state rapidly using the tools of capitalism to improve its economy and still buffering China, in spite of the communist win. The domino effect was limited to Laos and Cambodia, which had already been involved in the war.

Nobody has yet come up with a persuasive case for security interests promoted by the Iraq War, and the CIA and many others have suggested that intervening there ended up providing a recruiting tool for al Qaeda, decreasing overall US security, not improving it. Add to that the increased influence Iran now has due to Iraq's weakness, and the general damage done to American credibility and standing in the world. This is not even mentioning what happened to the Iraqis. Many of them would have questions whether being rid of Saddam compensates for the costs of the war and the present condition of their country.

One could make an idealistic case for all these wars, but no matter how desirable the outcome, there would still be the problem of persuading the listener that the benefits of the intervention exceeded the political, economic, and human costs it sustained for both the United States and the target country. In the case of the Philippines, it is true that the United States was a relatively enlightened colonial power and it quickly brought democracy and eventually independence to the Philippines. Such a reckoning, however, must also note that the Philippines is notorious in Southeast Asia for being ruled by a small set of elite families adverse to social democratic reform. The Americans never got over their original preference for working with the educated upper classes. Perhaps the legacy of a formal democracy with limited social-economic reform and considerable inequality is not that surprising, since US society itself tends to have that same structure. Given the implementation record in the other cases—Vietnam a failure; Iraq, failure followed by reform and tentative success; Afghanistan, still to be determined but not encouraging; and Bosnia, successful in stopping the violence—it would be hard to convince an idealistic proponent that intervention on humanitarian or idealistic grounds was wise in any of these cases except Bosnia. The costs so far exceeded the accomplishments in the others, with the possible exception of Afghanistan.

A question that might well be asked is: given that the United States does not fight low-intensity or irregular war well, how can one anticipate whether a particular intervention will involve fighting an irregular war? A number of interventions that did not involve fighting low-intensity war have gone smoothly. The Gulf War, the invasion of Panama and Grenada can be viewed as relatively successful. Obviously there is no magical formula that will allow decision makers to predict when low-intensity war will develop. A judgment call must be made, just as with most aspects of policy making. The presence of already organized insurgency movements (Vietnam), deeply split societies (Iraq), or previous anarchical conditions (Afghanistan) are obvious indicators that intervention may not be a smooth and wholly successful operation. Obviously intervention in circumstances that indicate a high likelihood of irregular war developing should not be undertaken except when security or humanitarian objectives are urgent, or when there is a high probability that the military is capable of waging effective counterinsurgency warfare. There is seldom a guarantee that warfare will not develop in the aftermath of an intervention. Unfortunately for the proponents of aggressive intervention policies, it is probable that in most cases considered for intervention, some of the conditions mentioned—or equally serious problems—will exist. It is, after all, almost always the defects in the preinvasion social-political-cultural structure that make it necessary to intervene in the first place, and that will complicate the postintervention violence.

In the implementation phase, four out of the five cases reveal that policy makers had considerable difficulty in initially adjusting to the kind of warfare that was needed. In the cases of Afghanistan and Iraq, however, there is evidence of the kind of innovation that could transform the way the United States approaches interventions involving irregular war. In Iraq, following four years of war and disastrous results, a change in war strategy transformed the situation and has allowed the Americans to move to the sidelines of military activity, pending a complete withdrawal. While the cost of the intervention, both to the United States and to the Iraqis still makes the intervention a questionable decision, the ability of the military to adjust the strategy indicates real progress in implementation of counterinsurgency and opens the possibility of successfully incorporating counterinsurgency into the US arsenal of war strategies and tactics. If done successfully, it would be a historic first.

Attempts to apply the same basic approach in Afghanistan have been less successful, primarily because of the three factors that have dogged the US effort since 2001: the initial abandonment of Afghanistan after the initial success in favor of Iraq, the continued involvement of Pakistan in supplying and supporting the insurgents, and an incompetent and corrupt Karzai government that does not have the confidence of the populace. In spite of these obstacles, the overall approach to prosecuting the war in Afghanistan remains basically transformed from earlier conflicts such as Vietnam. Following the turn around in Iraq, one recent visitor to Afghanistan noted a definite new receptivity among the US military to and acceptance of the need for counterinsurgency, which is also reflected in McChrystal's report on the situation there (Brooks, 2009; McChrystal, 2009). Whether the military is yet ready to focus on, retain, and expand this knowledge is still a big unknown. The changes in the international system discussed in Chapter 1 regarding how large powers relate to one another and the increased relevance of counterinsurgency warfare may lead to more receptivity within the United States to the kind of perspective that General Petraeus and others have presented and used with such deftness in Iraq. This kind of acceptance and acknowledgement of its utility is required for developing a reliable and ongoing counterinsurgency capability.

The Philippine War, even though it occurred nearly a half-century before the United States emerged as a superpower, was a precursor of the need for counterinsurgency skills in order to defeat the enemy. The Americans had some successes in using counterinsurgency in the Philippines, no doubt at least partly because the army still retained experience and expertise in those who had fought in earlier similar wars. The war was fought using both conventional and unconventional warfare and several generals in particular showed themselves adept at counterinsurgency. But while the United States learned a great deal about counterinsurgency warfare in the Philippines, it made little effort to retain the lessons derived there. The army and navy both longed for the larger, more conventional war as a milieu in which they could prove their mettle. The marines' *Small Wars Manual*, written in the 1930s, did capture some of the Philippine counterinsurgency experiences but by the time of WWII, they had mostly been forgotten (Boot, 2002:283).

In the case of Vietnam, there never was a government in power in the south that possessed the competence and the legitimacy to serve as an effective force against the nationalist credentials, the ideology and the organization skills possessed by the north, and the northern-influenced troops operating in South Vietnam. These facts were repeatedly conveyed to US leaders by people with knowledge of the country and what was transpiring there, from the early 1950s on. These facts made little impression on most of the US leadership during the period of active US involvement. Nor was there any serious effort to implement counterinsurgency within the country. The other two wars, the conventional ground war and the air war, were for the most part irrelevant to the communist Vietnamese leaders that were determined to unite the country under the communist ideology and were prepared to persist indefinitely and pay a great price to do so. The ineffectiveness and irrelevance of the war ensured that the United States would eventually dissipate its political capital and withdraw, clearing the way for a communist victory. In spite of President Kennedy's attempt to develop counterinsurgency skills, little was accomplished.

PREPARING FOR INTERVENTION

CREATING A POLITICAL PARADIGM

When deciding whether to intervene or how to fight a war, it is crucial to have a political paradigm or perspective that allows the proper decisions to be made in the context of and in relation to facts, evidence, and preferences. A historical perspective is necessary, and close attention needs to be paid to the relationship between the political and military means to accomplish the objectives. A proper political perspective allows one to view the problem in a long-term perspective. Solving problems politically rather than militarily usually takes more time, but military "solutions" not placed in the proper political context are not likely to endure. Military solutions are often a "last chance" effort to solve a problem. Since governments, like most organizations, are notoriously bad at long-range planning and action, by default particularly thorny problems often end up with the government attempting to apply a military solution. In the modern world of irregular war, the symbiotic relationship between these two spheres is closer and more crucial than in the wars of attrition the United States has traditionally fought. An illustrative example of this is the war in Afghanistan. The Soviet War with Afghanistan was particularly debilitating to the society. There was tremendous destruction of property and many casualties. The aid to the Afghan jihadis fighting for control of the country turned into the biggest US covert operation since WWII. Among those receiving US aid was Osama bin Laden. When the cold war superpower contest was finished, the superpower belligerents walked away from the "great game" wreckage, but did nothing to diminish the opportunity for the "lesser game" jihadis and their neighbors to finish the destruction of the society of Afghanistan. The Afghan people became a "forgotten people," the remnants of the "forgotten war" (Jalali, 2007:26). It did not take a lot of insight at the end of the 1980s to guess that this scene, where multiple players participated in a vicious and unfettered civil war, was likely to have unfortunate effects further down the road. Rather than simply walking away, it would have been sensible for the United States to exercise some diplomatic clout to try to dampen the fighting and help develop a procedure to find a solution. Since nothing was done then, the results came back to haunt the United States with the 9/11 incident. The same argument can be made for the support the United States gave Saddam Hussein in the 1980s. Not only did it encourage a war with Iran that produced a million casualties, but the United States ended up consorting with a vicious dictator who used poison gas against his own people as well as committing many other atrocities. Ironically, the same person that served as a liaison with Saddam in 1980, Donald Rumsfeld, ended up being the defense secretary who conducted the war against him in 2003. It is too much to hope that governments will spend a lot of time planning for hypothetical issues that might happen years in the future, but there are situations where a little low-cost preventative action may have a substantial payoff in the future.

These cases seem to support the conclusions of a previous study of intervention: a common assumption, except for Bosnia, is that there is more to be lost by not intervening than by intervening. In the decisions to intervene, the burden of proof was on those opposed to intervention rather than those in favor of the action (Levite et al., 1992). This inversion of the "default" option reflects a failure to think through the political implications of intervention and to set political priorities. Given all the history, risks, and uncertainties of interventions, it would appear the burden of proof should rest with the proponents of intervention.

In all of our cases, with the possible exception of Bosnia, more attention to political issues might have avoided the necessity of using military means. The Philippine struggle was an offshoot of the Spanish-American War. While it would be wrong to claim that much thought was given to the conduct of that war as a whole, even less was given to the Philippine part of it. As a consequence the initial confrontations were decided in the American favor since the Spanish empire was teetering on its last legs, but when the Americans were confronted with the Philippine uprising against the new would-be colonial power, they were both unprepared and not entirely sure why they were there. The American public, which had been so adamant about annexing the Philippines, soon lost interest and the acquired islands were seen as more of a liability than an asset.

Other cases show similar costs when the political framework in which a conflict is fought is not sufficiently analyzed or understood. In Vietnam, the United States would have been well advised to consider more carefully the chances of triumphing on the ground when there was no government, nor the prospect of creating one, that would have the legitimacy and the anticolonial credentials to rival those of Ho Chi Minh's movement. For that matter, it would have also been useful to give some attention to the French experience, why they lost, and how a client state of the United States would be able to compete when the Americans were viewed as the successor to the French effort. By ignoring or deemphasizing these questions, the United States set itself up for a military commitment that accomplished little but had tremendous costs to both sides.

In Afghanistan, there was inadequate discussion on the context of the proposed war during the stage prior to the attack, that is, consideration of what kind of reprisal would make the most sense when the main actors were not representatives of a state but of a transnational organization. And while the decision makers were sensitive to the difference between the Taliban and al Qaeda, there was apparently no discussion of a more limited attack that might have left the Taliban regime intact instead of deposing it. And while President Bush expressed a preference for a substantive policy rather than a symbolic one, one can't help but conclude that the need for a demonstration of the US determination to retaliate hurried the decision-making process and truncated a thorough discussion of alternatives in the new world of transnational actors. Further, once a decision was made to dethrone the Taliban, then the follow-on decision to refocus attention, priorities, troops, and supplies on Iraq rather than to concentrate on Afghanistan was a mistake.

In the case of Iraq, the problem of Saddam had long existed and the existing paradigm for handling the problem was judged unsuitable by the Bush administration. But the replacement framework for viewing the problem was also unsuitable. The decision to attack Iraq, as we have seen, was inadequately thought through with (purposely) poor communication throughout the bureaucracy, and the administration was able to prevail in public opinion only by using devious and misleading methods and ignoring information that was readily available. Worst of all, the effort ended up siphoning men and materials from Afghanistan. This resulted in a disastrous situation in both countries. The Vice President's beloved "demonstration effect" ended up demonstrating the wrong lesson, and created even more recruits for al Qaeda.

Many people have long recognized that the budget of the State Department, aid agencies, and other government departments get too little funding in relation to defense. The funding priorities reflect the policy priorities. According to a recent report, even senior Defense Department officials recognize that this is the case, and are supporting a new review to examine what changes should be made (Shanker, 2009). While the problem is above all conceptual, there is no doubt that additional funding for nondefense departments would be helpful in shifting toward a more balanced political-military approach to sound defense policy.

A second issue for which a more complete political paradigm would be helpful is that of determining the objectives of the intervention and the identity of the enemy. One constantly recurring problem in American intervention has been determining the objectives of the intervention. This suggests that accepting at face value the purpose or rationale for intervention may often be misleading. Particular care must be taken when using large n studies citing security rationales for intervention (Meernik, 2004:11), since the gap between the policy maker's and the analyst's conclusions regarding the legitimacy of security justifications for intervention may be great. Only in-depth study of each case can provide this information.

This problem is counterintuitive, since one would like to believe that if a situation is serious enough to take one to war, then the identity of the enemy should be obvious. But what is forgotten is that these wars are not conventional wars like WWII, the Korean War, or the Gulf War. It is the often confusing nature of unconventional wars that leads to problems with such elemental functions as deriving a clear and precise identity for the enemy. Ironically, in what was arguably the most confusing conflict in these case studies, the one in Bosnia, the United States fared well in picking the "correct" enemy at an early stage. It was Britain, especially, that maintained its traditional attachments to Serbia and tended to treat all parties as equally guilty of contributing to violence. This was a stance that could not be maintained over time. The difficulty the United States had was mustering the will to pay the political costs of intervention and then persuading the Europeans to cooperate in a joint effort. After a four-year period when US rhetoric often did not match actions, the Contact Group was able to mobilize and bring about negotiations, relying mostly on the threat of American bombing and changes brought about on the battlefield by Croatia and Bosnia. There was also difficulty in identifying the enemy in the Philippines, although the confusion was quickly remedied there. The Americans, intent on eliminating the Spanish presence in the Philippines, were surprised when military resistance to their presence developed among the Filipinos. This in turn was a function of another difficulty in the American approach to war that has also appeared in the later cases, an inability to appreciate fully the importance of nationalist motivation. Once the extent of Philippine resistance became clear and the Spanish were no longer around, it was easy to focus on going after Aguinaldo and his men, although there was still a problem of exactly what kind of war should be waged against them. Both this and the problems of nationalism are discussed below.

In Vietnam, the identification of the enemy was more difficult. The shifting nature and composition of the "communist bloc" and its impact on the war was never really discussed in any detail. I have argued that this was a major flaw in the official analysis of the war that had a major impact on whether and how the war should be fought. There was a failure to adjust the rationale for the war to the developing split between China and the Soviet Union that opened up the possibility of Vietnam becoming an "Asian Tito," which the United States could best encourage, not by assaulting North Vietnam, but rather by concentrating its vigilance and pressure on the larger powers. The major obstacle to grappling with this change (Kail, 1973:Chapter 2) reflects the administration's failure to update its view of the ideology and organization of China, the Soviet Union, and North Vietnam, and to adapt its strategy accordingly. This crucial information should have been the key to choosing to intervene and determining how to intervene. Intervention at all was a mistake, but close monitoring of events analyzed in the framework of the split in the communist bloc would have provided abundant evidence that whatever the initial justification for the conflict, it had now become anachronistic.

In both Afghanistan and Iraq, difficulties also existed in deciding on the enemy. In Afghanistan, there was no doubt that al Qaeda was an important target of intervention since it was the organization responsible for the 9/11 attacks. The difficulty lay in deciding the proper stance toward the Taliban, which was sheltering al Qaeda. The decision was to team with a proxy—the Northern Alliance—and topple the Taliban government. The difficulties in nation-building that have followed from that decision suggest that a more narrow intervention that concentrated more single-mindedly on al Qaeda would have had significant advantages. Certainly this was a judgment call, but the issue deserved more discussion. Regarding Iraq, there still exists considerable bafflement as to why Iraq was singled out for attack at the very time when the United States should have been occupied with the Afghan War. Many have argued that the net effect of the war has been negative for dealing with the threat from terrorists, since US involvement there acted as an effective recruiting tool for al Qaeda as well as strengthening Iran. So many things were wrong with the way the Iraqi decisions were made that it is difficult to choose the central problem. Rigid ideological thinking is perhaps the main culprit.

PAROCHIALISM, ETHNOCENTRISM, AND MESSIANIC TENDENCIES

These cases provide plenty of evidence of American ethnocentrism and parochialism in the formulation of foreign policy and intervention, what one scholar calls "cultural insularity" (Van Evera, 2008:26). Parochialism is isolation from and ignorance of norms and facts widely available in the outside world. Both arrogance and ignorance derived from this state of affairs have been too much in evidence in American foreign policy in the post-WWII period. An ideal policy would replace these counterproductive traits with more humility and increased effectiveness.

Racism has an extended heritage in American foreign policy and that heritage was very much on display from the American approach to the Philippines at the turn of the century. The United States treated the Filipinos as disqualified for self-government and the attitudes and policies of its officials and soldiers reflected blatant racism and contempt for their culture. This attitude was not uncommon at the time among Western powers, and some of the more blatant judgments and beliefs were modified as the Americans prepared to grant independence and Americans had increased contacts with Filipinos.

A different kind of parochialism, but one no less debilitating for effective foreign policy, could be viewed in US policy toward Vietnam. There the United States, especially during the Johnson administration, took little note of the knowledge and experience the French could offer the Americans, experience that was extremely relevant to potential involvement in Vietnam. Moreover, the administration was so threatened by de Gaulle that it went out of its way to discredit him and his views on the war. Indeed as we have seen, most of the rest of the world was not only against the war but had strong views on the chances of the US effort succeeding and plenty of advice to offer on what the problems were. Instead of learning from these reactions and asking about the significance of the fact that most of our friends and allies were carefully erecting a wall between themselves and any involvement in our effort in Vietnam, the Americans persisted in staying the course. US officials for the most part either ignored or discredited the outside perspectives and sometimes tried to browbeat allies into making a greater contribution. It is remarkable that 40 years later when preparations were being made for the Iraq War, a chief opponent of the US insistence that Iraq must be attacked was, again, France. No doubt some of the US attitude toward France in 2003 reflected the commonly held belief that the French specialized in being difficult and that frequently one motivation of French policy is to deviate from US policy enough to give the French some leverage and influence (Cogan, 2003). But in both cases the French had valuable insights into the proposed action, and in both cases they were proved right. The rationales on which the French and German pleas for moderation in the stance toward Iraq were based were:

(1) there was insufficient evidence that the threat posed by Saddam was imminent;
(2) the goal of building democracy was going to be infinitely more difficult, long, and bloody than anticipated; and
(3) the resulting occupation would enflame anti-Western passions throughout Islam (Merry, 2005:246).

Iraq gave President Chirac an opportunity that de Gaulle longed for but never got; a chance to directly oppose the United States on a major issue, and with strong German backing (Mead, 2005:142). In the case of both Vietnam and Iraq, it turns out, the French had valuable insights into basic issues regarding the interventions that the Americans would have done well to heed. Instead, both presidents Johnson and Bush and their supporters contemptuously dismissed their warnings and plunged ahead. Both would later pay the price for this indiscretion.

We have also seen in this analysis that the American attitude toward Hans Blix and UNMOWIC in the run-up to the attack on Iraq showed a number of officials to have a petty prejudice toward Blix and the commission, based on the belief that Swedes were likely to lack objectivity in evaluating the presence of WMD. Needless to say, the shortfall in objectivity was shown decisively to lie with the American side.[2]

It is interesting that the Bosnia case seems to be relatively free of cultural blinders that impeded US effectiveness there. Perhaps this reflects the common Western heritage, even if that heritage does have a little different twist in the Balkans. Aside from the first Bush administration being slow to take the full measure of the situation there and especially the need for decisive action, the end result was an effective blend of force and diplomacy that decisively stopped the violence. Richard Holbrooke proved a fitting match for the three Balkan leaders once US policy got serious about ending the conflict. If the United States is to be an effective actor in the world, especially in situations involving low-intensity war, then it must avoid ethnocentrism and parochialism. Interestingly the current president Obama has a family and residence background unlike anyone previously elected to the office, leading one to expect that some of the narrow perspectives that have affected US policy in the past may be corrected during his term.

Reinhold Niebuhr wrote that

> [o]ne of the most pathetic aspects of human history is that every civi-lization expresses itself most pretentiously, compounds its partial and universal values most convincingly, and claims immortality for its finite existence at the very moment when the decay that leads to death has already begun.
>
> Niebuhr. 1955:39

If Niebuhr's statement is true, after reading the fervent and fantastical pronouncements of the George W. Bush administration for eight years, one would have to conclude that the demise of the "finite existence" of the United States might be near. But perhaps Niebuhr was too pessimistic. After all, the United States, the "crusader state" has had an inflated view of what it could accomplish in the world for many decades, at least since the events of 1898 chronicled in this book (McDougall, 1997:206). This book is about presumed national interests, but researching the facts and imbibing the rhetoric of US foreign policy in these five studies cannot but suggest to the reader that often it is America's messianic tendencies rather than a cold cal-culation of security interests that sets the pattern for American intervention. In three of the five cases (Philippines, Vietnam, and Iraq) here examined, I have found that the security interests were anything but coldly and care-fully calculated. In all three cases there was a great outpouring of messianic verbiage that promised salvation for the targeted state. In the case of Iraq, especially, the president and the neoconservatives repeatedly invoked the virtue of overthrowing Saddam in terms of the benefit to Iraqis. One com-mentator notes that the best explanation of the war is "power, opportunity, and devotion to the democratic dogma, America's oldest secular religion" (Joffe, 2006:50). Who can imagine a more laudable foreign policy objective than overthrowing Saddam Hussein? It was only in the implementation of the policy that the United States failed badly (Mead, 2005:122). But this is one of the chief characteristics of a messianic approach. It is not difficult to think up lists of laudable foreign policy goals; the difficulty lies in carrying them out, and the former is by far the easier. One cannot help but suspect that the missionary errand of the United States is at least an unconscious factor at work in motivating many US interventions. The rhetoric of the Philippine and Vietnam wars nearly equaled that of Iraq in intensity and verbosity. When the same uplifting claims repeatedly dot the explanations of US motivations, one must at least entertain the fact that the pontificating official believes it and that to some degree it motivates foreign policy. Robert McNamara assured us that in Vietnam "the ultimate goal of our country . . . in Southeast Asia is to help maintain free and independent nations there in which the people can develop politically and socially according to patterns of their own choosing." He goes on to further assure us: "That's our objective. That's our only objective" (Kail, 1973:70). The cynic will respond that this is only window dressing, that more callow national interests are at base the motivators of US policy. My preference is to believe that after a while, politicians and other spokesmen tend to believe their own rhetoric and to equate their status as liberators to the florid rhetoric they utter.

An alternative is to view policy makers as using ideals to generate public support for the policies that would otherwise not be supported. Certainly it is easier to argue that most often the use of these fiery phrases and pronouncements represents not the motivating beliefs of the official, but her use of rhetoric to influence the public and sell her policy. Almost everybody will admit that this use of ideals to promote policies takes place. In practice it is difficult to distinguish empirically between rhetoric as motivation and rhetoric as sales tool. Liberal democratic ideals as a sales tool may appear more frequently than liberal democratic ideals as motivation for the choice of policy—but it is easy to believe that frequently ideals play roles.

One may be tempted to suggest that "the United States ought simply to close its Meliorist shop and abolish all its do-gooder agencies" (McDougall, 1997:210). But this would be throwing the good out with the bad. There is a role for a superpower that occasionally intervenes. The trick is to intervene when necessary, with an understanding of the dynamics of the situation and with a commitment based upon an accurate cost-benefit analysis. In one case, that of the genocide in Rwanda, many believe that intervention would have been relatively risk-free, but would have saved hundreds of thousands of lives (Dallaire, 2003). Interventions where costs are likely to be high and benefits marginal should be abandoned, but those that promise substantial rewards but at a reasonable cost should be made. No doubt readers and policy makers alike will have widely varying perspectives on policies and on which decisions will be appropriate when implemented as US foreign policy.

The intervention cases studied here have shown influences from a variety of pressures from the domestic realm, namely, public opinion, personality, and bureaucratic inertia. In the Philippines, public opinion appears to have been a key factor in McKinley's decision to take over the islands. In Afghanistan as well, it is clear from Woodward's book that public pressure for a quick response to 9/11 was an important consideration in President Bush's response. Vietnam and Iraq required more effort at building public support, with such efforts often relying heavily on messianic themes. In Bosnia, public opinion was an obstacle to intervention, not an inducement. Public pressure may or may not be a force for intervention, depending on the specifics of the situation.

The personality of the president appears to have been important in two interventions: Vietnam and Iraq, although such a statement is controversial and there are supporters on both sides of the argument. Ascertaining whether Kennedy would have made the decisions on Vietnam that Johnson did has been controversial. Some maintain that Kennedy was more flexible, with a greater tolerance for argumentative debates where all sides of the issue were debated. Johnson, on the other hand, tended to surround himself with cheerleaders rather than critics. Inexperienced in international politics, he was particularly concerned that he not be seen to be "losing" Vietnam when he, as an heir to the Kennedy mandate, had a special obligation to see it through. It is very tempting to see George W. Bush's decision to go into Iraq as reflecting his own idiosyncratic beliefs and temperament. Reflecting the messianic tendencies of his Texas power base and his inexperience in foreign affairs, he was willing to take risks other presidents would have shied away from. He adopted the cause of Iraq as his own, but because of the appallingly bad administration of the war, the costs mounted steadily and only a drastic change of strategy made an outcome of a stable Iraq a possibility. Bad administration, as illustrated in Afghanistan, Iraq, and the aftermath of Katrina, suggests that administrative problems were more the norm than the exception during his two terms.

Obstacles to Successful Intervention

The Quagmire Phenomenon

The quagmire phenomenon, where the intervening government is stuck with the client government of the state in which it has intervened, has been a recurring theme in these cases, highlighting the difficulties facing an intervening power. The intervening power is very dependent on the client government in power in the target state, and once the intervention has taken place, it is neither easy to change the client government nor to disengage. In a situation where the intervening power is dependent on a client state, wielding influence over the client is almost always difficult. The client state wants to preserve its influence, but if it has not already succeeded in establishing a legitimate and popular government, it probably needs assistance to do so. If the client government is left alone to improve its position, it is unlikely to be successful. If on the other hand, the intervening government plays a strong role in promoting reforms or even taking over some of the functions of the client government, then the client state will have compromised its legitimacy, its capabilities, and its standing with the populace. It will have been shown to lack nationalist motivation and credentials and to be a neocolonialist lackey or some equally infamous type of actor. Since these sorts of dilemmas are almost impossible to resolve, it suggests that a power contemplating intervention should not intervene unless one of two conditions exists. Either a legitimate and capable government is already functioning, in which case the intervention may not be necessary, or there exists an overwhelming security interest that justifies high-risk intervention. In the case of Vietnam, there existed a relatively quiet time in the late 1950s when, if progress were going to be made in bolstering the support and legitimacy of the Saigon government, it should have occurred. Even during the first few years of the 1960s the situation might still have been turned around without excessive American involvement. Again it was not, but again the United States persisted. There seemed to be a US determination, in the face of evidence that the South Vietnamese government could not be reformed, to redouble the effort. The attempt to fix the problem through a coup against Ngo Dinh Diem was even less successful, since it further destabilized the situation. Other coups followed, but there was little progress in improving the legitimacy of the government. Interestingly, in Bosnia the government in Sarajevo, whatever its shortcomings, improved its performance and became an asset in the pre-Dayton period when it was able to take advantage of its ability to get arms through the embargo lines (with US help) and acquitted itself quite well militarily in the closing period of the war. This was an assist in meeting the US Dayton objective of a viable and self-sufficient Muslim state and reflects a kind of learning and performance not often seen in a client state.

The quagmire problem was also present in Iraq and Afghanistan. In Iraq, the Baghdad government was originally predominantly Shiite, even extreme Shiite. This made it difficult to provide a government acceptable to the Kurds, but especially not to the Sunnis. In this case, American pressure and progress in nation-building did improve the political base of the government. Whether it will be sufficient to maintain the peace after US troops are drawn down is still to be determined. The United States faces the quagmire phenomenon in its starkest form in Afghanistan, where the Karzai government has shown itself from early on unable or unwilling to perform needed government functions and bolster its legitimacy by fighting corruption and decreasing warlord influence although it is certainly true that it was often encouraged in this by the Americans. As Condoleezza Rice points out, today it is often weak and poorly governed states that are the cause of international problems and the principal cause of international crisis, not the strong, aggressive states (Ikenberry et al., 2009:21–22). The most effective way to avoid the quagmire phenomenon is to find an alternative to military intervention. Before committing military force, US leaders should be "very confident that the peoples of the nation we're trying to help will fight harder for their own freedom than our armed forces will" (Gelb, 2009:165). Otherwise, we risk being caught in a dilemma that can be resolved only at very high cost.

NATIONALIST RESISTANCE AND UNILATERALISM

Chapter 1 discussed the power of nationalism and its growing influence since the end of WWII. This is a phenomenon to which the United States seems particularly deaf. It has been an important phenomenon in all the conflicts in this study and US officials typically underrate its importance. In the Philippines, nationalism was important, even though Aguinaldo did not draw much on the lower levels of society, and his rebellion preceded most of the more vociferous anticolonial movements outside of Latin America. In Vietnam, nationalism was an important phenomenon from the French period through to the North Vietnamese takeover. More important than communist ideology, nationalism was the spark plug of Ho Chi Min's revolution. In Afghanistan and Iraq, nationalism has been a crucial force in the resistance.

Why does the United States underrate the impact of nationalism? Lyndon Johnson seemed to absorb very little of its impact on the Vietnamese movement. He thought he could buy Ho Chi Minh off with a TVA-like offer of aid and development, unaware that a leader and a movement that had sustained a movement for years and defeated the French were after something much grander than a TVA project. The George W. Bush administration ignored the impact of nationalism in Iraq, expecting to be greeted with open arms, and to have an easy task in dealing with further developments. American officials were more cognizant of its potential in Afghanistan as suggested by their sensitivity

about how fast the Northern Alliance progressed and the need to minimize the American presence. Adverse nationalist reactions are the first
thing the officials of an intervening country should look for. It is the
rare military intervention that does not provoke a nationalist reaction.
Nationalism was an obstacle to the US intervention in the Philippines, a
decisive obstacle in Vietnam, and an important factor in both Iraq and
Afghanistan. In Bosnia, it was the key motivating element of the war
among all the parties.

"The United States does not need the world's permission to act, but
it does need the world's support to succeed." This quote from Richard N.
Haas could be no better illustrated than in Afghanistan (Joffe, 2006:207).
The Europeans immediately offered help under NATO after 9/11, invoking Article 5, which stipulated that an attack on one member obligated
the other members to assist. This offer the United States for the most part
spurned in favor of doing things its own way. Years later, after things had
gone askew there, the United States was busy lecturing the Europeans
on their duty to assist the Americans to help fight the insurgency in
Afghanistan, and all under the same administration. The more cooperative and interdependent nature of the world, previously noted, is now very
much in evidence, even to the rugged individualists in the United States.
This truth is clearly evident in our sample of interventions. The one
relatively successful intervention, Bosnia, became successful only after the
Contact Group was able to stitch together a perspective to which all members could subscribe, including not only Europe and the United States, but
Russia as well. This reminds us that "multilateralism is not cost free" (Haas,
1994:143). In addition to adding legitimacy and strength to an intervention, it can also slow down intervention. In general, the advantages will
outweigh the drawbacks. Vietnam suffered all along from being essentially
a one-country show, that is, an operation conceived and implemented by
the United States. The same was certainly true of Iraq, but here NATO was
sidelined in an even more defiant manner. And the neoconservative idea
that once the United States was successful in its unilateral efforts everybody
else would fall in line behind it was proved deficient.

In spite of these setbacks, the United States is not the indispensable
nation, as former Secretary of State Albright has said, but its services
are in demand. The reason is simple. The United States is often trusted
in a way that other leading powers are not. Countries do not take their
problems to other great powers. No other major power has played an
important role in orchestrating a settlement between Israel and Palestine
or provided cover for what will someday probably be a gradual integration
of Taiwan into mainland China. Europe failed to solve its own problem with
Bosnia. Despite the shortcomings and imperfections, the United States is

still regarded as the closest country to an honest broker, one that will come close to upholding the common good while also providing benefit for the client state. The world may chafe under US leadership, but it would rather "have a voice in Washington than entrust the world to China, Russia, India, Japan or France, or any combination thereof" (Joffe, 2006:219). With the Obama administration, it is clear that much of the world is hoping for a restoration of a more judicious America, better attuned to the needs and preferences of the rest of the world. There is a hope that new US policies will correct the tangents on to which the Americans have veered during the past few years and restore an equilibrium more acceptable to the global order. Consulting more with allies on interventions would almost certainly provide more selectivity in choosing interventions—meaning there would be fewer interventions—and more effectiveness in prosecuting those interventions that are undertaken.

WAGING THE WRONG KIND OF WAR

Fighting unconventional war is clearly a problem for the United States, since it has not done well in that type of battle. The preference of most of the armed services not to fight low-intensity war, and instead to prefer "real" war, is therefore understandable. Max Boot argues that military personnel prefer to pit their fighting skills against other professionals. They favor conventional conflicts where the battles display the martial skills of the participants in a "pure" form, without the complication of political considerations. The primary problem with low-intensity wars is that "there is no obvious field of battle; there are only areas to be controlled, civilians to be protected, hidden foes to be subdued. Soldiers must figure out who the enemy is before killing him." Soldiers find much less satisfaction in this kind of war (Boot, 2002: 282). The preference to fight more traditional wars is both a cause and a consequence of the lack of success with unconventional war, part of a vicious circle. Americans tend to think low-intensity war is inconsequential; it is not glamorous and does not provide advancement—therefore they avoid studying it and are not very good at it. Because they are not very good at it, they focus on the more successful and well-known conventional wars and spend little time learning counterinsurgency.

The turnaround in Iraq confirms the adage that necessity is the mother of invention. The desperate plight of the United States in Iraq forced a turnaround and generals Petraeus, Odierno, and others were able to move the military in the direction of counterinsurgency, a move that was long overdue. In general, counterinsurgency war, properly executed, has the potential to make conflict less costly in human terms. A war of attrition has as its goal attrition, or the destruction of the enemy. Counterinsurgency has as its goal winning the support of the population so as to make violence unnecessary. Successful counterinsurgency therefore is a route to stability and away from violence and chaos. A recent argument that counterinsurgency wars have been won less often starting with the last quarter of the nineteenth century due to the increased mechanization of warfare, which diminishes soldier contact with the population and leads to less intelligence, strengthens the argument made here. What is frequently needed is a counterinsurgency that is less technological and more political (Lyall and Wilson, 2009).

Even if a civil/military leadership excels at counterinsurgency, it still should be applied only when it is feasible, and when it is tailored to the situation. Traditional wars between the United States and a major power, such as a war in the Taiwan Strait, or even another gulf war, are still possible, but appear to be increasingly rare. There is currently a battle going on for the heart and soul of the Pentagon, between what can loosely be called the conventional technology and attrition orientation to war, and the new emphasis on unconventional war to which the US military has been forced by recent events (Jaffe, 2009). Exactly how that battle, in all its complexity, will play out will tell a lot about the future of US intervention.

REALISM, IDEALISM, EMPIRE?

Realism provides guidelines for intervention, thus providing a valuable service. The guidelines used here suggest that realism can be useful as a check on American activity abroad. Too often, the United States has gone abroad with too little awareness of just what the goal was or how exactly such a goal could be obtained. Noting that states "often fight for stakes that seem meager in comparison to the costs of the struggle," Jack Snyder calls this one of the key puzzles of international relations. Even status quo states carry out aggressive foreign policies, and empires still more often make the same mistakes (Jervis and Snyder, 1991:4). This study provides only partial and tentative answers to the puzzle, but it certainly confirms the assertion. In all of our cases except Bosnia, the costs were very high and the benefits meager. George W. Bush, after throwing out the "standard foreign-policy playbook" and conducting a "grand experiment" during his first administration, returned to a more realist approach and much more orthodox policies for his second term. Realism has been touted as the antidote to the excesses of idealism. The realists come in and clean up after the exuberance of the more reckless and flamboyant idealists (Rose, 2004; 2005). Here I have suggested the United States needs a policy that puts security first. Realist criteria are a good starting point, then, since no approach to foreign policy puts a greater emphasis on security than realism.

But do the idealists have a place at the decision making table? Most assuredly they do. The cursory attention given here to humanitarian intervention suggests it may be a more appropriate mission for US interventions, since interventions to support national security goals have often been misdirected and unsuccessful. Humanitarian missions are often more limited and less likely to lead to serious complications. The idealist missions must be done carefully, however. What is wanted is a "better understanding of the relation between ideals and actions" (Haley, 2006:212).[3] In short, we need knowledge of the rest of the world; we need careful analysis of what the goals of US policy are and how they might be accomplished and then a calculation of the likely costs as compared to the likely benefits. It sounds simple, but these basic considerations seem to be missing from many of the decisions taken for military intervention over the past century. Following Morgenthau, we need more emphasis on empirical analysis than we have had in the past. We need discussions that get down to specific actions and likely consequences. We need less use of vague abstractions like the "domino theory," the perfect example of a prescientific, nonempirical approach to international relations. As Morton Halperin and Arnold Kanter note, as an issue is perceived to be of increasing importance, it passes from the "scrutiny of experts up to the politically appointed generalists, who are less inclined toward empirically determined solutions" (Booth, 1979:29). We usually need more area experts, not fewer, to be involved in decision making on intervention.

At this point in history, there seems to be widespread support for "disavowing the crusader state" (Merry, 2005; Johnson, 2000; McDougall, 1997). The idealist that is wanted is a sober, tempered, and reflective idealist that will create less noise and more effective results. Missions and crusades without a firm grounding in the realities of the international system are extravagant luxuries we cannot afford. As David M. Kennedy says, "When American diplomacy has been most effective is when it has tempered ideology with interest, aspiration with practicality, and universalistic yearnings with frank acknowledgement of nationalist particularities" (Kennedy, 2008:159).

Even those favorable to an American empire now have their doubts. From suggesting at the turn of the century that the United States should devote a larger portion of its vast resources to making "the world safe for capitalism and democracy," Niall Ferguson still believed in 2004 that the world needs a "liberal empire" managed by the United States, but doubts that the United States has the will and the inclination to do it. A bad case, among both liberals and conservatives, of "imperial denial" casts doubt on the future ability of the United States to undertake the task of empire. This is a task for which the Americans lack the economy, the manpower, or the attention to operate abroad with the persistence and the agility required for effectiveness (Ferguson, 2004). Americans fundamentally dislike long sojourns abroad, Ferguson says. They are not suited to empire, since they prefer staying at home. Another critic notes the willingness of the Americans to fight wars and conquer countries, but they are done in by the "crippling ambivalence of occupiers who refuse to govern" (Luttwak, 2007). This assessment is supported by the current fatigue connected to the wars in Afghanistan and Iraq. None other than Secretary of Defense Robert Gates, the man who oversaw the reversal of course in those two countries and the attempts to pull the looming disasters out of the fire, has stated that any future defense secretary "who advises the president to again send a big American land army into Asia or into the Middle East or Africa" should have his head examined (Gates, 2011).

The current economic downturn is even more likely to diminish the US role in the world. The economic slump not only debilitates the world economy, but saps the enthusiasm left among Americans for a vigorous world role. In the new economy-dominated world, economic leadership by the United States will likely be less effective, but still needed. President Obama has indicated that the US economy can no longer be the sole engine of global growth (Faiola, 2009). More priority to political and economic activities and less to military intervention is the right strategy for effectively accomplishing security objectives.

NOTES

1. Hans Morgenthau, on his first visit to Vietnam, made observations that paralleled those of my Polish friend (see, 2001:423).
2. Other examples of post–cold war intervention can be found in Haass (1994: Chapter 2). A comprehensive list of US interventions from 1789 to 1993, major to miniscule, is Collier (1993).
3. These criteria of evaluation are similar to those suggested by Joseph Nye, who posits motives, means, and consequences as key elements of assessing a policy's worth (Nye, 1993).
4. Despite the many discrepancies between the two areas of inquiry, however, there is an overlapping of interests. As Colin Elman predicted, study of deterrence and bipolarity were "policy needs" of the cold war and interest in them decreased with the end of the bipolar stand-off (Elman, 1996). On the other hand, the study of terrorists and terrorism increased dramatically after 9/11.

CHAPTER 1

1. "Although economic interests have always influenced the course of international politics, they are of greater consequence in the modern era. Whereas other ages were dominated by religious and political passions, today economic interests and calculations have an enhanced role in the determination of foreign policy" (Gilpin, 1981:68).
2. It is important to remember that not all of the traditional wars of attrition are predictable. Prior to the Gulf War, there was much apprehension about high casualties and prolonged conflict, but the outcome was a six-week air campaign and a 100-hour ground war in which the United States lost only 146 soldiers (Sullivan, 2007:517–18).
3. This discussion of the developments leading to fourth generation warfare, and the stages that preceded it, relies on Lind et al. (1989) and Hamme (2006).
4. An extreme view, perhaps, but illustrative of the problem were the values expressed by an anonymous senior US Army officer, who, when pressed to adapt his approach to Vietnamese conditions, stated: "I'll be damned if

I will permit the United States Army, its institutions, its doctrine, and its traditions to be destroyed just to win this lousy war" (Nagl, 2005:172).

5. But some, including Secretary of Defense Rumsfeld, preferred a less traditional approach to the invasion, using fewer US troops and relying more on Iraqi forces for "liberation," similar to what was done in the early stages in Afghanistan (Arquilla, 2008:216).

CHAPTER 2

1. "Remember," Kennan stated at a National War College talk in October 1947, "that . . . as things stand today, it is not Russian military power which is threatening us, it is Russian political power . . . If it is not entirely a military threat, I doubt that it can be effectively met entirely by military means." Emphasizing that it was not communism but Russia that was the problem, he added that communism was not the disease, it was a complication (Gaddis, 2005:35, 39).

2. McGeorge Bundy called the offshore islands "trivial bits of land" (McMahon, 1991:461).

3. Analysis of the Eisenhower administration's interest in and responses to evidence of Sino-Soviet tensions is in Mayers (1986).

4. Two studies of the imposition of democracy by force are Peceny (1999) and Von Hippel (2000).

5. In the off-year 2010 election, Republicans frequently alluded to what they believed was the Democratic denial of American exceptionalism. In a news conference shortly after the election, Senate Minority Leader Mitch McConnell said that his only real disagreement with the president on foreign policy revolved around his denial of American exceptionalism, or going abroad and suggesting that the United States has been wrong on some things (McConnell, 2010).

6. Not everyone accepts Lipset's formulation of American exceptionalism. Victor Koschmann and Mary Nolan seem most disapproving of what they perceive of as Lipset's laudatory normative baggage—latent promotion of American cultural superiority—more than his analytic approach (Koschmann, 1997; Nolan, 1997). Lipset himself, however, sees his perspective on American uniqueness as a "double-edged sword," by no means only favorable or approving of American culture. Needless to say, this study concurs with that position.

7. Wilson's philosophy of democracy and the US role in promoting it was aptly summed up by this ambivalent quote: "*when properly directed,* there is no people not fitted for self-government" (emphasis added) (Smith, 1993:268).

8. Godfrey Hodgson makes some telling arguments that the United States' experience is not always as exceptional as exceptionalists maintain. The important point here, however, is that American beliefs about America's

exceptionalism, whatever their historical validity, have an important impact on foreign policy. As he himself states, "American history . . . [is] encrusted with accretions of self-congratulatory myth," myths that are specifically unique and applicable to the United States. (Hodgson, 2009:14).

9. The similarities between the ideas of Wilson and George W. Bush should not conceal the differences. As Anatol Lieven points out, one important difference is that Bush puts much less emphasis on the building of international institutions and exerting US power through those institutions than did Wilson, who, after all, conceived and promoted the League of Nations (Lieven, 2004:12).

10. Stanley Hoffmann points out that Americans often assume the ends of social actions are obvious; the question is how the actions should be executed. He quotes Kenneth Keniston: "Ours is a how-to-do-it society, and not a what-to-do society." American pragmatism assumes the ends are obvious; the question is one of choosing means. This in turn leads to an assumption that there is a "technical fix" for everything. But these US assumptions don't necessarily fit a foreign situation nor match foreign assumptions and values (Hoffmann, 1968b: 143–61). A discussion of the similarities and differences in the values of Wilson and George W. Bush is in Ikenberry et al. (2009).

11. "When the established faiths—political, social, religious—begin to grow stale, there is always another hot American revival in the wings" (Morone, 2003:497).

12. Benjamin Franklin said that native Americans were "barbarous tribes of savages that delight in war and take pride in murder." Thomas Jefferson and James Monroe believed the Indians should move on, "beyond the horizon of the Great Dessert." Krenn reports that "[by] the mid-1800s race was far from a trifling matter for the American people, and they were ready to put their racial ideas to the test beyond the U.S. borders" (Krenn, 2006:14, 11, 19; Drinnon, 1999).

13. David M. Barrett resists the conventional wisdom that Johnson's personality or feelings of inadequacy as an heir to the Kennedy presidency or intense concern about domestic consequences of giving up on the war distorted a rational decision-making process on Vietnam. He concludes rather that "tragic consequences can flow from the actions of rational, well-intentioned leaders pursuing a vision of world order" (Barrett, 1993:194).

14. Discussions of US security interests can be found in Blackwill (1993) and Neuchterlein (2001).

15. The increasing complexity of intervention decisions is indicated by the results of one study of intervention in international crises 1918–88, which found that in its sample there was not a "single case of major power military intervention in which the major power military coalition was at a decisive military disadvantage." The indicators for military strength were traditional: size of armed forces, military expenditures, and expenditures per soldier (Huth, 1998). Using those indicators, the

authors' results agree with mine as stated in the tables in the case study chapters, that is, the United States always had a military advantage. But if the actual results on the battlefield are assessed, one of my five cases at the time of writing indicate military inferiority on the part of the United States (Vietnam), one approximate parity (Afghanistan), and three US superiority (Philippines, Iraq, and Bosnia).

16. Secretary of Defense Robert McNamara recounts how, in the context of the contradictory advice President Kennedy was getting on Vietnam, it fell to him and Secretary of State Dean Rusk to make recommendations to Kennedy on how to proceed. McNamara relates how they failed: "The dilemma Dean and I defined was going to haunt us for years. Looking back at the record of those meetings, it is clear our analysis was nowhere near adequate. We failed to ask the . . . most basic questions: Was it true that the fall of South Vietnam would trigger the fall of all Southeast Asia? Would that constitute a grave threat to the West's security? What kind of war—conventional or guerrilla—might develop? Could we win it with US troops fighting alongside the South Vietnamese? . . . It seems beyond understanding, incredible, that we did not force ourselves to confront such issues head-on. But then, it is very hard, today, to recapture the innocence and confidence with which we approached Vietnam in the early days of the Kennedy administration" (McNamara, 1995: 39).

CHAPTER 3

1. Emphasis in the original.
2. At the start of the Dien Bein Phu crisis, Kennedy remarked, "I am frankly of the belief that no amount of American military assistance in Indochina can conquer an enemy which is everywhere and at the same time nowhere, 'an enemy of the people,' which has the sympathy and covert support of the people" (Gelb and Betts, 1979:206).
3. Regarding that war, General Tony Zinni asserted that Desert Storm worked because "we managed to go up against the only jerk on the planet stupid enough to challenge us to refight World War II." Quoted in Helfers (2006:163).
4. Jonathan Caverley makes a convincing argument that another factor that encourages wealthy democracies to fight capital- and firepower-intensive strategies instead of counterinsurgency is that the political costs are more bearable. Since the troops for counterinsurgency would be drawn from the more numerous lower classes, it is best to avoid those political costs and rely on technology (Caverley, 2009). It is not clear, however, that such a strategy really is less costly politically, if it is ineffective.
5. It is noteworthy that much of the media coverage of the success in Iraq concentrates on the increased number of troops sent to Iraq (the "surge"), rather than the change in strategy and tactics to focus on counterinsurgency. This suggests it is not only the military that is resistant to acceptance of counterinsurgency war, but American culture as a whole.

CHAPTER 4

1. After the United States suddenly found itself in possession of the Philippines, McKinley reportedly told a group of Methodist missionaries in a quote, open to some question of its authenticity, that he walked the floor of the White House night after night trying to decide what to do with the Philippines. After much prayer it came to him that the United States had to educate and Christianize the Filipinos.

2. Taft went to the Philippines as head of the Taft commission, a body empowered with legislative authority regarding Philippine affairs: "Officials usually embark on missions with preconceived attitudes and Taft fit the pattern. He had already decided before reaching Manila . . . that Aguinaldo and his disciples were 'desperate men' fighting to convince the US public that the 'task of settling that country is hopeless.' Unless they were eliminated they would 'overawe the more peaceably inclined inhabitants and the better educated class' in the Philippines. Nothing he heard during his first few months in Manila changed his mind. He described the 'vast mass' of the natives as 'superstitious and ignorant' and unqualified for either universal suffrage or autonomy. 'They need the training of fifty or a hundred years before they shall even realize what Anglo-Saxon liberty is'" (Karnow, 1989:173).

3. McKinley, remembering the Civil War, said, "I shall never get into a war until I am sure that God and man approve. I have been through one war; I have seen the dead piled up; and I do not want to see another" (Trask, 1981:58).

4. The Conservative leader Antonio Canovas del Castillo (known as "the monster") stated, "The Spanish nation is disposed to sacrifice to the last *peseta* of its treasure and to the last drop of blood of the last Spaniard before consenting that anyone snatch from it even one piece of its sacred territory" (Trask, 1981:6).

5. According to Robert Dallek, the war was "a celebration of traditional virtues, the conflict expressed American wishes to meet current economic and social problems by returning to an older, simpler style of life" (Dallek, 1983:18). Dallek, like David F. Trask and Ernest R. May, has stressed the decisive impact of public opinion in bringing about the war, especially after the sinking of the Maine on February 15. At that time, "neighborhoods, suburbs, small towns, and rural communities simply caught fire. No section, no type of community, no occupational group was immune." May, as quoted in Trask (1981:xii).

6. "If old Dewey had just sailed away when he smashed the Spanish fleet," McKinley is reported to have said later, "what a lot of trouble he would have saved us." Quoted in Halle (1985:24).

7. Importing from home a tradition of using derogatory names for the native people, Americans called Filipinos "niggers" and "gugus," the latter an epithet derived from the tree bark the local women used as a shampoo. This tradition of using derogatory names continued in Vietnam, over a half-century later (Karnow, 1989:130–31).

8. Dewey had early expressed his confidence in Filipino abilities, at least in comparison to the Cubans, but he later reversed himself. The Schurman Commission concluded in the fall of 1899 that Filipinos believed that illiteracy, lack of political experience, and linguistic differences were obstacles to immediate self-government. If the United States withdrew, there would be anarchy that would lead to the intervention of other powers (Grunder and Livizey, 1951).

9. As Jorge I. Dominguez confirms, in some areas of the Philippines the colonial power had already been deposed. The United States' effort to turn back the clock, after both a war of independence and limited self-government, provoked the resistance (Dominguez, 1979).

10. Somewhat similar points are developed in Boudreau (2003:261). "Those Ilustrados [the upper propertied classes active in local government] who traveled to Europe in the late 1800s entered a cosmopolitan milieu considerably different than that encountered by Ho Chi Minh and Mohammad Hatta [Indonesian] a few decades later." Perhaps the closest parallel to the Philippine War was the Boer War in Africa where the Boers were fighting for their independence.

11. As one commentator put it, "The lack of class distinction, coupled with a refusal to tolerate religious instruction, provoked some opposition from the *principales* and clergy, but officers still believed that the schools were much appreciated" (Linn, 1989:128).

12. Funston showed awareness of the basic truth that in a war such as that in the Philippines, the army and its officers had to know and use far more the art of pacification than the art of war. There, the art of peace was four-fifths of the job and war making was only one-fifth (Linn, 1989:78).

13. In contrast, Louis J. Halle writes that given what the American nation was in 1898, its acquisition of an "unfortunate responsibility" appears to have been inevitable. "[B]ut surely it would not have been inevitable if it had been a nation of Talleyrands and Bismarcks" (Halle, 1985:15, xiii).

CHAPTER 5

1. A detailed account of the environment and the battle is given in Arnold (1991). See also Fall (1966).

2. A copy of the Final Declaration and the unilateral US statement is in the Pentagon Papers (1971a:570–73).

3. A comprehensive analysis of the validity of the domino theory is in Jervis (1997:165–76).

4. As Barbara Tuchman put it, "This melding of the several countries of East Asia as if they had no individuality, no history, no differences or circumstances of their own was the thinking, either uninformed and shallow or knowingly false, that created the domino theory and allowed it to become dogma" (1984:253). Donald Zagoria pointed out that

Vietnam was the only country in Africa, Asia, or Latin America in which communists had been able to seize control of a nationalist movement since the start of WW II (Fulbright, 1966:181).

5. The analysts of the Pentagon Papers note that as of 1954 the "domino theory" and the assumptions behind it were "never questioned. The homogeneity of the nations of Southeast Asia was taken as a given, as was the linkage in their ability to remain democratic, or at an acceptable minimum, non-communist, nations" (Pentagon Papers, 1971a:87).

6. Barbara Tuchman puts it thus: "The folly consisted not in pursuit of a goal in ignorance of the obstacles but in persistence in the pursuit despite accumulating evidence that the goal was unattainable . . . " (Tuchman, 1984:234). In testimony before the Senate in January 1962, US Ambassador to South Vietnam, Frederick E. Nolting, Jr., after relating the problems facing Vietnam and the increasing success of the communists since late 1959 and early 1960, was asked what the solution was. He replied, "I think it is to do what we are doing and do it better and harder" (US Congress, 1962).

7. In an article written in 1967, David Mozingo pointed out that indeed the main incentive to communist development has been "the existence of incompetence and corruption and the lack of a genuine, socially progressive, nation-building ethic within the non-Communist elite . . . " He further suggested that among Southeast Asian countries, close ties with the United States and the lack of an accommodationist policy toward China most clearly invited a Chinese call for revolution (Mozingo, 1967).

8. "The Sino-Soviet conflict has given the smaller parties unprecedented opportunities to increase their freedom of action. Examples could be multiplied almost indefinitely" (Zagoria, 1962:397).

9. The vicissitudes in relations between Hanoi and the two communist giants are traced through the years by Donald Zagoria (1967:99–124). The Vietnamese admired the Chinese model of revolutionary war and land reform, but as the war escalated, the Vietnamese badly needed the material assistance only the Soviets could provide. Douglas Pike (1966:318–43) looks at relations between the communist states as well as the complex nexus between the NLF and Hanoi.

10. Lawrence Freedman recounts that in the early 1960s most people who knew North Vietnam well believed that it might be interested in a deal with the South. One reason for their interest was that "Sino-Soviet acrimony was a burden," and would continue to be one as long as they had to fight the war (Freedman, 2000:382). J. Kenneth Blackwell, at the British consulate in Hanoi, in early 1963 also believed that Hanoi's aversion to China and consequent attraction to Moscow made it more willing to negotiate a face-saving exit for the Americans (Logevall, 1999:9–10).

11. Concurring with Morgenthau's view was, of all people, nationalist China's leader Chiang Kai-shek. He believed that American attempts

to save the French cause in Indochina was "a pure waste" and the final result would be the taking over of the area by the communists (Taylor, 2009:470–72, 495).

12. For an interesting argument that Kennedy had taken the measure of the Vietnam problem and had decided by the fall of 1961 that the United States would not get involved through inserting its own troops, see Blight et al. (2009). They argue that Kennedy had a very different perspective, personality, and background than did Lyndon Johnson.

13. Morgenthau's criticism of the war goes back a decade before his book appeared, to a visit he made to Vietnam in 1955, resulting in a *Washington Post* article on February 26, 1956. This was followed by criticism of developments in Vietnam in numerous other articles as well as his books. In the *Washington Post* article, he claimed that Diem was "building . . . a replica of the totalitarian regime" he claimed to oppose. Morgenthau has been called a "prophet without honor" for his early and prescient commentary on the war, and was ranked by his fellow intellectuals as the "second most influential figure in shaping their views on Vietnam." See Jennifer W. See's article (2001).

14. A second irony is the similarity of France's position on Vietnam compared to its position on the 2003 US incursion into Iraq. In both cases, the French leadership and the French people were adamantly opposed to US military action, and many would argue, in both cases they were right about the inadvisability of the undertaking.

15. Although de Gaulle thought Kennedy paid little attention to his June 1961 warnings on Vietnam, Kennedy invoked the French experience a few weeks later when arguing with his advisors against an escalation against the North (Freedman, 2000:318). On the other hand, he complained in September that the Americans were glad to get counsel, but after "carrying this load for eighteen years . . . we would like a little more assistance, real assistance" (Johnson, 1971:63).

16. De Gaulle was not the only French connection that was underused. Colin Powell is reported as believing that if American presidents had read Bernard Fall's work on Vietnam it might have changed American policy, since "Fall makes painfully clear that we had almost no understanding of what we had gotten ourselves into" in Vietnam (Powell, 1995:143). Robert McNamara, in his retrospective look at his years at Defense, alleged that, "[n]o Southeast Asian counterparts existed for senior officials to consult when making decisions on Vietnam" (McNamara, 1995:322). To this, Dorothy Fall, Bernard Fall's widow, responded that they lived ten miles away in the Washington, D.C. suburbs, but McNamara never called (Ruane, 2007). Paul Kattenburg, who was the Vietnam desk officer in the State Department, says that it is incorrect to say that the United States was ever without experts on Vietnam. He states that he could name at least a dozen officials and outsiders knowledgeable on Vietnam, even for the late 1940s and early 1950s (Kattenburg, 1980:170). Not only was Fall's expertise not used, but his

house was under surveillance by the FBI, presumably because the State Department considered him a "neutralist, crypto-communist."

17. What is more baffling than the silence of the policy makers on the Sino-Soviet dispute is that of the postwar analysts. David M. Barrett's book on Lyndon Johnson and his advisors on Vietnam, for instance, has not one index reference to the dispute. His index has one entry for "De Gaulle," but it has no relevance to Vietnam (Barrett, 1993). One analyst is a notable exception to the silence on the Sino-Soviet clash, devoting a whole chapter to it. Perhaps it is no accident that he is British (Freedman, 2000). See also Logevall (1999), Kail (1973), and Thomas C. Schelling in Hoffmann (1981).

18. According to Record, the factors contributing to US defeat included an ill-conceived-attrition strategy; an essentially superfluous bombing campaign; fractured command authority; self-defeating personnel rotation policies, and low combat-to-support ratios.

    French sociologist Michel Crozier describes a visit to South Vietnam just as the Americans were "taking over" from the French. He was shocked at the total ignorance of the Americans, combined with a marvelous self-confidence in being able to guide the country. The Americans refused to draw on any of the French expertise on the country. The French were regarded as "tainted" because they had lost their war (Hoffmann, 1981:13).

19. In addition to the ARVN's inability to communicate through organization, Lansdale pointed out that the government badly needed a broadcasting network that could compete with the North, and had needed it since 1954 (FRUS, 6/4/59). It was easier for troops and civilians to listen to Hanoi than to Saigon.

20. Komer's prescient analysis of what went wrong in Vietnam was said to be circulating among Americans in Iraq, where seemingly similar problems were plentiful. Komer, known for his optimism and outspokenness, had been in charge of pacification in Vietnam.

21. Thomas C. Schelling said: "If in 1964 one had added up what the United States was going to commit—everything from B-52s to the latest in fighter aircraft and ultimately 'smart bombs' and electronic fences—anybody would have said, 'you don't need sixty-four times as much as you think it will take.' We committed enough to sink the country . . . " (Hoffmann, 1981:9).

22. The irony is that even though the emphasis in Vietnam was on killing the enemy, much of the time US and ARVN soldiers couldn't find the enemy, as witnessed by the futility of many "search-and-destroy" missions (Nagl, 2005:115).

23. In August 1964, Sir Robert Thompson, who had advised the United States on Vietnam for two years and had been hopeful about the development of the situation, finally gave up and wrote a frank memorandum to London predicting defeat in the near term. See the account in (Logevall, 1999:222). For one US summary of Thompson's critique of the operation, see (FRUS, 4/6/62).

CHAPTER 6

1. Serbia's Milosevic and Croatia's Tudjman agreed in March 25, 1991, at Karadodevo and later at Tikves, that Bosnia should be divided between them, thus extending the borders of both of their countries, but endangering Bosnia and other multiethnic entities such as Macedonia as Yugoslavia continued to disintegrate (Mahmutcehajic, 2001:138).

2. A comprehensive summary of the results of elections in the various republics and the impact on the direction of regional events is given in Cohen (1995).

3. Of the 160,000 Muslims, 2,000 died at the hands of Croats, the rest were killed by Serbs. Of the 30,000 Croats, an estimated 2, 000 were killed by Muslims, the rest by Serbs. Of the 25,000 Serbs dead, one-half were by Croats, one-half by Muslims. The data are by the Zagreb demographer, Vladimir Zerjavic, and given in Ramet (2002:239).

4. Susan L. Woodward was one of the most vocal proponents of a US interest in maintaining the alliance as a vital US interest. She deplored the fact that the United States focused on humanitarian justifications for its actions in Bosnia instead of explaining the US security interests that should have underlain a more vigorous US presence in the area (Woodward, 1995:11, 324–25, 398). See also Lewis (1995).

5. Hoffmann's argument is a refutation of the attack on "foreign policy as social work" by Michael Mandelbaum (Hoffmann, 1996; Mandelbaum, 1996).

6. Eagleburger himself admitted that he had misjudged Milosevic, believing him someone with whom the United States could do business (Cohen, 1995:218). At times, his comments bordered on the incoherent: "It is difficult to explain, but this war is not rational. There is no rationality at all about ethnic conflict. It is gut; it is hatred; it's not for any common set of values or purposes; it just goes on. And that kind of warfare is most difficult to bring to a halt" (US Department of State, 1992b).

7. See Brzezinski (1994), Perle (1994), and Odom (1994).

8. Robert W. Merry provides an American perspective favoring partition as "the only solution that could have seriously addressed the Balkan agonies" and "proved successful" (Merry, 2005:140–41).

9. In defense of the Clinton administration, it should be pointed out that V-O caught them just coming to power, and preceded their ground-up review of their whole policy toward Bosnia. On this and for more detail on V-O, see Bert (1997:Chapter 11).

10. David Owen quoted Vuk Draskovic, the main opposition figure in Belgrade, as saying that the Americans took the worst possible course. They refused to get serious about V-O, but they also declined to take military action (Bert, 1997:195).

11. Discussion of figures and sources is in Bert (1997:255–57) and Burg and Shoup, (1999:131–39).

12. Two interpretations of the dissolution of Yugoslavia more favorable to the Serbs than most are Boyd (1995) and Woodward (1995).

13. A notable exception to the timidity—sometimes the result of a lack of armor—of many UNPROFOR personnel was one Swedish Colonel Ulf Hendrikson whose battalion had arrived at Tuzla with Leopard II tanks in June 1993. When he arrived at checkpoints where soldiers refused to remove mines blocking the way, he said, "I have told the soldiers if they don't move the mines we'll blow their heads off," and, he added with satisfaction that he had "always gotten through" (Gow, 1997:129).

14. "Rarely, if ever, in history can so much time, energy, manpower, finance and diplomatic attention have been applied to a conflict with so little reward . . . only after four years of individual and collective effort had failed, was the war stopped" (Gow, 1997:2).

15. As Richard Holbrooke put it, "The Bosnian Serbs, poorly trained bullies and criminals, would not stand up to NATO air strikes the way the seasoned and indoctrinated Vietcong and North Vietnamese had. And, as we had seen in the Krajina, Belgrade was not going to back the Bosnian Serbs the way Hanoi had backed the Vietcong." He also quoted General Morillon, a former commander of U.N. forces in Bosnia saying, "Hit them the first time they challenge you and they won't respond again" (Holbrooke, 1998:93: 218).

16. Many people in the United States were delighted that a meaningful response was finally being made. Holbrooke asked his colleagues why this was being done now when it had not happened in the past. The best explanation seemed to be that US officials had finally reached the end of the line. The president and everybody else had had enough. Key Republicans, however, showed little enthusiasm for sending troops to Bosnia to enforce the settlement. Moreover, a year before the presidential election, 70 percent of the public did not want American troops sent to Bosnia under any circumstances (Holbrooke 1998: 103, 173, 219). An account of the bombing is also in Holbrooke.

CHAPTER 7

1. A tribute to the power of Afghan nationalism, the anniversary of this British rout is "one of the few official celebrations that successive Afghan regimes seem to have in common" (Johnson and Leslie, 2004:57). A very readable account of this incident is in Hopkirk (1992:230–69).

2. "Afghans today remain deeply bitter about their abandonment by the USA, for whom they fought the Cold War. In the 1980s the USA was prepared to 'fight till the last Afghan' to get even with the Soviet Union, but when the Soviets left, Washington was not prepared to help bring peace or feed a hungry people. Regional powers took advantage of the political vacuum the US retreat created, saw an opportunity to wield influence and jumped into the fray" (Rashid, 2000:209).

3. This is not to minimize the coordination, innovation, and even brilliance of the organization and planning that went into the attack. See Posen (2001/02).

4. "Leadership involves not so much marching gloriously at the head of the parade as paying quietly for the parade permit and the cleanup afterward. Leading the world means acting not as its commander in chief but as its concierge" (Mandelbaum, 2002:66).

5. Here Leslie Gelb's advice that before undertaking military action, a president needs to take her time and be as convinced as possible that the action is appropriate and no reasonable alternative exists. If necessary, "[t]ell those who demand instant action to go to hell" (Gelb, 2009:186).

6. "Our security establishment and senior elected leaders all think in terms of nations, not networks . . . The vast majority of the world's violence is now being perpetrated by networks of substate factions rather than the nations themselves" (Arquilla, 2008).

7. Another relevant argument for a policy maker considering military strategy is made by Fawaz A. Gerges, that the jihadi movement was badly split between those who wanted to concentrate on the "near enemy," their own governments, versus those who favored attacking the "far enemy," as happened in 9/11 (Gerges, 2005).

8. These questions perhaps belong as much to the intelligence agencies as to policy makers. Still, what is striking about the discussion of how to go into Afghanistan is the seeming lack of curiosity about these issues, which are not broached even in passing. An example of consideration of such issues in the CIA is in Coll (2004:Chapter 14).

9. The two movements and leaders were bound by mutual ideology and respect in a tight alliance. The Taliban would do anything for al Qaeda, Mullah Omar—the leader of the Taliban—declared to Western reporters in 2001. "Half my country was destroyed by 23 years of war. If the remaining half of Afghanistan is destroyed in trying to save Bin Laden, I am ready" (Byman and Pollack, 2007:111). See also Rais (2008:107, 118).

10. "Before 9/11, Pakistan's ties to the Taliban were extensive and well documented; despite Islamabad's claims to the contrary, there was at best a short hiatus in the relationship after 9/11" (Byman, 2008:53).

11. One international relations specialist was proffering exactly the needed advice at the time: "The United States should accompany its incentives to the Pakistani regime with sticks—for example, pressuring its military leaders to end their policy of exporting jihad to Indian Kashmir and to persuade them to transfer power to civilian hands through free and fair national elections by the October 2002 deadline set by Pakistan's Supreme Court. . . . Continued international pressure will force the regime to hold elections" (Walt, 2001/02:91).

12. An aide to former senator Joe Biden reports that four months after 9/11 and with the Taliban on the run after the US attack on Afghanistan, Senator Biden visited Kabul and met with the Afghan minister of education. To a question of what he most needed to do his job, instead of listing educational supplies or buildings, the minister replied that he needed just three things: security, security, security (Kurz, 2009).

13. A perspective from another angle is given by a civilian volunteer and former NPR reporter in Afghanistan, Sarah Chayes, who observed that in the whole American embassy, there was only one diplomat who spoke an Afghan language, learned 30 years earlier as a peace corps volunteer in Iran. Called up out of retirement, he lasted six weeks at the embassy. Most others lasted two or three weeks. "The significance of such a rapid changeover was that the United States had, in effect, no policy in Afghanistan. During that crucial window of time that could make or break the future of the country, America's sails were luffing . . . no guidance was coming from Washington. It was as though it had never occurred to anyone to think about what would happen once the Taliban were defeated . . . US action was slipshod and haphazard, just when Afghanistan needed legibility, direction, and consistency" (Chayes, 2006:151).

14. Sarah Chayes details the steps in the developing emergence of the Taliban, beginning about six months after the invasion. Starting with simply showing their turbaned heads, threats progressed to "night letters," or written threats, then a bomb or gunfire where the aim was bad, followed by the same when the aim was good (Chayes, 2006:Chapter 18).

15. Vivid examples of how corruption and warlord greed sapped the resources that should have gone for education and other vital causes are in Chayes (2006:Chapter 20).

16. According to Richard A. Clarke, on September 4, 2001, at a meeting discussing the threat from al Qaeda Powell laid out an aggressive strategy for inducing Pakistan to side with the Americans against al Qaeda and the Taliban. There were no funds, however. Rumsfeld, meanwhile, seemed more concerned with other alleged sources of terror such as Iraq (Clarke, 2004:237).

CHAPTER 8

1. On the demise of a bill aimed at imposing sanctions on Iraq for its use of gas on the Kurds and the Reagan administration's silence on Saddam's use of chemical weapons, see Galbraith (2006).

2. W. Patrick Lang, who served in various intelligence positions in the Defense Department, tells a revealing story about a conversation with Douglas Feith in 2001. Upon learning that Lang was an Arabist, Feith asked "Is it really true that you really know the Arabs this well, and that you speak Arabic this well? Is that really true?" When Lang answered that it was, Feith replied, "That's too bad." As Lang explained it, the neoconservatives hired people with similar political views, not people with specialized expertise. They had disregard for bureaucratic and professional authority (Wedel, 2009:180).

3. In Wolfowitz's words, "The truth is that for reasons that have a lot to do with the U.S. government bureaucracy we settled on the one issue that everyone could agree on which was weapons of mass destruction as the

core reason, but . . . there have always been three fundamental concerns. One is weapons of mass destruction, the second is support for terrorism, the third is the criminal treatment of the Iraqi people" (Galbraith, 2006:78–79).

4. Interestingly, when in an interview with C-SPAN in 1994 Dick Cheney was asked if the decision not to depose Saddam was a mistake, he indicated it was not. He stated that the occupation of Baghdad would have resulted in a "quagmire" and could have destabilized the entire region (Ferguson, 2008: 573). But Cheney also was complicit in an alternative plan to remove Saddam from power during the Gulf War (Western, 2005:186–87).

5. "From the day of our founding, we have proclaimed that every man and woman on this earth has rights and dignity and matchless value because they bear the image of the maker of heaven and earth. Across the generations, we have proclaimed the imperative of self-government, because no one is fit to be a master, and no one deserves to be a slave" (Bush, 2005). Rice also maintains that "American values are universal" (Kaplan, 2008:120). "If freedom is mankind's natural state," Fred Kaplan writes, "it's worth asking why it took until the eighteenth century—several millennia into civilization's development—for the concept to gain philosophical traction" (Kaplan, 2008:193).

6. As A. Trevor Thrall points out, prior to 9/11 the country suffered from the opposite problem, threat *deflation*, when people didn't worry about terrorism, defining it as something that "happens over there to other people" (Thrall, 2007:487).

7. The Iraq Liberation Act stated that "[i]t should be the policy of the United States to support efforts to remove the regime headed by Saddam Hussein from power in Iraq" (Iraq Liberation Act, 1998).

8. The effectiveness and morality of the trade embargo vs. the arguments for an invasion was discussed by Michael Walzer at the Brookings Institution prior to the beginning of the war. In retrospect the argument for regime change as a moral alternative to continuing the embargo seems shaky. One report notes that before the invasion 19 percent of children were malnourished, a frequently cited criticism of the embargo. In 2007, 28 percent of Iraqi children were malnourished (Greenwell, 2007).

9. An often overlooked point admitted by George Tenet is that there was no "technically collected" evidence on Iraq's WMD program. The intelligence services were basing every claim of current programs on information from defectors. This fact obviously diminished reliability of the information (Cramer, 2007:506).

10. One account describes meetings between US officials and Blix's weapons inspectors. Instead of the Americans querying the inspectors about their findings, they lectured the inspectors, who after all were the ones who had been out in the field, on how they should perform their job (Wedel, 2009).

11. It is well-known that the confidence of many administration officials in both Hans Blix and most inspectors was limited, although Blix had long

experience in the weapons control and inspection business and had a good reputation. Perhaps the looniest sentiment came from Karl Rove, a Norwegian-American, who "was convinced of the historical duplicity of the Swedes, who had invaded Norway in 1814 and ruled the country until 1905. There was a long-standing grudge" (Woodward, 2004:176, 224, 240, 250; Blix, 2004:12–13). If one discounted all nationalities whose country had participated in imperialist adventures or aggression, the roster of reliable potential weapons inspectors would indeed be short. According to one commentator, not only Bush the Younger, but his father as well as President Clinton all had little faith in the reliability of the inspectors (Davis, 2006:3).

12. An alternate take on the Iraq conflict can be found in Byman (2008a).

13. In addition to the state and Army War College studies already mentioned, there was a heavily researched study by James Fallows of the *Atlantic Monthly*, a study by Anthony Cordesman entitled "Planning for Peace as a Self-Inflicted World," a briefing by Roberto M. Perito given in February to the Defense Policy Board and other studies by other parts of the government, universities and think tanks. For the most part, "these analyses agreed both on what the principal challenges of occupied Iraq would be and on how to handle them" (Ferguson, 2008:44–45; Gordon and Trainor, 2006).

14. Bremer's calendar for achieving representative democracy was: (1) start with the Americans appointing a governing council, (2) June 2004—sovereignty would be returned to Iraq with an appointed interim government, (3) January 2005—national election to be held to determine an interim national assembly that would draft a constitution and select an acting government, (4) October 2005—vote on the constitution—if it passed, and (5) December 2005—there would be another national election to select a permanent government (West, 2008a:39).

15. It is telling of how deep into the American grain the idea of exporting democracy is embedded, that an article by Douglas A. Ollivant and Eric D. Chewning published in *Military Review* that is alleged to be the foundation of Petraeus's Baghdad security plan cites "liberal democracy and free-market capitalism" as the "competing cause" that is crucial to fighting a counterinsurgency war (Ollivant and Chewning, 2006). Building a market economy was an integral part of democratization in Iraq, in the American view. As Bremer said when asked about the wisdom of privatizing all the state-owned enterprises, "If we don't get their economy right, no matter how fancy our political transformation, it won't work" (Chandrasekaran, 2006:62).

16. Robert Hutchings, chairman of the NIC, refers to the intelligence assessments and the reactions to them in an interview with Charles Ferguson (Ferguson, 2008:346–48).

17. For accounts of the reclaiming of Baghdad neighborhoods that had become havens for the Sunni insurgency using Petraeus's strategy, and the positive results, see Robinson (2008).

CHAPTER 9

1. As indicated by presidential candidate John McCain's statement that Vietnam was a "noble cause," made in the 2008 campaign.

2. The sheer ignorance of some in the Bush administration was perhaps best symbolized by Press Secretary Dana Perino, who admitted that when the subject of the 1962 Cuban missile crisis came up at a White House briefing, she "really [didn't] know about . . . the Cuban Missile Crisis . . . It had to do with Cuba and missiles, I'm pretty sure" (Baker, 2007). A woman working next to the president wasn't aware of the moment in history, less than 50 years previously, when a massive nuclear exchange that could have destroyed much of the industrialized world was only narrowly avoided.

3. I. William Zartman argues that in many cases early (nonmilitary) intervention could have prevented a failed state or saved lives or economic value. Because there was no early intervention, at a later date military intervention became necessary, or at least was undertaken. Many of his examples would not have justified intervention on security grounds as defined here (Zartman, 2005).

REFERENCES AND FURTHER READING

ABC News. 1994. Peter Jennings Reporting, "While Americans Watched: The Bosnian Tragedy," Shows #ABC-51, March 17.

Adelman, Ken. 2002. "Cakewalk in Iraq," *The Washington Post*, February 13, A27.

Ajami, Fouad. 2006. *The Foreigner's Gift: The Americans, the Arabs, and the Iraqis in Iraq* (New York: Free Press).

Al-Khalil, Samir. 1989. *Republic of Fear: The Inside Story of Saddam's Iraq* (New York: Pantheon Books).

Anderson, John Ward. 2007. "NATO Conflicted over Afghanistan," *The Washington Post*, October 21, A21.

Anderson, Jon Lee. 2002. *The Lion's Grave: Dispatches from Afghanistan* (New York: Grove Press).

Anonymous. 2004. *Imperial Hubris: Why the West Is Losing the War on Terror* (Washington, D.C.: Brassey's).

Arnold, James R. 1991. *The First Domino: Eisenhower, the Military, and America's Intervention in Vietnam* (New York: William Morrow).

Arquilla, John. 2008. *Worst Enemy: The Reluctant Transformation of the American Military* (Chicago: Ivan R. Dee).

Bacon, Kenneth H., and Kristele Younes. 2008. "Outside and Inside Iraq's Borders, a Forgotten Exodus," *The Washington Post*, January 20.

Baker, James A, III. 1995. *The Politics of Diplomacy: Revolution, War and Peace, 1989–1992* (New York: G. P. Putnam's Sons).

Baker, Peter. 2007. "Bush Knows Well the Hazards of the Trail," *The Washington Post*, December 10.

Barber, Benjamin R. 1996. *Jihad vs. McWorld: How Globalism and Tribalism Are Reshaping the World* (New York: Ballantine Books).

Barrett, David M. 1993. *Uncertain Warriors: Lyndon Johnson and His Vietnam Advisers* (Lawrence: University Press of Kansas).

Bearden, Milton. 2001. "Afghanistan, Graveyard of Empires," *Foreign Affairs* 80, no. 6:17–30.

———. 2009. "Curse of the Khyber Pass," *The National Interest*, no. 100, March/April, 4–12.

Beckett, Ian F. W. 1988. "The United States Experience," in his ed., *The Roots of Counterinsurgency: Armies and Guerrilla Warfare, 1900–1945* (New York: Blandford).

Beisner, Robert L. 1968. *Twelve against Empire: The Anti-Imperialists, 1898–1900* (New York: McGraw-Hill).

Bell, Coral. 1999. "American Ascendancy and the Pretense of Concert," *The National Interest*, no. 57:55–63.

Bensahel, Nora et al. 2008. *After Saddam: Prewar Planning and the Occupation of Iraq* (Santa Monica: RAND).

Bergen, Peter. 2009. "The Battle for Tora Bora," *The New Republic*, December 30.

Berlin, Isaiah. 1993. *The Hedgehog and the Fox* (Chicago: Elephant Paperbacks).

Bert, Wayne. 1997. *The Reluctant Superpower: United States' Policy in Bosnia, 1991–95* (Basingstoke: Macmillan).

Betts, Richard K. 1994. "The Delusion of Impartial Intervention," *Foreign Affairs* 73, no. 6:20–33.

Blackwill, Robert D. 1993. "A Taxonomy for Defining US National Security Interests in the 1990s and Beyond," in *Europe in Global Change: Strategies and Options for Europe,* ed. Werner Weidenfeld and Josef Janning (Gutersloh: Bertelsmann Foundation Publ.).

Blight, James G., Janet M. Lang, David A. Welch. 2009. *Vietnam If Kennedy Had Lived: Virtual JFK* (Lanham: Rowman & Littlefield).

Blix, Hans. 2004. *Disarming Iraq: The Search for Weapons of Mass Destruction* (London: Bloomsbury).

———. 2008. Interview on Diane Rehm Show, NPR, April 10.

Boehlert, Eric. 2006. *Lapdogs: How the Press Rolled over for Bush* (New York: Free Press).

Boot, Max. 2002. *The Savage Wars of Peace: Small Wars and the Rise of American Power* (New York: Basic Books).

Booth, Ken. 1979. *Strategy and Ethnocentrism* (New York: Holmes and Meier).

Bose, Meena. 2006. "What Makes a Great President? An Analysis of Leadership Qualities in Fred I. Greenstein's The Presidential Difference," in *The Art of Political Leadership: Essays in Honor of Fred I. Greenstein,* ed. Larry Berman (Lanham: Rowman and Littlefield).

Boucher, Richard. 2001. Daily Press Briefing, US Department of State, November 21.

Boudreau, Vince. 2003. "Methods of Domination and Modes of Resistance: The US Colonial State and Philippine Mobilization in Comparative Perspective," in *The American Colonial State in the Philippines: Global Perspectives,* ed. Julian Go and Anne L. Foster, (Durham: Duke University Press).

Boyd, Charles G. 1995. "Making Peace with the Guilty," *Foreign Affairs* 74, no. 5: 22–38.

Bradsher, Keith. 2009. "In Downturn, China Sees Path to Growth," *The New York Times (NYT)* online, March 16).

Brands, H. W. 1998. "Exemplary America versus Interventionist America," in *At the End of the American Century: America's Role in the Post-Cold War World,* ed. Robert L. Hutchings (Baltimore: Johns Hopkins University Press).

Bremer, L. Paul III, with Malcolm McConnell. 2006. *My Year in Iraq: The Struggle to Build a Future of Hope* (New York: Threshold Editions).

Brooks, David. 2009 Comments, Jim Lehrer News Hours, March 27.

Brown, Seyom. 1992. *International Relations in a Changing Global System* (Boulder, CO: Westview Press).

———. 1994. *The Faces of Power: Constancy and Change in United States Foreign Policy from Truman to Johnson* (New York: Columbia University Press).

Brzezinski, Zbigniew. 1994. "NATO: Expand or Die?" *NYT*, December 28, A15.

Bumiller, Elisabeth. 2010. "Intelligence Report Offers Dim Views of Afghan War," *NYT* online, December 14.

Burg, Steven L., and Paul S. Shoup. 1999. *The War in Bosnia-Herzegovina: Ethnic Conflict and International Intervention* (Armonk, NY: ME Sharpe).

Bush, George W. 2002a. "West Point Commencement Speech," in *America and the World: Debating the New Shape of International Politics* (New York: Council on Foreign Relations).

———. 2002b. "President Outlines War Effort," Speech at Virginia Military Institute, April 17.

———. 2005. "There is no Justice without Freedom," Second Inaugural Address, January 21.

Buzan, Barry. 1991. *People, States, and Fear: An Agenda for International Security Studies in the Post-Cold War Era* (Boulder, CO: Lynne Rienner).

Buzan, Barry, and Ole Waever. 2003. *Regions and Powers: The Structure of International Security* (Cambridge: Cambridge University Press).

Buzan, Barry, Ole Waever, and Jaap de Wilde. 1998. *Security: A New Framework for Analysis* (Boulder, CO: Lynne Rienner).

Byman, Daniel. 2008a. "An Autopsy of the Iraq Debacle: Policy Failure or Bridge Too Far?" *Security Studies* 17:599–643.

———. 2008b. 'Rogue Operators," *The National Interest*, no. 96:52–59.

Byman, Daniel L., and Kenneth M. Pollack. 2001. "Let Us Now Praise Famous Men: Bringing the Statesman Back In," *International Security* 25, no. 4:107–46.

———. 2007. *Things Fall Apart: Containing the Spillover from an Iraqi Civil War* (Washington, D.C.: Brookings Institution).

Byman, Daniel L., Kenneth Pollack, and Gideon Rose. 1999. "The Rollback Fantasy," *Foreign Affairs* 78, no.1:24–41.

Campbell, James H., and Michael E. O'Hanlon. 2008. "The State of Iraq: An Update," Brookings Institution, Washington, D. C., June 22.

Campbell, Jason, Michael O'Hanlon, and Amy Unikewicz. 2008. "The State of Iraq: An Update," *NYT* online, December 28.

Caverley, Jonathan D. 2009. "The Myth of Military Myopia: Democracy, Small Wars, and Vietnam," *International Security* 34, no. 3:119–57.

Chandrasekaran, Rajiv. 2006. *Imperial Life in the Emerald City: Inside Iraq's Green Zone* (New York: Alfred A. Knopf).

Chayes, Sarah. 2006. *The Punishment of Virtue: Inside Afghanistan after the Taliban* (New York: Penguin).

Chollet, Derek. 2005. "Dayton at Ten: A Look Back," in *The Tenth Annivrsary of the Dayton Accords and Afterwards: Reflections on Post-Conflict State- and Nation-Building*, ed. Nida Gelazis (Washington, D.C.: Woodrow Wilson International Center for Scholars).

CIA. 2002. Iraq National Intelligence Estimate (declassified sections) in Public Affairs Reports, *The WMD Mirage: Iraq's Decade of Deception and America's Fake Premise for War* (Cambridge, MA: Public Affairs, 2005).

Cigar, Norman, Branka Magas, and Ivo Zanic. 2001. "Introduction," in *The War in Croatia and Bosnia-Hercegovina,* ed. Magas and Zanic (London: Frank Cass).

Cirincione, Joseph et al. 2004. *WMD in Iraq: Evidence and Implications* (Washington, D.C.: Carnegie Endowment for International Peace).

Clarke, Richard A. 2004. *Against All Enemies: Inside America's War on Terror* (New York: Free Press).

Clinton Iraq Policy Letter. 1998 at http://www.newamericancentury.org/iraqclintonletter.htm.

Cogan, Charles. 2003. *French Negotiating Behavior: Dealing with La Grande Nation* (Washington, D.C.: United States Institute of Peace).

Cohen, Lenard J. 1995. *Broken Bonds: Yugoslavia's Disintegration and Balkan Politics in Transition,* second edition (Boulder, CO: Westview Press).

Cohen, Michael A., Maria Figueroa Kupcu, and Parag Khanna. 2008. "The New Colonialists," *Foreign Policy,* July/August, 74–79.

Coll, Steve. 2004. *Ghost Wars: The Secret History of the CIA, Afghanistan, and Bin Laden, From the Soviet Invasion to September 10, 2001* (New York: Penguin).

Collier, Ellen C. 1993. "Instances of Use of United States Forces Abroad, 1798–1993," *CRS Issue Brief* (Washington, D.C.: Congressional Research Service) at http://www.fas.org/man/crs/crs_931007.htm, last accessed August 4, 2009.

Collier, Paul. 2005. "The Market for Civil War," in *International Politics: Enduring Concepts and Contemporary Issues,* ed. Robert J. Art and Robert Jervis (New York: Longman).

Collins, Alan. 2003. *Security and Southeast Asia: Domestic, Regional, and Global Issues* (Boulder, CO: Lynn Rienner).

Committee on Armed Services. 1994. US Senate, 103rd Congress, second session, June 23.

Cordesman, Anthony. 2009. "Sanctum FATA," *The National Interest,* no. 101: 28–38.

Craig, Gordon A., and Alexander L. George. 1990. *Force and Statecraft: Diplomatic Problems of Our Time,* second edition (New York: Oxford, 1990).

Cramer, Jane Kellett. 2007. "Militarized Patriotism: Why the Marketplace of Ideas Failed Before the Iraq War," *Security Studies* 16, no. 3:489–524.

Crnobrnja, Mihailo. 1994. *The Yugoslav Drama* (Montreal: McGill-Queen's University Press).

Cullinone, Michael. 2003. *Ilustrado Politics: Filipino Elite Responses to American Rule, 1898–1908* (Manila: Ateneo de Manila University Press).

Daalder, Ivo H., and James M. Lindsay. 2003. *America Unbound: The Bush Revolution in Foreign Policy* (Washington, D.C.: Brookings Institution).

Dallaire, Romeo. 2003. *Shake Hands with the Devil: The Failure of Humanity in Rwanda* (Toronto: Random House Canada).

Dallek, Robert. 1983. *The American Style of Foreign Policy: Cultural Politics and Foreign Affairs* (New York: Oxford University Press).

Davis, John. 2006. *Presidential Policies and the Road to the Second Iraq War: From Forty One to Forty Three* (Burlington, VT: Ashgate).

de Gaulle, Charles. 1971. *Memoirs of Hope: Renewal and Endeavor* (New York: Simon and Schuster).

de Tocqueville, Alexis. 2002. *Democracy in America* (Chicago: University of Chicago Press).

DeYoung, Karen. 2007. "Iraq War's Statistics Prove Fleeting," *The Washington Post*, March 19, A1.

Diamond, Larry. 2005. *Squandered Victory: The American Occupation and the Bungled Effort to Bring Democracy to Iraq* (New York: Henry Holt).

Divjak, Jovan. 2001. "The First Phase, 1992–1993: Struggle for Survival and Genesis of the Army of Bosnia-Herzogovina," in *The War in Croatia and Bosnia-Herzogovina,* ed. Magas and Zanic.

Dobbins, James F. 2008. *After the Taliban: Nation-Building in Afghanistan* (Washington, D.C.: Potomac Books).

Dobbins, James, John G. McGinn, Keith Crane, Seth G. Jones, Rollie Lal, Andrew Rathmell, Rachel Swanger, and Anga Timilsina. 2003. *America's Role in Nation-Building: From Germany to Iraq* (Santa Monica: RAND).

Dominquez, Jorge I. 1979. "Responses to Occupations by the United States: Caliban's Dilemma," *Pacific Historical Review* 48:591–605.

Donia, Robert J., and John V. A. Fine, Jr. 1994. *Bosnia and Hercegovina: A Tradition Betrayed* (New York: Columbia University Press).

Dorronsoro, Gilles. 2005. *Revolution Unending Afghanistan: 1979 to the Present* (London: Hurst and Co.).

Drinnon, Richard. 1999. "The Metaphysics of Empire: American Imperialism in the Age of Jefferson and Monroe," in Krenn, *The Impact of Race on US Foreign Policy.*

Duiker, William J. 1994. *U.S. Containment Policy and the Conflict in Indochina* (Stanford: Stanford University Press).

Edwards, George C. III, and Desmond S. King, eds. 2007. *The Polarized Presidency of George W. Bush* (Oxford: Oxford University Press).

Eisenhower, Dwight D. 1963. *Mandate for Change: The White House Years, 1953–1956* (New York: Doubleday).

Ekbladh, David. 2010. *The Great American Mission: Modernization and the Construction of an American World Order* (Princeton, NJ: Princeton University Press).

Elliott, David W. P. 2007. *The Vietnamese War: Revolution and Social Change in the Mekong Delta 1930–1975,* concise edition (Armonk, NY: M. E. Sharpe).

Elman, Colin. 1996. "Horses for Courses: Why Not Neorealist Theories of Foreign Policy?" *Strategic Studies* 6, no. 1: 7–53.

Ewans, Martin. 2002. *Afghanistan: A Short History of Its People and Politics* (New York: Perennial).

Faiola, Anthony. 2009. "US Signals New Era for Global Economy," *The Washington Post,* April 2.

Fall, Bernard B. 1966. *Hell in a Very Small Place: The Siege of Dien Bien Phu* (New York: Random House).

Fallows, James. 2006. *Blind into Baghdad: America's War in Iraq* (New York: Vintage).

Ferguson, Charles H. 2008. *No End in Sight: Iraq's Descent into Chaos* (New York: Public Affairs).

Ferguson, Niall. 2004. *Colossus: The Rise and Fall of the American Empire* (New York: Penguin).

Fick, Nathaniel, and John Nagl. 2009. Letters, *Foreign Policy,* March/April, 8.

Filkins, Dexter. 2008. *The Forever War* (New York: Alfred A. Knopf).

———. 2010. "With U. S. Aid, Warlord Builds Afghan Empire," *NYT* online, June 6, 1.

———. 2011. "The Afghan Bank Heist," *The New Yorker,* February 14 and 21.

Fogarty, Brian E. 2009. *Fascism: Why Not Here?* (Washington, D.C.: Potomac Books).

Freedman, Lawrence. 1994. "Why the West Failed," *Foreign Policy,* no. 94:53–69.

———. 2000. *Kennedy's Wars: Berlin, Cuba, Laos, and Vietnam* (New York: Oxford University Press).

Foreign Relations of the United States (FRUS) (2/24/51) Heath to Acheson, 1951, Asia and Pacific, vol. VI, part I, p. 384 at (1994). http://digital.library.wisc.edu/1711.dl/FRUS.FRUS1951v06p1, accessed 12/9/09.

———. (3/20/51) NIE 20, 1951, Asia and Pacific, vol. VI, part I, pp. 27–28.

———. (5/17/51) NSC 48/5, 1951, Asia and Pacific, vol. VI, part I, p.56.

———. (6/29/51) Memorandum Heath to Acheson, 1951, Asia and Pacific, vol. VI, part I, pp. 432–37.

———. (9/20/51) Record of Meeting at Pentagon, 1951, Asia and Pacific, vol. VI, part I, pp. 517.

———. (1/3/55) Memorandum Lansdale to Collins, 1955–57, Vietnam, vol. I, pp. 3–7.

———. (6/7/56) Paper, Radford (Chair, Joint Chiefs of Staff), 1955–57, Vietnam, vol. 1, p. 705.

———. (5/14/57) NIE 63.2–57, doc. 383, 1955–57, Vietnam, vol. I, p. 818.

———. (6/4/58) Operations Plan for Viet-nam, doc. 17, 1958–60, vol. I, Vietnam, pp. 44–45.

———. (11/17/58) Memorandum of Conversation, Department of State, 1958–60, Vietnam, vol. 1, p. 101.

———. (5/26/59) NIE 63–59, 1958–60, Vietnam, vol. I, p. 202.

———. (6/4/59) Lansdale to O'Donnell, 1958–60, Vietnam, vol. I, pp. 204–06.

———. (12/7/59) Despatch [sic] Durbow (Ambassador in Vietnam) to Department of State, doc. 97, 1958–60, Vietnam, vol. I, pp. 256, 262.

———. (1/4/62) Talking Paper, Levy, Joint Chiefs of Staff, doc. 6, 1961–63, vol. II, Vietnam, 1962.

———. (1/11/62) Memorandum Johnson (Policy Planning) to Rostow, doc. 12, 1961–63, Vietnam, vol. II.

———. (1/16/62) Memorandum of Conversation, Fishel, doc. 24, 1961–63, Vietnam, vol. II.

———. (1/19/62) Letter Martin to Cottrell, doc. 29, 1961–63, Vietnam, vol. II.

———. (2/2/62) Paper, Hilsman, doc. 42, 1961–63, Vietnam, vol. II.

———. (2/6/62) Editorial Note, doc. 50, 1961–63, Vietnam, vol. II.

————. (3/23/62) Airgram, Embassy to Department of State, doc. 127, 1961–63, Vietnam, vol. II.

————. (4/6/62) Memorandum Cottrell to Harriman, doc. 149, 1961–63, Vietnam, vol. II.

————. (5/11/62) Memorandum Wood to Harriman, doc. 188, 1961–63, Vietnam, vol. II.

Fulbright, J. William. 1966. *The Arrogance of Power* (New York: Random House).

Gaddis, John Lewis. 2005. *Strategies of Containment: A Critical Appraisal of American National Security Policy during the Cold War* (New York: Oxford University Press).

Galbraith, Peter W. 2006. *The End of Iraq: How American Incompetence Created a War without End* (New York: Simon and Schuster).

Gall, Carlotta. 2008. "Afghan Leader Criticizes U.S. on Conduct of War," *NYT* online, April 26.

Garofano, John. 2002. "Tragedy or Choice in Vietnam? Learning to Think Outside the Archival Box: A Review Essay," *International Security* 26, no. 4:143–68.

Gates, Robert. 2011. Speech at West Point, February 25.

Gelb, Leslie. 2009. *Power Rules: How Common Sense Can Rescue American Foreign Policy* (New York: Harpers).

Gelb, Leslie H., and Richard K. Betts. 1979. *The Irony of Vietnam: The System Worked* (Washington, D.C.: The Brookings Institution).

Gelman, Barton. 2008. *Angler: The Cheney Vice Presidency* (New York: Penguin).

Gerges, Fawaz A. 2005. *The Far Enemy: Why Jihad Went Global* (Cambridge: Cambridge University Press).

George, Alexander L., and Juliette L. George. 1964. *Woodrow Wilson and Colonel House: A Personality Study* (New York: Dover).

Gholz, Eugene, Daryl G. Press, Harvey M. Sapolsky. 1997. "Come Home, America: The Strategy of Restraint in the Face of Temptation," *International Security* 19, no. 4:5–48.

Gilpin, Robert, 1981. *War and Change in World Politics* (New York: Cambridge University Press).

Giustozzi, Antonio. 2008. *Koran, Kalashnikov, and Laptop: The Neo-Taliban Insurgency in Afghanistan* (New York: Columbia University Press).

Glad, Betty, and Kenneth Kitts. 2006. "Sidestepping the Hawks: Eisenhower, the Solarium Study, and the Hungarian Crisis of 1956," in *The Art of Political Leadership: Essays in Honor of Fred I. Greenstein,* ed. Larry Berman (Lanham: Rowman and Littlefield).

Goldstein, Gordon M. 2008. *Lessons in Disaster: McGeorge Bundy and the Path to War in Vietnam* (New York: Times Books).

Gopal, Anand. 2010. *The Battle for Afghanistan: Militancy and Conflict in Kandahar* (Washington, DC: New America Foundation), November.

Gordon, Michael R., and Bernard E. Trainor. 2006. *Cobra II: The Inside Story of the Invasion and Occupation of Iraq* (New York: Pantheon).

Gordon, Philip H. 2003. "Bush's Middle East Vision," *Survival* 45, no. 1:155–64.

Gow, James. 1997. *Triumph of the Lack of Will: International Diplomacy and the Yugoslav War* (New York: Columbia University Press).

Gow, James, and Ivan Zverzhanovski. 2006. "The Milosevic Trial: Purpose and Performance," in *Conflict in Southeastern Europe at the End of the Twentieth Century: A "Scholars" Initiative Assesses Some of the Controversies,* ed. Thomas Emmert and Charles Ingrao (London: Routledge).

Graham, Bob. 2004. *Intelligence Matters: The CIA, the FBI, Saudi Arabia, and the Failure of America's War on Terror* (New York: Random House).

Gray, Colin S. 2005. "The American Way of War: Critique and Implications," in Anthony D. McIvor, ed., *Rethinking the Principles of War* (Annapolis: Naval Institute Press).

Green, Joshua. 2007. "The Rove Presidency," *The Atlantic Monthly,* September: 52–72.

Greenstein, Fred I., and John P. Burke et al. 1989. *How Presidents Test Reality: Decisions on Vietnam, 1954 and 1965* (New York: Russell Sage).

Greenwell, Megan. 2007. "A Dismal Picture of Life in Iraq," *The Washington Post,* July 31, A14.

Grunder, Garel A., and William E. Livezey. 1951. *The Philippines and the United States* (Norman: University of Oklahoma Press).

Gurtov, Melvin. 1967. *The First Vietnam Crisis: Chinese Communist Strategy and United States Involvement, 1953–1954* (New York: Columbia University Press).

Haass, Richard N. 1994. *Intervention: The Use of American Military Force in the Post-Cold War World* (Washington, D.C.: Carnegie Endowment).

Haley, P. Edward. 2006. *Strategies of Dominance: The Misdirection of US Foreign Policy* (Baltimore: Johns Hopkins Press, 2006).

Hall, Rodney Bruce. 1999. *National Collective Identity: Social Constructs and International Systems* (New York: Columbia University Press).

Halle, Louis J. 1985. *The United States Acquires the Philippines: Consensus vs. Reality* (New York: University Press of America).

Hammes, Thomas X. 2006. *The Sling and the Stone* (Minneapolis: Zenith Press).

———. 2008. "The Art of Petraeus," *The National Interest,* no. 98:53–59.

Hartz, Louis. 1955. *The Liberal Tradition in America: An Interpretation of American Political Thought since the Revolution* (New York: Harcourt, Brace).

Hashim, Ahmed S. 2006. *Insurgency and Counter-Insurgency in Iraq* (Ithaca, NY: Cornell University Press).

Heilbrunn, Jacob. 2008. "The Shadow President," *New York Times Book Review,* October 10.

Helfers, John. 2006. "Hearts and Minds in 2025: How Foreign and Domestic Culture Will Shape the Future Battlefield," in *Beyond Shock and Awe: Warfare in the 21st Century,* ed. Eric L. Haney and Brian M. Thomsen (New York: Berkley Caliber).

Hiltermann, Joost. 2010. "Iraq: The Impasse," *The New York Review of Books,* August 19.

Hirsh, Michael. 2001. "America Adrift: Writing the History of the Post Cold Wars," *Foreign Affairs* 80, no. 6:158–64.

Hodgson, Godfrey. 2009. *The Myth of American Exceptionalism* (New Haven, CT: Yale University Press).

Hoffman, Bruce, and Seth G. Jones. 2008. "Cellphones in the Hindu Kush," *The National Interest* 96:42–51.

Hoffmann, Stanley. 1968a. "The American Style: Our Past and Our Principles," *Foreign Affairs* 46, no. 2:362–76.

———.1968b. *Gulliver's Troubles or the Setting of American Foreign Policy* (New York: Council on Foreign Relations).

———. 1996. "In Defense of Mother Teresa: Morality in Foreign Policy," *Foreign Affairs* 75, no. 2:172–75.

———. et al. 1981. "Vietnam Reappraised," *International Security* 6, no. 1: 3–27.

Hofstadter, Richard. 1964. *The Paranoid Style in American Politics and other Essays* (New York: Vintage Books).

Holbrooke, Richard. 1998. *To End a War,* revised edition (New York: Modern Library).

Holsti, Kalevi J. 2006. "The Decline of Interstate War: Pondering Systemic Explanations," in *The Waning of Major War: Theories and Debates,* ed. Raimo Vayrynen (New York: Routledge).

Honey, P. J. 1963. *Communism in North Vietnam: Its Role in the Sino-Soviet Dispute* (Cambridge, MA: MIT Press).

Hopkirk, Peter. 1992. *The Great Game: The Struggle for Empire in Central Asia* (New York: Kodansha International).

Hunt, Michael H. 1987. *Ideology and American Foreign Policy* (New Haven, CT: Yale University Press).

Huntington, Samuel P. 1993. "Why International Primacy Matters," *International Security* 17, no. 4:68–83.

———. 1999. "The Lonely Superpower," *Foreign Affairs* 78, no. 5:28–49.

Huth, Paul K. 1998, "Major Power Intervention in International Crises, 1918–1988," *Journal of Conflict Resolution* 42, no. 6:744–70.

ICG (International Crisis Group). 2003. "Bosnia's Nationalist Governments: Paddy Ashdown and the Paradoxes of State Building," Europe Report No. 146, July 22.

———. 2004. "EUFOR: Changing Bosnia's Security Arrangements," Europe Briefing No. 31, June 29.

———. 2005. "Bosnia's Stalled Police Reform: No Progress, No E.U.," Europe Report No. 164, September 6.

———. 2007a. Comments, National Public Radio, July 12.

———. 2007b. "Ensuring Bosnia's Future: A New International Engagement Strategy," Europe Report No. 180, February 15.

Ignatius, David. 2008. "The Iran Problem," *The Washington Post,* April 9, A19.

IISS (International Institute for Strategic Studies) (1994) *Strategic Survey, 1993–4* (London: Brassey's).

Ikenberry, G. John. 1996. "The Myth of Post-Cold War Chaos," *Foreign Affairs* 75, no. 3: 79–91.

———. 2002. "America's Imperial Ambition," *Foreign Affairs* 81, no. 5:44–60.

————. 2004. "The End of the Neo-Conservative Moment," *Survival* 46, no. 1: 7–22.

Ikenberry, G. John, Thomas J. Knock, Anne-Marie Slaughter, and Tony Smith. 2009. *The Crisis of American Foreign Policy: Wilsonianism in the Twenty-First Century* (Princeton, NJ: Princeton University Press).

Imbrahim, Raymond. 2007. *The Al Qaeda Reader* (New York: Broadway Books).

Iraq Liberation Act (1998) HR 4655.

Isikoff, Michael, and David Corn. 2006. *Hubris: The Inside Story of Spin, Scandal, and the Selling of the Iraq War* (New York: Crown Publishers).

Jacobson, Gary C. 2007. "The Public, the President, and the War in Iraq," in Edwards King, *The Polarized Presidency of George W.*

Jaffe, Greg. .2009. "Short '06 Lebanon War Stokes Pentagon Debate," *The Washington Post,* April 6, A1.

Jaffe, Greg, and Shailagh Murray. 2009. "Gates Seeks Sharp Turn in Spending," *The Washington Post,* April 7, A1.

Jalali, Ali A. 2003. "Afghanistan in 2002: The Struggle to Win the Peace," *Asian Survey* 43, no. 1:174–85.

————. 2007. "The Legacy of War and the Challenge of Peace Building," in *Building a New Afghanistan,* ed. Rotberg (Washington, D.C.: Brookings).

Jentelson, Bruce W. 2002. "The Need for Praxis: Bringing Policy Relevance Back In," *International Security* 26, no. 4:169–83.

Jervis, Robert. 1991. "Domino Beliefs and Strategic Behavior," in *Dominoes and Bandwagons: Strategic Beliefs and Great Power Competition in the Eurasian Rimland,* ed. Jervis and Snyder (New York: Oxford University Press).

————. 1994. "Leadership, Post-Cold War Politics and Psychology," *Political Psychology,* 15:769–77.

————. 1997. *System Effects: Complexity in Political and Social Life* (Princeton, NJ: Princeton University Press).

Jervis, Robert, and Jack Snyder, eds. 1991. *Dominoes and Bandwagons: Strategic Beliefs and Great Power Competition in the Eurasian Rimland* (New York: Oxford University Press).

Joffe, Josef. 2006. *Uberpower: The Imperial Temptation of America* (New York: W. W. Norton).

Johnson, Chalmers. 2000. *Blowback: The Costs and Consequences of American Empire* (New York: Henry Holt).

Johnson, Chris, and Jolyon Leslie. 2004. *Afghanistan: The Mirage of Peace* (New York: Zed Books).

Johnson, Lyndon Baines. 1971 *The Vantage Point: Perspectives on the Presidency 1963–1969* (New York: Holt, Rinehart, and Winston).

Johnson, Thomas H., and M. Chris Mason. 2008. "No Sign Until the Burst of Fire: Understanding the Pakistan-Afghanistan Frontier," *International Security* 32, no. 4 (Spring) 41–77.

Jones, Ann. 2006. *Kabul in Winter* (New York: Metropolitan Books).

Jones, Howard. 2001. *Crucible of Power: A History of U.S. Foreign Relations since 1897* (Wilmington, DE: Scholarly Resources).

Jones, Seth. 2008a. "The Rise of Afghanistan's Insurgency: State Failure and Jihad," *International Security* 32, no. 4:7–40.

———. 2008b. *Counterinsurgency in Afghanistan* (Santa Monica: RAND).

Jones, James L., and Thomas R. Pickering. 2008. *Afghan Study Group: Revitalizing Our Efforts, Rethinking Our Strategies,* January 30.

Kagan, Frederick W. 2003. *Commentary* 115, no. 3, March: 39–45.

———. 2008. Comments, Chairlie Rose Show, March 20.

Kagan, Robert. 2006. *Dangerous Nation: America's Place in the World from Its Earliest Days to the Dawn of the Twentieth Century* (New York: Knopf).

———. 2009. "Disturber of the Peace," *The Washington Post,* April 2, A21.

Kail, F. M. 1973. *What Washington Said: Administration Rhetoric and the Vietnam War, 1949–1969* (New York: Harper & Row).

Kaldor, Mary. 2001. *New and Old Wars: Organized Violence in a Global Era* (Stanford: Stanford University Press).

Kaplan, Fred. 2008. *Daydream Believers: How a Few Grand Ideas Wrecked American Power* (Hoboken, NJ: John Wiley & Sons).

Kapstein, Ethan B., and Michael Mastanduno, eds. 1999. *Unipolar Politics: Realism and State Strategies after the Cold War* (New York: Columbia University Press).

Karnow, Stanley. 1989. *In Our Image: America's Empire in the Philippines* (New York: Random House).

———. 1997. *Vietnam: A History* (New York: Penguin).

Karzai, Hamid. 2009. Interview, Jim Lehrer News Hour, Public Broadcasting Service, March 18.

Kattenburg, Paul M. 1980. *The Vietnam Trauma in American Foreign Policy, 1945–75* (New Brunswick: Transaction).

Kaufmann, Chaim. 2004. "Threat Inflation and the Failure of the Marketplace of Ideas: The Selling of the Iraq War," *International Security* 29, no. 1:5–48.

Keegan, John. 2001. "If America Decides to Take on the Afghans, This is How to Do It," *Daily Telegraph,* September 20.

Kegley, Charles W., Jr. 1995. *Controversies in International Relations Theory: Realism and the Neoliberal Challenge* (New York: St. Martins Press).

Kennan, George F. 1947. "The Sources of Soviet Conduct," The History Guide: Lectures on Twentieth Century Europe, at www.historyguide.org/europe/Kennan.html, accessed March 8, 2011.

———. 1951. *American Diplomacy 1900–1950* (New York: Mentor Books).

Kennedy, David M. 2008. "Two Concepts of Sovereignty," in *To Lead the World: American Strategy after the Bush Administration,* ed. Melvyn P. Leffler and Jeffrey W. Legro (New York: Oxford University Press).

Kennedy, Paul. 1987. *The Rise and Fall of the Great Powers: Economic Change and Military Conflict from 1500 to 2000* (New York: Random House).

Keohane, Robert O. 1984. *After Hegemony: Cooperation and Discord in the World Political Economy* (Princeton, NJ: Princeton University Press).

Keohane, Robert O., and Joseph S. Nye. 1977. *Power and Interdependence: World Politics in Transition* (Boston: Little, Brown).

Kinzer, Stephen. 2006. *Overthrow: America's Century of Regime Change from Hawaii to Iraq* (New York: Henry Holt).

Kirshner, Jonathan. 2008. "Globalization, American Power, and International Security," *Political Science Quarterly* 123:363–89.

Kissinger, Henry. 1994. *Diplomacy* (New York: Simon and Schuster).

Kitson, Frank. 1971. *Low Intensity Operations: Subversion, Insurgency, Peace-Keeping* (Harrisburg, PA: Stackpole Books).

Komer, R. W. 1972. *Bureaucracy Does Its Thing: Institutional Constraints on US-GVN Performance in Vietnam* (Santa Monica: RAND).

Koschmann, J. Victor. 1997. "Review Essay: The Nationalism of Cultural Uniqueness," *American Historical Review* 102:758–68.

Krause, Peter John Paul. 2008. "The Last Good Chance: A Reassessment of US Operations at Tora Bora," *Security Studies* 17:644–84.

Krauthammer, Charles. 1990–91. "The Unipolar Moment," *Foreign Affairs* 70, no. 1, 23–33.

Krenn, Michael L., ed. 1999. *The Impact of Race on U.S. Foreign Policy: A Reader* (New York: Garland).

———, 2006. *The Color of Empire: Race and American Foreign Relations* (Washington, D.C.: Potomac Books).

Krepinevich, Andrew F., Jr. 1986. *The Army and Vietnam* (Baltimore: Johns Hopkins University Press).

Kugler, Richard L. with Marianna V. Kozintseva. 1996. *Enlarging NATO: The Russia Factor* (Santa Monica, CA: RAND).

Kupchan, Charles A., and Peter L. Trubowitz. 2007. "Dead Center: The Demise of Liberal Internationalism in the United States," *International Security* 32, no. 2:7–44.

Kurth, James. 2008. "Boss of Bosses," in *To Lead the World: American Strategy after the Bush Doctrine,* ed. Leffler and Legro (New York: Oxford University Press).

Kurz, Norman J. 2009. "Biden's Afghan Journey," *The Washington Post,* October 8, A29.

LaFeber, Walter. 1998. *The New Empire: An Interpretation of American Expansionism 1860–1898* (Ithaca, NY: Cornell University Press).

Langston, Thomas S. 2007. "'The Decider's' Path to War in Iraq and the Importance of Personality," in *The Polarized Presidency of George W. Bush,* ed. Edwards and King.

Layne, Christopher. 2009. "The Waning of US Hegemony—Myth or Reality? A Review Essay," *International Security* 34, no. 1:147–72.

Lears, T. J. Jackson. 2009. *Rebirth of a Nation: The Making of Modern America, 1877–1920* (New York: Harper).

Lebow, Richard Ned. 2003. *The Tragic Vision of Politics: Ethics, Interests and Orders* (New York: Cambridge University Press).

Lebow, Richard Ned, and Thomas Risse-Kappen. 1995. *International Relations Theory and the End of the Cold War* (New York: Columbia University Press).

Leffler, Melvyn P., and Jeffrey W. Legro, eds. 2008. *To Lead the World: American Strategy after the Bush Doctrine* (New York: Oxford University Press).

Levite, Ariel E., Bruce W. Jentleson, and Larry Berman, eds. 1992. *Foreign Military Intervention: The Dynamics of Protracted Conflict* (New York: Columbia University Press).

Lewis, Anthony. 1995. "Abroad at Home; The Speech Not Given," *NYT*, June 2, A29.

Lewy, Guenter. 1978. *America in Vietnam* (New York: Oxford University Press).

Lieven, Anatol. 2004. *America Right or Wrong: An Anatomy of American Nationalism* (New York: Oxford University Press).

———. 2011. "A Mutiny Grows in Punjab," *The National Interest*, no. 112: 15–24.

Lind, William S. et al. 1989. "The Changing Face of War: Into the Fourth Generation," *Marine Corps Gazette,* October, accessed June 4, 2009 at http://www.d-n-i.net/fcs/4th_gen_war_gazette.htm.

Linn, Brian McAllister. 1988. "Intelligence and Low Intensity Conflict in the Philippines War, 1899–1902," Third USAWC International Conference on Intelligence and Military Operations, May.

———. 1989. *The US Army and Counterinsurgency in the Philippine War, 1899–1902* (Chapel Hill: University of North Carolina Press).

———. 2000. *The Philippine War 1899–1902* (Lawrence: University of Kansas Press).

———. 2007. *The Echo of Battle: The Army's Way of War* (Cambridge, MA: Harvard University Press).

Lipset, Seymour Martin. 1996. *American Exceptionalism: A Double-Edged Sword* (New York: W. W. Norton).

Lister, Sarah, and Hamish Nixon. 2007. "The Place of the Province in Afghanistan's Subnational Governance," in *Building a New Afghanistan,* ed. Rotberg.

Lobell, Steven E., Norrin M. Ripsman, and Jeffrey W. Taliaferro. 2009. *Neoclassical Realism, the State, and Foreign Policy* (New York: Cambridge University Press).

Lock-Pullan, Richard. 2006. *US Intervention Policy and Army Innovation: From Vietnam to Iraq* (New York: Routledge).

Logan, Lara. 2009. Interview, Charlie Rose Show, October 6.

Logevall, Fredrik. 1999. *Choosing War: The Lost Chance for Peace and the Escalation of War in Vietnam* (Berkeley: University of California Press).

Londono, Ernesto. 2010. "Anxiety along Iraq's Border with Iran," *The Washington Post,* December 1, A6.

Long, Austin. 2006. *On "Other War" Lessons from Five Decades of RAND Counterinsurgency Research* (Santa Monica: RAND).

Luttwak, Edward. 1985. *Strategy and History: Collected Essays, Volume 2* (New Brunswick: Transaction Books).

———. 2007. "Dead End: Counterinsurgency Warfare as Military Malpractice," *Harper's,* February.

Lyall, Jason, and Isaiah Wilson III. 2009. "Rage against the Machines: Explaining Outcomes in Counterinsurgency Wars," *International Organization* 63, no. 1: 67–106.

Macdonald, Douglas J. 1991. "The Truman Administration and Global Responsibilities: The Birth of the Falling Domino Principle," in *Dominoes and Bandwagons,* ed. Jervis and Snyder.

Magas, Branka, and Ivo Zanic, eds. 2001. *The War in Croatia and Bosnia-Herzegovina 1991–1995* (London: Frank Cass).

Mahmutcehajic, Rusmir. 2001. "The Road to War," in *The War in Croatia and Bosnia-Herzegovina,* ed. Magis and Zanic.

Maliniak, Daniel, Amy Oakes, Susan Person, and Michael J. Tierney. 2007. "Inside the Ivory Tower," *Foreign Policy,* March/April, 63–68.

Mandelbaum, Michael. 1996. "Foreign Policy as Social Work," *Foreign Affairs* 75, no. 2:16–32.

———. 2002. "The Inadequacy of American Power," *Foreign Affairs* 81, no. 5: 61–73.

Mann, James. 2004. *Rise of the Vulcans: The History of Bush's War Cabinet* (New York: Viking).

Mastanduno, Michael. 1997. "Preserving the Unipolar Moment: Realist Theories and US Grand Strategy after the Cold War," *International Security* 21, no. 4:49–88.

May, Ernest R. 1968. *American Imperialism: A Speculative Essay* (New York: Atheneum).

May, Glenn A. 1983. "Why the United States Won the Philippine-American War, 1899–1902," *Pacific Historical Review* 52:353–77.

Mayers, David Allan. 1986. *Cracking the Monolith: US Policy against the Sino-Soviet Alliance, 1949–1955* (Baton Rouge: Louisiana State University Press).

Mazzetti, Mark, and David Rohde. 2008. "Amid Policy Disputes, Qaeda Grows in Pakistan," *NYT,* June 30.

McAlister, John T., Jr. 1971. *Vietnam: The Origins of Revolution* (New York: Doubleday).

McChesney, R. D., ed. 1999. *Kabul under Siege: Fayz Muhammad's Account of the 1929 Uprising* (Princeton, NJ: Mark Wiener).

McChrystal, Gen. Stanley A. 2009. *COMISAF Initial Assessment* (Unclassified) http://www.washingtonpost.com/wp-dyn/content/article/2009/09/21/AR2009092100110.html accessed September 30, 2009.

McConnell, Mitch. 2010. Speech at the Heritage Foundation, Washington, D.C., November 4.

McDougall, Walter A. 1997. *Promised Land, Crusader State: The American Encounter with the World since 1776* (New York: Houghton Mifflin, 1997).

McKechnie, Alastair J. 2007. "Rebuilding a Robust Afghan Economy," in *Building a New Afghanistan,* ed. Rotberg.

McMahon, Robert J. 1991. "Credibility and World Power: Exploring the Psychological Dimension in Postwar American Diplomacy," *Diplomatic History* 15:455–71.

McMahon, Patrice C., and Jon Western. 2009. "The Death of Dayton," *Foreign Affairs* 88, no. 5:69–83.

McNamara, Robert S. 1995. *In Retrospect: The Tragedy and Lessons of Vietnam* (New York: Random House).

Mead, Walter Russell. 2005. *Power, Terror, Peace and War: America's Grand Strategy in a World at Risk* (New York: Vintage).

Mearsheimer, John J. 2001. *The Tragedy of Great Power Politics* (New York: W. W. Norton).

Mearsheimer, John J., and Stephen Walt. 2003. "An Unnecessary War," in *The Iraq War Reader: History, Documents, Opinions,* ed. Micah L. Sifry and Christopher Cerf (New York: Simon and Schuster, 2003).

Meernik, James David. 2004. *The Political Use of Military Force in US Foreign Policy* (Burlington, VT: Ashgate).

Meier, Viktor. 1995, 1999. *Yugoslavia: A History of its Demise* (New York: Routledge).

Mercer, Jonathan. 1996. *Reputation and International Politics* (Ithaca, NY: Cornell University Press).

Merry, Robert W. 2005. *Sands of Empire: Missionary Zeal, American Foreign Policy and the Hazards of Global Action* (New York: Simon and Schuster).

Mojares, Resil B. 1999. *The War against the Americans: Resistance and Collaboration in Cebu, 1899–1906* (Manila: Anteneo de Manila University Press).

Morgenthau, Hans J. 1965. *Vietnam and the United States* (Public Affairs Press).

———. 1967. *Politics among Nations: The Struggle for Power and Peace,* fourth edition (New York: Alfred A. Knopf).

Morone, James A. 2003. *Hellfire Nation: The Politics of Sin in American History* (New Haven, CT: Yale University Press).

Mozingo, David P. 1967. "Containment in Asia Reconsidered," *World Politics* 19, no. 3:361–77.

Mueller, John. 1989. *Retreat from Doomsday: The Obsolescence of Major War* (New York: Basic Books).

———. 1995. *Quiet Cataclysm: Reflections on the Recent Transformation of World Politics* (New York: HarperCollins).

———. 2006. *Overblown: How Politicians and the Terror Industry Inflate National Security Threats, and Why We Believe Them* (New York: Free Press).

———. 2009. "War Has Almost Ceased to Exist: An Assessment," *Political Science Quarterly* 124:297–321.

Muravchik, Joshua. 1996. *The Imperative of American Leadership: A Challenge to Neo-Isolationism* (Washington, D.C.: AEI Press).

Nagl, John A. 2005. *Learning to Eat Soup with a Knife: Counterinsurgency Lessons from Malaya and Vietnam* (Chicago: University of Chicago Press).

Nasr, Vali. 2010. "Ramadan," *Foreign Policy,* July/August.

Nautilus. 2011. Institute for Security and Sustainability, at www.nautilus.org/publications/books/australian-forces-abroad/afghanistan/opium prod.

Neuchterlein, Donald E. 2001. *America Recommitted: A Superpower Assesses Its Role in a Turbulent World* (Lexington: The University Press of Kentucky).

NYT. 1992. *The New York Times,* August 23, A16.

———. 1994. *The New York Times,* November 27.

———. 2007. Editorial, August 20.

Niebuhr, Reinhold. 1955. *Beyond Tragedy: Essays on the Christian Interpretation of History* (New York: Charles Scribner's Sons).

Nolan, Cathal J. 2006. "Learning to Lead: Theodore Roosevelt, Woodrow Wilson, and the Emergence of the United States as a World Power," in *Artists of Power: Theodore Roosevelt, Woodrow Wilson, and Their Enduring Impact on*

US Foreign Policy ed. William N. Tilchin and Charles E. Neu (Westport, CT: Praeger Security International).

Nolan, Mary. 1997. "Review Essay: Against Exceptionalisms," *American Historical Review* 102:769–74.

Nye, Joseph S. 1993. "Ethics and Intervention," in *Ideas and Ideals: Essays on Politics in Honor of Stanley Hoffmann,* ed. Linda B. Miller and Michael Joseph Smith (Boulder, CO: Westview).

———. 2009. "Scholars on the Sidelines," *The Washington Post,* April 13, A15.

Odom, William E. 1994. "Invade, Don't Bomb," *The Wall Street Journal,* February 18, A12.

Ollivant, Douglas, and Eric D. Chewning. 2006. "Producing Victory: Rethinking Conventional Forces in COIN Operations," *Military Review,* July-August.

O'Reilly, K. P. 2007. "Perceiving Rogue States: The Use of the "Rogue State" Concept by U.S. Foreign Policy Elites," *Foreign Policy Analysis* 3:298.

Osgood, Robert E. 1953. *Ideals and Self-Interest in America's Foreign Relations: The Great Transformation of the Twentieth Century* (Chicago: University of Chicago Press).

Owen, David. 1996. *Balkan Odyssey: A Personal Account of the International Peace Efforts Following the Breakup of the Former Yugoslavia* (New York: Houghton Mifflin).

Packer, George. 2005. *The Assassins' Gate: America in Iraq* (New York: Farrar, Straus, and Giroux).

Pape, Robert A. 2005. *Dying to Win: The Strategic Logic of Suicide Terrorism* (New York: Random House).

Papp, Daniel S., John Endicott, and Loch K. Johnson. 2004. *American Foreign Policy: History, Politics, and Policy* (New York: Longman).

Peceny, Mark. 1999. *Democracy at the Point of Bayonets* (University Park, PA: Pennsylvania State University).

Pei, Minxin (2003) "The Paradoxes of American Nationalism," *Foreign Policy,* May/June, 31–37.

Pentagon Papers: The Defense Department History of United States Decisionmaking on Vietnam, Vol. I. 1971a. Senator Gravel Edition (Boston: Beacon Press).

———. The Defense Department History of United States Decisionmaking on Vietnam, Vol. II. 1971b. Senator Gravel Edition (Boston: Beacon Press).

———. The Defense Department History of United States Decisionmaking on Vietnam, Vol. III. 1979. Senator Gravel Edition (Boston: Beacon Press).

Perle, Richard. 1994. *The Wall Street Journal,* December 8, A19.

Pike, Douglas. 1966. *Viet Cong: The Organization and Techniques of the National Liberation Front of South Vietnam* (Cambridge, MA: MIT Press).

Podhoretz, Norman. 1983. *Why We Were in Vietnam* (New York: Simon and Schuster).

Pollack, Kenneth. 2002. *The Threatening Storm: The Case for Invading Iraq* (New York: Random House).

Porter, Gareth. 2005. *Perils of Dominance: Imbalance of Power and the Road to War in Vietnam* (Berkeley: University of California Press).

Posen, Barry R. 2001/02. "The Struggle against Terrorism: Grand Strategy, Strategy, and Tactics," *International Security* 26, no. 3:39–55.

Powell, Colin. 1995. *My American Journey* (New York: Ballantine Books).

Powers, Thomas. 2007. "What Tenet Knew," *The New York Review of Books,* July 19, 71.

Race, Jeffrey. 1972. *War Comes to Long An: Revolutionary Conflict in a Vietnamese Province* (Berkeley: University of California Press).

Rais, Rasul Bakhsh. 2008. *Recovering the Frontier State: War, Ethnicity, and State in Afghanistan* (Lanham: Lexington Books).

Ramet, Sabrina P. 1994. "The Yugoslav Crisis and the West: Avoiding 'Vietnam' and Blundering into 'Abyssinia,'" *East European Politics and Society* 8, no. 1: 189–219.

———. 2002. *Balkan Babel: The Disintegration of Yugoslavia from the Death of Tito to the Fall of Milosevic* (Boulder, CO: Westview Press).

Rapport, Aaron. 2008. "Unexpected Affinities: Neoconservatism's Place in IR Theory," *Security Studies* 17:257–93.

Rashid, Ahmed. 2000. *Taliban: Militant Islam, Oil and Fundamentalism in Central Asia* (New Haven, CT: Yale University Press).

———. 2008. *Descent into Chaos: The United States and the Failure of Nation Building in Pakistan, Afghanistan and Central Asia* (New York: Viking).

Rathbun, Brian C. 2008. "Does One Right Make a Realist? Conservatism, Neoconservatism, and Isolationism in the Foreign Policy Ideology of American Elites," *Political Science Quarterly* 123:271–99.

Record, Jeffrey. 1998. *The Wrong War: Why We Lost in Vietnam* (Annapolis: Naval).

———. 2004. *Dark Victory: America's Second War against Iraq* (Annapolis: Naval Institute Press).

Renshon, Stanley. 1998. *The Psychological Assessment of Presidential Candidates* (New York: Routledge).

Rice, Condoleezza. 2000. "Promoting the National Interest," *Foreign Affairs* 79, no. 1:45–62.

Ricks, Thomas E. 2006. *Fiasco: The American Military Adventure in Iraq* (New York: Penguin).

Rieckhoff, Paul. 2006. *Chasing Ghosts, Failures and Facades in Iraq: A Soldier's Perspective* (New York: Nal Caliber).

Rieff, David. 2003. "Blueprint for a Mess," *The New York Times Magazine,* November 2.

Robichaud, Carl. 2007. "Buying Time in Afghanistan," *World Policy Journal* 24, no. 2:1–10.

Robinson, Edgar E., and Victor J. West. 1917. *The Foreign Policy of Woodrow Wilson, 1913–1917* (New York: Macmillan).

Robinson, Linda. 2008. *Tell Me How This Ends: General David Petraeus and the Search for a Way Out of Iraq* (New York: Public Affairs Press).

Rodman, Peter W. 2009. *Presidential Command: Power, Leadership, and the Making of Foreign Policy from Richard Nixon to George W. Bush* (New York: Alfred A. Knopf).

Rohde, David, and David E. Sanger. 2007. "How a 'Good War' in Afghanistan Went Bad," *NYT,* August 12, 2007.

Rose, Gideon. 1998. "Neoclassical Realism and Theories of Foreign Policy," *World Politics* 51:144–72.

———. 2004. "The Empire Strikes Out," *Washington Monthly* online, April 9.

———. 2005. "Get Real," *NYT* online, August 18.

Rosenburg, J. Philipp. 1986. "Presidential Beliefs and Foreign Policy Decision-Making: Continuity during the Cold War Era," *Political Psychology* 7: 733–51.

Rosecrance, Richard. 1999. *The Rise of the Virtual State: Wealth and Power in the Coming Century* (New York: Basic Books).

———. 2001. "Has Realism Become Cost-Benefit Analysis? A Review Essay," *International Security* 26, no. 2:132–54.

Rotberg, Robert I. 2007. *Building a New Afghanistan* (Washington, D.C.: Brookings).

Ruane, Michael E. 2007. "A Triangle Comes Full Circle," *The Washington Post,* November 17.

Rubin, Barnett R. 2006. *Afghanistan's Uncertain Transition from Turmoil to Normalcy,* CSR No. 12, Council on Foreign Relations, March.

———. 2007. "Saving Afghanistan," *Foreign Affairs* 86, no. 1:57–78.

Russett, Bruce. 1985. "The Mysterious Case of Vanishing Hegemony, or is Mark Twain Really Dead?" *International Organization* 29:207–31.

Said, Edward W. 1978. *Orientalism* (New York: Vintage Books).

———. 1993. *Culture and Imperialism* (New York: Alfred A. Knopf).

Schlesinger, Arthur M. 1986. *The Cycles of American History* (Boston: Houghton Mifflin).

Schmidt, Brian C., and Michael C. Williams. 2008. "The Bush Doctrine and the Iraq War: Neoconservatives Versus Realists," *Security Studies* 17:191–220.

Schmitt, Eric. 2010. "U.S. Envoy's Cable Shows Concern on Afghan Plans," *NYT* online, January 25.

Schweller, Randall L. 1998. *Deadly Imbalances: Tripolarity and Hitler's Strategy of World Conquest* (New York: Columbia University Press).

Scott, James C. 1976. *The Moral Economy of the Peasant: Rebellion and Subsistence in Southeast Asia* (New Haven, CT: Yale University Press).

Scowcroft, Brent. 2002. "Don't Attack Saddam," *The Wall Street Journal* online, August 15, at http://www.opinionjournal.com/editorial/feature.htm?id=110002133, accessed October 4, 2008.

See, Jennifer W. 2001. "A Prophet without Honor: Hans Morgenthau and the War in Vietnam, 1955–1965," *Pacific Historical Review* 70, 419–47.

Semple, Kirk. 2007. "Citing Taliban Threat, Afghan Ex-Militia Leaders Hoard Illegal Arms," *NYT,* October 28, 18.

Serbian Academy of Arts and Sciences. 1986. "Memorandum 1986 (the Greater Serbian Ideology)" Belgrade, September 24.

Shadid, Anthony. 2007. "With Iran Ascendant, U.S. Is Seen at Fault," *The Washington Post,* January 30, A1.

Shanker, Thom. 2009. "Pentagon Rethinking Old Doctrine on 2 Wars," *NYT,* March 15.

Sheehan, Neil. 1988. *A Bright Shining Lie: John Paul Vann and America in Vietnam* (New York: Random House).

Shelton, Hugh. 2010 Remarks on Charlie Rose Show, December 30.

Sheridan, Mary Beth. 2008a. "US Troops in Baghdad Take a Softer Approach," *The Washington Post,* November 20, A1.

———. 2008b. "Iraq Security Pact Highlights Battle Between US, Iran," *The Washington Post,* October 28, A10.

Silber, Laura, and Allan Little. 1995. *Yugoslavia: Death of a Nation* (New York: TV Books).

Simon, Herbert A. 1997. *Administrative Behavior: A Study of Decision-Making Process in Administrative Organizations* (Free Press).

Slater, Jerome. 1993–94. "The Domino Theory and International Politics: The Case of Vietnam," *Security Studies* 3, no. 2:186–224.

Smith, Joseph. 1994. *The Spanish-American War: Conflict in the Caribbean and the Pacific 1895–1902* (New York: Longman).

Smith, Steve, and Michael Clarke. 1985. *Foreign Policy Implementation* (Boston: Allen & Unwin).

Smith, Tony. 1993. "Woodrow Wilson and the Election of Good Men in Latin America," in *Ideas and Ideals: Essays on Politics in Honor of Stanley Hoffmann,* ed. Linda B. Miller and Michael Joseph Smith (Boulder, CO: Westview).

Stewart, Rory. 2006. *The Prince of the Marshes and other Occupational Hazards of a Year in Iraq* (New York: Harcourt).

Stone, Robert. 2007. "The Unconscionable War," *The New York Review of Books,* November 22.

Sullivan, Patricia L. 2007. "War Aims and War Outcomes: Why Powerful States Lose Limited Wars," *The Journal of Conflict Resolution* 51:496–524.

Summers, Harry G., Jr. 1982. *On Strategy: A Critical Analysis of the Vietnam War* (Novato, CA: Presidio).

Suskind, Ron. 2004. "Faith, Certainty and the Presidency of George W. Bush," *New York Times Magazine,* October 17.

Switzer, Warren H. 2001. "International Military Responses to the Balkan Wars: Crisis in Analysis," in *The War in Croatia and Bosnia-Herzegovina,* ed. Magas and Zanic.

Taylor, Jay. 2009. *The Generalissimo: Chiang Kai-shek and the Struggle for Modern China* (Cambridge, MA: Harvard University Press).

Terdoslavich, William. 2006. "From Shock and Awe to Aw Shucks," in *Beyond Shock and Awe: Warfare in the 21st Century,* ed. Eric L. Haney and Brian M. Thomsen (New York: Berkley Caliber).

Thomson, James C. et al. 1981. *Sentimental Imperialists: The American Experience in East Asia* (New York: Harper and Row).

Thompson, Sir Robert. 1968. "Squaring the Error," *Foreign Affairs* 46:442–53.

Thrall, A. Trevor. 2007. "A Bear in the Woods? Threat Framing and the Marketplace of Values," *Security Studies* 16, no. 3:452–88.

Tierney, John J. Jr. 2006. *Chasing Ghosts: Unconventional Warfare in American History* (Washington, D.C.: Potomac Books).

Trask, David F. 1981. *The War with Spain in 1898* (New York: Macmillan).

Tuchman, Barbara W. 1984. *The March of Folly: From Troy to Vietnam* (New York: Knopf).

Tumulty, Karen. 2010. "Conservatives' New Focus: America, the Exceptional," *The Washington Post,* November 29, A1.

Tus, Anton. 2001. "The War in Slovenia and Croatia up to the Sarajevo Ceasefire," in *The War in Croatia and Bosnia-Herzegovina,* ed. Magas and Zanic.

Tyler, Patrick E., and Elisabeth Bumiller. 2001. "Bush Offers Taliban 2nd Chance to Yield," *NYT* online, October 12.

Ucko, David H. 2009. *The New Counterinsurgency Era: Transforming the US Military for Modern Wars* (Washington, D.C.: Georgetown University Press).

US Army/Marine Corps. 2007. *Counterinsurgency Field Manual* (Chicago: University of Chicago Press).

US Congress. 1962. Testimony of Ambassador Frederick E. Nolting, Jr., Subcommittee on Far Eastern Affairs, US Senate, 87th Congress, Second Session, January 12.

———. 1996. *U.S. Role in Iranian Arms Transfers to Bosnia and Croatia,* Committee on International Relations, House of Representatives, One Hundred Fourth Congress, Second Session, May 8.

US Department of State. 1992a. *Department of State Dispatch Supplement,* December.

———. 1992b. Department of State Dispatch Supplement, September.

United States-Vietnam Relations 1945–1967. 1971. Study prepared by the Department of Defense for the House Committee on Armed Services, 92nd Congress, 1st Session.

Van Evera, Stephen. 2008. "A Farewell to Geopolitics," in *To Lead the World,* ed. Leffler and Legro.

Von Hippel, Karin. 2000. *Democracy by Force: US Military Intervention in the Post-Cold War World* (New York: Cambridge University Press).

Walt, Stephen M. 1987. *The Origins of Alliances* (Ithaca, NY: Cornell University Press).

———. 2001/02. "Beyond bin Laden: Reshaping US Foreign Policy," *International Security* 26, no. 3:56–78.

Waltz, Kenneth. 1979. *Theory of International Politics* (Menlo Park, CA: Addison-Wesley).

———. 2000. "Structural Realism after the Cold War," *International Security* 25, no. 1:5–41.

Wedel, Janine R. 2009. *Shadow Elite: How the World's New Power Brokers Undermine Democracy, Government, and the Free Market* (New York: Basic Books).

Weisberg, Jacob. 2008. *The Bush Tragedy* (New York: Random House).

Welch, Richard E., Jr. 1979. *Response to Imperialism: The United States and the Philippine-American War, 1899–1902* (Chapel Hill: University of North Carolina Press).

West, Bing. 2008. *The Strongest Tribe: War, Politics, and the Endgame in Iraq* (New York: Random House).

Western, Jon. 2005. *Selling Intervention and War: The Presidency, the Media, and the American Public* (Baltimore: Johns Hopkins Press).

Weston, Rubin Francis. 1998. "Racism and the Imperialist Campaign," in *Race and US Foreign Policy in the Ages of Territorial and Market Expansion, 1840–1900*, ed. Michael L. Krenn (New York: Garland Publishing).

White House. 2002 *The National Security Strategy of the United States of America*, September.

———. 2010. *National Security Strategy*, May.

Wilkinson, David. 1999. "Unipolarity without Hegemony," *International Studies Review* 1, no. 2:141–72.

Will, George F. 2008. "Steady Hand at Defense," *The Washington Post*, December 11, A25.

Witte, Grif. 2009. "Taliban Shadow Officials Offer Concrete Alternative," *The Washington Post*, December 8, A1.

Williams, Brian Glyn. 2009. Interview, Charlie Rose Show, October 9.

Wohlforth, William C. (1994–95) "Realism and the End of the Cold War," *International Security* 19, no. 3:91–129; and "Correspondence," *International Security* 20 no. 2:185–87.

Wohlstetter, Albert. 1968. *On Vietnam and Bureaucracy* (Santa Monica: Rand Corporation, July 17, at http://www.rand.org/publications/classics/wohlstetter/D17276.1/D17276.1.html, accessed December 7, 2007.

Wolff, Leon. 1961. *Little Brown Brother: How the United States Purchased and Pacified the Philippine Islands at the Century's Turn* (New York: Doubleday).

Woodward, Bob. 2002. *Bush at War* (New York: Simon and Schuster).

———. 2004. *Plan of Attack* (New York: Simon and Schuster).

———. 2006. *State of Denial: Bush at War, Part III* (New York: Simon and Schuster).

———. 2008. *The War Within: A Secret White House History 2006–2008* (New York: Simon and Schuster).

Woodward, Susan L. 1995. *Balkan Tragedy: Chaos and Dissolution after the Cold War* (Washington, D.C.: Brookings Institution).

Wright, Donald P., and Timothy R. Reese. 2008. *On Point II, Transition to the New Campaign: The United States Army in Operation Iraqi Freedom, May 2003–January 2005* (Washington, D.C.: Government Printing Office).

Zagoria, Donald S. 1962. *The Sino-Soviet Conflict: 1956–1961* (Princeton, NJ: Princeton University Press).

———. 1967. *Vietnam Triangle: Moscow, Peking, Hanoi* (New York: Pegasus).

Zartman, I. William. 2005. *Cowardly Lions: Missed Opportunities to Prevent Deadly Conflict and State Collapse* (Boulder, CO: Lynne Rienner).

Zegat, Amy. 2008. "The Legend of a Democracy Promoter," *The National Interest*, no. 97:43–53.

Zunec, Ozren. 2001. "Operations Flash and Storm," in *The War in Croatia and Bosnia-Hercegovina*, ed. Magas and Zanic.

INDEX

Abdur Rahman, Pakistan General
Akhtar, 149
Abizaid, General John (CENTCOM
Commander 2003–2007), 186
Abrams, General Creighton, emphasis
on counterinsurgency, 49, 95
Abu Ghraib prison, 190
Acheson, Secretary of State Dean, 20–21
Adelman, Kenneth
attack on Iraq as cakewalk, 164–165
friend of Rumsfeld, 179
Afghanistan War, x, 11, 27, 175
Afghanistan on sociopolitical
indexes, 127–130
Ambassador Eikenberry's view of
Karzai, 148
and narcotics, 128, 148
bin Laden
why did he attack America?,
134–135
Bonn agreement, 142
British historical experience, 128
ethnocentric approach to
development, 192–193
fall of Kandahar, 141
inappropriate development strategies
impact of NGOs, 152
overwhelming foreign presence,
152–153
influence of warlords, 147–148,
231 (n15)
insufficient resources for task, 144
Karzai's popularity, 148
lack of access to Kabul by Ghiljais
tribe, 146

lack of institutions and legitimacy,
128–130
neutrality proposal, 150
Northern Alliance, 137, 141–142,
146, 152, 206
Pakistan's role
aid to Taliban under Benazir
Bhutto, 140
Armitage demands on Pakistan, 139
Pashtun social code, 150
relations with Afghanistan and
aid to insurgents, 149–51
reintegration of insurgents, 148, 154
resources diverted to Iraq, 143
suicide attacks and bombing
imported from Iraq, 147
support for minimal project in
Afghanistan, 143–144
US attack on Afghanistan, 141
US security interests
and baiting by bin Laden, 132
chaos and early support for
mujaheddin, 130–131
failure to apprehend bin Laden
at Tora Bora, 138–39
lack of military targets, 134
need for urgency, 132–133
no plans existed for attacking
Afghanistan, 134
questions on Iraq, 133
US decision making and
conventional thinking, 131–139,
230 (nn6, 8)
who should run the country?, 142
Aguinaldo. See Philippine War

Albanians (Kosovo), 104
al Qaeda, xv, 133–39, 140, 145, 148–49,
    154, 162, 167–68, 172, 191,
    198–99, 191, 203–06
al-Sistani, Grand Ayatolla Ali. *See*
    Iraq War
Alsop, Joseph, 81
aluminum tubes, 170
American exceptionalism,
    Americans as creators of turmoil, 32
    Bush, George W., and, 32
    meliorism, 28
    public self-perceptions, 30
    religiosity, 30
    Republican Party focus on, 220 (n5)
    Wilsonianism, 29
American style of war, 43–45, 50–51
Anan, Kofi, 189
Anbar, 191
Armey, House Majority Leader Dick,
    164
Army War College, 176
assessing policy, 219 (n3)
Atta, Mohammad, 169
Azziz, Iraqi Deputy Prime Minister, 158

Baath Party, 160, 181, 184
Baker, Secretary of State, James, 106,
    159, 164. *See also* Iraq War
    statement in Belgrade, 108
Bakir Hakim, Ayatollah Mohammed.
    See Iraq War
balance of power, 16, 40–42
balance of threat, 17
bandwagoning, 77
Bell, General J. Franklin, 67–68
Beveridge, Senator Albert, 16, 33, 62
Biden, Vice President Joseph, 153
bin Laden, 131–135, 137–139, 142,
    148, 153, 169, 202
Bismarck, xvi
Blair, British Prime Minister Tony, 133
Blix, Hans, 170–171, 207
Boban, Mate, 114
Bodine, Ambassador Barbara, on
    looting, 179

Boucher, Richard, 140
Bosnian War, x, xi, xiii, 175
    and US public opinion, 117–118
    arms embargo, 109
    Bosnian referendum on autonomy,
        105, 110
    Bush, George H. W., 26–27, 112
        US refusal to send signal on
            Dubrovnik, 120
        US wary of "middle way," 120,
            228 (n6)
    Clinton, William, 26–27, 112
        divided advisors, 118
        lack of fit between aspirations
            and political costs, 118
    Contact Group and push for
        settlement, 114, 205
    credibility of NATO, 110
    Croats
        played both sides of the fence,
            110
        responsibility for war, 116
        slow to respond to provocations,
            104
    Dayton accords (Dayton Peace
        Agreement)
        Croat strike in Krajina crucial to
            Dayton, 121, 122
        defects of agreement, 123–24
        groundwork carefully prepared
            by Holbrooke, 123
        West's agreement on use of force,
            122–123, 228 (nn15, 16)
    Dubrovnik, assault on, 109
    EC and US recognition of Bosnia,
        109
    ethnic cleansing, 115, 228 (n3)
        massacre in Srebrenica, 115
        Serbs with worst reputation, 115
    ethnic mix in Bosnia, 103
    Europe, hour of, 105
    Federation of Croatia and Bosnia-
        Herzegovina, 114, 121
    free elections in 1990, 104
    ineffectiveness of Bosnian Serb
        forces, 121–122

Izetbegovic, Bosnian President
Alija, 105, 108
accused of Islamic extremism,
116
commitment to multicultural
society diminished, 116
Karadzic, Radovan, 114
Kosovo, 110
lift and strike
Americans divided on, 119
at heart of differences with
Europe, 118
promoted in Europe by
Christopher, 118
Serbs say will not negotiate
without military equal, 119
Macedonia, 106, 108
Markovic, Yugoslav Prime Minister
Ante, 108
Milosevic, Serbian President
Slobodan
and Arkin (Zeljko Raznjatovic),
116
extent of control over Serbian
military forces, 116
played role of villain with
panache (Greater Serbia),
116, 117
sought gains in Bosnia and
Croatia (with Tudjman), 116,
228 (n1)
partitioning as solution, 112–114,
228 (n8)
British preference for, 113
role of United Nations
Secretary General's lack of
enthusiasm for war, 117
UNHCR's superior reputation
for action, 117, 228 (n13)
UNPROFOR and humanitarian
deliveries, 109, 117
U.N. veto on NATO use of
force, 117
Serbia
British and French preference
for, 116–117

demonstrations, 104
nationalism, 104, 106
Slovenia
allowed to exit federation, 109
amended constitution to allow
succession, 104
Tudjman, Croatian President
Franjo, 105
values-interest distinction in US
policy, 41, 111, 228 (n4)
Vance-Owen proposed settlement,
113–114
Vukovar (destruction of), 115
Bremer, L. Paul, 177, 180–182, 185,
188–189
Bretton Woods, 7
Britain, 15, 144. *See also* Bosnian War
Bulatovic, Montenegrin President
Momir, 114
Bundy, McGeorge, x, 90
Bush, President George W., 18, 148,
151, 153–154, 158, 160,
170–171, 173, 175, 184, 203,
210, 212. *See also* Iraq War
as strong leader, 35
bland initial agenda, 27
Bush doctrine, 19
ethnocentrism, 37–38, 207
ideologically rigid, 165–168
implementation of policy. *See*
intervention
invading Afghanistan, 132–134,
141–143
post 9/11 national security strategy, 27
Bush, President George H. W., 127,
158, 168. *See also* Bosnian War
and Gulf War, 162
and Somalia, 26
as "master of his own brief," 38
policy in Bosnia, 35
Byrd, Senator Robert, 173

Canadians, 145
Carter, President Jimmy, 24, 130
Casey, Lt. General George, 186–187,
190

Chalabi, Ahmed, 183–184
Cheney, Vice President, 19, 159, 204
  as influential adviser on Iraq, 162, 168
  believed US would get warm greetings from Iraqis, 164
  events originated with states, not transnational actors, 133
  made speeches alleging Iraq had WMD and developing nuclear, 170
Chiang Kai-shek opposed to Vietnam War, 225 (n11)
Chiarelli, Major General Peter, 186
China, 13
  as financier of US, 7
  as perceived military threat, 7
  as potential Yugoslavia, 20
  US reluctance to fight there, 23
CIA, xv, 132, 138, 164, 199
CIA NIE—2002, 169–170
Clark, General Wesley K., 119
Clarke, Richard A., 231 (16), 172–173
Clausewitz, Carl von, ix
Clifford, Clark, 85
Clinton, President William, 158–160, 175. See also Bosnian War
  foreign policy as social work, 27
  policies toward Somalia and Rwanda, 26
  policy in Bosnia, 35
  search for post–cold war strategy, 26
  strengthened alliance with Japan, 26
cold war, end of, 4, 7, 26
containment policy, 19–24. See also George F. Kennan
cost-benefit analysis, xiii
counterinsurgency, 214–215. See also Iraq War
  British experience, 51
  early attempts at institutionalization, 48–51
CPA, 177, 185
Crocker, Ambassador Ryan, 184
Crook, Major General George C., 46

crusader state, 208
Cuba, 15
culture insularity, 206
Curveball, 171

Daudzai, Mohammad Umer, 127
de Lattre de Tassigny, General, 77
de Mello, Sergio Vieira, 181
de Tocqueville, Alex, Americans' talkative patriotism, 31
Dewey, Admiral, role in Philippine War, 58
Diamond, Larry, 185, 189, 193
Diem, Ngo Dinh. See Vietnam War
Dien Bien Phu, 22
Dobbins, Special Envoy to Afghanistan James, 144, 179
Dominican Republic, xii
Donovan, "Wild Bill," and counterinsurgency in WWII, 47
Dulles, Secretary of State John Foster, 22–23
  and Dien Bien Phu, 80
  US possessing "moral excellences," 38

Eagleburger, Deputy Secretary of State Lawrence, 108, 114, 159
Edelman, Eric S., 43
Eikenberry, Ambassador Karl W., view of Karzai, 148
Eisenhower, President Dwight D. See also Vietnam War
  and Hungarian uprising, 39–40
  and importance of organization, 39–40
  and importance of resolve, 22
  implementation of policy. See intervention
  intervention under, 22, 24
  open decision-making style, 37
  organization and decision making, 39–40
  reliance on nuclear weapons, 23
  reluctance to intervene, 23
ethnocentrism, 7

Fall, Bernard. *See* Vietnam War
Fallujah, 188
FBI, 132, 164, 169
Feith, Douglas, 159, 174, 184
flexible response, 23
France, 15, 214
  positions on Vietnam and Iraq
    Wars, 91–92, 207, 226 (n14)
Franks, General Tommy (CENTCOM
    Commander 2000–2003),
    135, 143, 174, 186
Funston, General "Fighting Fred"
  capture of Aguinaldo, 68
  successful counterinsurgent, 68–69,
    224 (n12)

Ganic, Ejup, 119
Garner, Jay M., 174
  argued for limiting de-bathification,
    retaining infrastructure,
    180–181
  belief in quick exit, 183–184
  surprised by extent of looting, 178
Gates, Secretary of Defense Robert,
    131, 145, 150
  on counterinsurgency, 51
  on need for restraint in
    intervention, 217
Gelb, Leslie, 15, 125
geopolitics, importance of, 3
Gerson, Michael, 166
Glaspie, April, and support for
    Saddam, 158
globalization, 4
  definition of, 6
Gorbachev, Mikhail, 25
Graham, Senator Bob, 143
great game, 128, 202
Gresham, Secretary of State Walter
    Q., 55
Gulf War, x, xii, 8, 158, 164, 199,
    204, 219 (n2)

Haass, Richard N., 143, 157, 213
Hadley, Stephen, 174, 181
Hagel, Senator Chuck, 160

Haiti, xi, xii
Hamilton, Representative Lee, 119
Haqani, Jalaluddin, 131
Ho Chi Minh, 11, 76, 203, 212
Holbrooke, Richard, 154, 208. *See
    also* Bosnian War
Hoopes, Townsend, 98
Hungarian uprising, 22, 39

idealism, 16–19
India, 149–150
interdependence, growth of, 5
Inter-Services Intelligence, 137
intervention
  cost and success of, xiii–xvi, 41–42
  implementation of, xiii–xv, 39–40
  legitimacy of, xiii
  public support for, xiv
Iran, 150, 160, 164, 172–173, 199.
    See also Iraq War
Iraq Liberation Act, 27
Iraq War, 27
  Americans as liberators or
    occupiers?, 182–183, 189
  Bakir Hakim, Ayatollah
    Mohammed, 186
  Bush, George W.
    approval numbers, 172
    unique beliefs, 19, 165–167,
      231 (n5)
  civilian casualties, 188
  controversy over responsibility for
    disbanding of army, 180–182
  decision to intervene, x
  Democratic support for war, 160
  developing civil war, 188
  disbanding of army justified for
    placating Kurds, 182
  failure to appreciate Grand
    Ayatollah Ali al-Sistani, 189
  ignorance of Americans about Iraq,
    185
  incoherence of Bush's beliefs, 167
  insurgency as fourth generation
    war, 10
  isolation of green zone, 185

Iraq War – *continued*
   negative perspectives on Bremer, 185
   Petraeus as champion of new
      strategy, 191
   politicization of effort in Iraq,
      192–193, 231 (n2)
   poor strategies and mismatched
      personnel, 185–187
   promotion of stability or
      democracy?, 183–184
   rationale for war, 160–165
      Iraq connections with terrorists,
        162–163
      the aftermath of the Gulf War,
        164–165
      WMD rationale for war, 162,
        231 (nn3, 9)
   Reagan administration early
      support of Saddam, 158–159,
      231 (n1)
   significance and cost of looting,
      176–179
   success of "surge," 222 (n5)
   transition from attrition strategy to
      counterinsurgency, 189–192
   US attempts to balance Iran, 157
   US perspective on Middle East, 163
irregular war, 45. *See also*
     unconventional war
   American experience in, 45–47
Israel, 162, 213

Jalali, Ali A., 146
Japanese, 11
Johnson, President Lyndon
   and Vietnam, 23, 76, 207, 210
   as strong leader, 35
   craved approval of Kennedy
      people, x
   leader with rigid personality,
      ethnocentrism, 36–37
Johnston, Lt. William, 65

Kabul, 130, 146, 151–152, 155
   as only lit city in Afghanistan, 128
   Northern alliance entered, 142

   projecting influence to countryside,
     143, 154
Kagan, Frederick W., 137, 190
Kaldor, Mary, and "new war," 12, 125
Karzai, Hamid, 154, 212
   complained of excessive use of
     force by US, 151–152
   US reliance on warlords for order,
     145–149
Kay, David, 171
Keane, General Jack, 190
Keegan, John, 136
Kennan, George F., 16
   and containment, 19–24
   and "natural forces of resistance," 20
   emphasis on political aspects of
     containment, 220 (n1)
   support for Korean War, 20–21
Kennedy, President John, 210
   and flexible response, 23
   and nuclear test ban treaty, 23
   attempts to develop
     counterinsurgency, 48
   attitude on Indochina, 222 (n2),
     226 (n12)
   decision making in Cuban missile
     crisis, 39
   implementation of policy. *See*
     intervention
Khalilzad, Zalmay, 159
Kieu Cong Cung, 82–83
Kissinger, Henry
   ending war in Vietnam, 71
Komer, R. W., 98
Korean War, xii, 8, 20–22, 44, 73,
   76, 204
Kosovo, xi, 175
Kristol, William, 159
Kucan, Slovenian President Milan, 108
Kuwait, 160, 164, 168

Lebanon, 22
Leclerc, General Philippe, 71
Le Duc Tho, 71
Lewy, Guenter, 93
liberal-democratic ideals, xiv, 25–26

Lippmann, Walter, 38
Lord Axleworthy, xv
low-intensity war, 44. *See*
    unconventional war

Machiavelli, 16
Maliki, Nouri al-, 184, 189–190, 192
Mao Zedong, 11
Marion, Francis, 45
Matsu, 22
Mazar-e Sharif taken, 141
McCarthur, General Douglas, and
    counterinsurgency, 47
McCarthy, Joseph, 23
McChrystal, General Stanley A.
  and counterinsurgency, 50, 151,
    155, 200
McFaul, Michael, 160
McGovern, George, 25
McKiernan, General David, 154
McKinley, President William, 16, 62,
    223 (nn 1, 3), 198, 210
  as serious statesman, 57, 60
  weak leader in Philippine case, 35
McMaster, H. R., 190
McNamara, Secretary of Defense
    Robert, 209
  failure to ask important questions
    on Vietnam, 222 (n16)
McNeill, General Dan, 145
Mead, Walter Russell, 197
Miles, Colonel Nelson A., 46
militarist fantasy, 16
Morgenthau, Hans, 3, 16, 17, 216
  comments on Vietnam, 88, 91,
    219 (n1), 226 (n13)
Musharraf, Pakistani President, 138–139,
    140–141, 149, 151
Myers, chairman of the joint chiefs of
    staff Richard, 173, 181

Nagle, John, 186
National Intelligence Council, 188,
    233 (n16)
nationalism, 7
  as motivator of insurgencies, 8

reason for Sino-Soviet dispute, 8
  US underestimation of, 212–213
National Security Council, 132–133,
    142, 182–183
NATO, 144, 149–150, 154
neoconservative ideas, 7, 16–19, 159,
    165
Netherlands, 145
Nicaragua, xi
Niebuhr, Reinhold, 208
Nitze, Paul, 22
Nixon, President Richard
  and Chile, 24
  opened relations with China, 23
NSC-68, 20
nuclear revolution, 3

Obama administration, 151, 155, 214
O'Hanlon, Michael, 160
On Strategy, 49
ORHA, 174
O'Sullivan, Meghan, 174–175
Otis, Major General Elwell S., 66

Pace, Marine General Peter, 173
Pakistan, 130, 138–139, 140, 149,
    154, 231 (n16). *See also*
    Afghanistan War
Panama, invasion of, xi, xii
parochialism in US policy, 206
Pashtuns, 137, 141, 150–151
Pearl Harbor compared to 9/11, 131
Perle, Richard, 19, 159
Petraeus, General David, 12, 214
  concern over killing of Afghan
    civilians, 155
  success of clear, hold, and build,
    189–192
Philippine War, xi, 15
  accomplishments in
    counterinsurgency, 69–70
  Aguinaldo, Emilio, 56, 62, 205
    elitist nature of movement, 63–65
    into exile and return, 56
    strengths and weaknesses of his
      forces, 63–65

Philippine War – *continued*
  ethnic tension, 64–65
  humanitarian efforts, 67
  in context of Spanish-American
      War, 56–58
  insurgency for independence, not
      reform, 58, 66, 224 (n9)
  katipunan (Society of Sons of the
      People), 56
  obstacles to success, 65–69
  other interested powers, 60–61
  racism and war, 59, 62, 223 (n7)
  second thoughts on war, 69, 223 (n6)
  Spanish abuse of Filipinos, 56–57
  supporters and opposition, 59–60
  US security interests, 58–61
Pillar, Paul, 169
Podhoretz, Norman, 93
Poland, ix
policy vs. theoretical concerns, xvi
Powell, Colin, 231 (n16), 168, 171, 183,
      189. *See also* Afghanistan War
  agreed to DoD lead in Iraq
      reconstruction, 174
  discrepancy between Powell's and
      DoD's views on Iraq, 174
  initial enthusiasm for Vietnam
      War, 93
  initially favored diplomatic pressure
      on Taliban, 138
  proposal for assistance to Pakistan,
      143
  reservations on Iraq intervention,
      133, 160
  stresses importance of Pakistan, 139

Quantrill, William, 47
Quemoy, 22
Quezon, Manual, 70

racism, 33–34, 206
Ramadi, 188
Reagan, President Ronald, 141. *See
      also* Iraq War
  as crusader, 24
  negotiations with Gorbachev, 24

realism, 16–19, 25–26, 215
  classical realism, 16
  neoclassical realism, 17
  neorealism, 17
Rice, Secretary of State and NSA
      Condoleezza, 19, 127, 143,
      151, 170, 174, 181, 184,
      189, 212
  on prospects for democracy in Iraq,
      38
Roosevelt, President Franklin, 19
Roosevelt, President Theodore, 16,
      198
  role as advocate of war, 57–58
Rostow, W. W., 78
Rumsfeld, Secretary of Defense
      Donald, 134–135, 138, 145,
      162, 174–175, 180–182,
      184, 189, 202, 220 (n5), 231
      (n16)
  Afghanistan as vindication for
      streamlined military,
      141–142
  and looting, 179
  and urgency in attacking
      Afghanistan, 132
  as practitioner of neoconservatism,
      19
  denial of insurgency situation in
      Iraq, 50
  need for Afghanistan to organize
      on its own, 143
  raised issue of attacking Iraq, 133
  reluctance to cooperate on Iraqi
      postconflict planning, 175
Russia, 150
Rwanda, genocide there, xii, 209

Saddam Hussein, 18, 28, 157–165,
      167–169, 171, 177, 179–180,
      183–184, 187, 193, 202, 204,
      222 (n3)
Samarra, 184
Sanchez, Lt. General Ricardo S.,
      185–186
Saudi Arabia, 162, 173, 192

Scowcroft, National Security Advisor
     Brent, 108, 159
  dissent on Iraq intervention, 160
security, as rationale for intervention,
     xiii–xv
  definition of, xiv–xv
Seminole war, 46
Shelton, chairman of the joint chiefs
     of staff Hugh, 133, 143
Shiites, 173, 178, 182–184, 187–188,
     190–191, 211
Shinseki, General Eric, 175, 178
Silajdzic, Bosnia Foreign Minister
     Haris, 108
Smith, General Jacob H. (Hell-Roaring
     Jake), 68
Somalia, 11
South Vietnam, 21, 23
Spain, 15, 16
Sumaidaie, 183
Summers, Harry G., and
     counterinsurgency, 100
Sunnis, 178, 180–181, 182, 184,
     188, 190–192, 211

Taft, William Howard, president's
     emissary to Philippines, 56,
     223 (n2)
Taliban, 128, 136–138, 140, 145–148,
     149, 152–155, 203
Taylor, General Maxwell, 94
Tenet, CIA Director George, 133, 169
Thompson, Robert
  and lack of US direction in
     Vietnam, 101
  comments there is no channel for
     criticism of war effort, 95
  gives up on war effort, 227 (n23)
Thucydides, 16
Tito, 23
Tomasky, Michael, 160
Toynbee, Arnold, 5
Truman, President Harry, 19, 20

Uday Hussein, 178
Ul-Haq, Pakistan General Zia, 149

Umer Daudzai, Mohammad, 127
unconventional war, definition of, xi
United Nations, 40, 150, 152
United States
  as dominant power, 5
  as virtual state, 6
  debate over post–cold war strategy,
     24–28
  emergence as world power, 55
  primacy of, 24
UNMOVIC, 168, 171, 207
UNSCOM, 169
US Defense Department, 142, 148, 204
US special forces, 132, 141
US State Department, 20, 142, 144,
     170, 174, 176, 204

Venezuela, 16
Vietminh (Vietnam Independence
     League), 72
Vietnam War, 9, 21, 23, 35, 219
     (n4)
  and American ignorance of
     Southeast Asia, xv
  and China, 71–73
  and domino theory, 76–80
     loss of Japan and India, 77
     NIE, 79
     questions about, 78–80
  and excess military emphasis, 86
  and Korean War, 73, 87
  and National Liberation Front, 77
  and US aid program, 73
  Bao Dai's views, 73
  Bernard Fall
     not consulted by Washington,
        226 (n16)
     on land reform, 82
  CIA views on prospects of Saigon,
        84–85
  Dien Bein Phu and Geneva
        Conference, 73–75
  Eisenhower's refusal to intervene,
        73–75
  failure to implement
        counterinsurgency, 94–100

Vietnam War – *continued*
  comparing a Catholic village
    (Luong Hua) and communist
    movement, 98
  conceptual vacuum, 96–97
  Saigon's lack of reform and
    nationalist thinking, 96–97
  mindset of US policy makers,
    90–93
  and Charles de Gaulle, 90–92
  lack of foreign support, 91
  mix of ideals and security concerns,
    93–94
  nationalism and, ix
  President Ngo Dinh Diem
    and ARVN, 83, 95
    and civic action teams, 82
    and John Paul Vann, 83
    as fervent reactionary, 82
    deposed by coup d'etat, 80, 211
  Sino-Soviet dispute, 86–90
    and Yugoslavia, 87–88
    Ho Chi Minh as Asian Tito, 88
    official attitudes toward the split,
      88–90
  US reluctance to intervene
    post-Vietnam (Vietnam
    syndrome), 26
Vojvodina, 104

Waller, Major, 68
war
  declining utility of, 4–5
  fourth generation war

as people's war, 11
  winning legitimacy and popular
    support, 11
  frequency of, 4
  war of attrition, 44
War of 1812, 15
Warwick, Thomas, 174–175
weapons of mass destruction, 3, 158,
    167, 169–172, 207
Weidenbaum, Murray on "small wars
    and big defense," 44
Weinberger, Secretary of
    Defense, support for
    counterinsurgency, 49
White House, 142, 175
Wilson, President Woodrow, 16–19,
    29
Wolfowitz, Paul D., 19, 133, 142, 178
  believed no extra troops necessary
    for postinvasion phase, 175
  favored Chalabi government in
    Iraq, 184
  influence on Iraq decision, 162
  long history working with other
    neoconservatives, 159
  on terrorist/government
    cooperation, 164
  thought Iraqis would welcome
    Americans, 183

Young, General Samuel, 65

Zimmermann, Warren, 103
Zinni, General Anthony, 179, 222 (n2)